# WINNING
# RESUMES

## SECOND EDITION

## ROBIN RYAN

John Wiley & Sons, Inc.

Published by John Wiley & Sons, Inc., Hoboken, New Jersey.
Published simultaneously in Canada.

For general information on our other products and services please contact our
Customer Care Department within the U.S. at (800) 762-2974, outside the United
States at (317) 572-3993 or fax (317) 572-4002.

Wiley also publishes its books in a variety of electronic formats. Some content that
appears in print may not be available in electronic books.

***Library of Congress Cataloging-in-Publication Data:***

Ryan, Robin, 1955-
    Winning resumes / Robin Ryan.—2nd ed.
        p. cm. — (Career coach)
    Includes index.
    ISBN 0-471-26365-6 (pbk. : alk. paper)
    1. Râsumâs (employment)  I. Title.

HF5383 .R934 2002
650.14'2—dc21                                                    2002068994

Printed in the United States of America.

10 9 8 7 6 5 4 3 2

*To my husband Steven*
*and my son Jack*

*and*

*all the clients and job hunters*
*I've had the privilege of guiding*
*toward a better job*

# CONTENTS

# ACKNOWLEDGMENTS

I'm indebted to all the hiring managers who responded to my survey for this book. Many gave freely of their time and insights so you could benefit. I'm grateful to all the clients who so graciously helped, too.

I deeply appreciate the efforts of Lisa O'Toole, Steve Ryan, Tracy White, and Sandy DeHan, who read the manuscript and offered valuable suggestions to improve it. Dawnie Thompson made a tremendous contribution, as she typed and formatted many pages of this book. Adam Zoll and Janet Nelson were also a big help with typing revisions and changes. Paysha Stockton, with flexibility and terrific skills, typed and improved many pages. I owe her a big thank-you. Sandy Dehan and other HR Managers offered special help and shared invaluable professional insights with me.

I want to thank Mike Hamilton, my editor, and everyone at Wiley for allowing me to create a book that will help so many people find more rewarding work.

My husband and son were also supportive, letting mommy work when deadlines got tight. Our nanny, Patty Lowe, has proven herself a godsend. She gave me the time I needed to make this book a reality. Lastly, I must also thank my mom for her supportive way and numerous long-distance phone calls to listen, understand, and give me encouragement when I needed it. She's the best mother any woman could ever have.

# BEAT THE COMPETITION WITH THE GOLDMINING TECHNIQUE™

" **A**mazing—I've sent out 10 resumés and got 10 interviews. That's a 100% success rate. I would never have believed I could be in such demand," said Tom, a real estate executive and one of my career counseling clients. "In fact, the old resumé I had been sending out for months before we redid it, got *no* response. But this new one made a big difference for me—it pointed out my unique strengths and demonstrated accomplishments. Now I know that's exactly what employers want to read. My field is jam-packed with executives looking for jobs, but that was no deterrent for me once I had the right resumé. Employers saw me as a top candidate coming in the door. Now I've had the luxury to evaluate several job offers that came as a result," he concluded.

Anne, an advertising executive and career counseling client, wrote to report about her success. "We've done such a fantastic job on my new resumé that the managers and executives who interviewed me actually commented that my resumé was excellent—easy to follow, and provided details in a clear and brief manner. One manager picked out my resumé from among 300+ she received and commented on how good it was. A great resumé sure helped when I'm trying to beat the odds. Who would have thought that I would get a new job this fast?"

Jack, chief financial officer and seminar participant, wrote to say, "Previous to your job search seminar, I virtually never got a response to any resumé that I sent out. However, subsequent to your seminars, I seem to have had about one interview per week either on the phone or in person. Interviewers in the Portland area tell me that they receive about 100 to 400 resumés for each position. To stand out in such a crowd was a result of your seminars, and I now hold a superior new job to prove it."

The Goldmining Technique—that's how each of these people wrote their resumé and subsequently got their new jobs. Client after client had similar success and got the job they wanted. *Proven, market-tested resumés that were successful with employers*—that's all you'll see in this book. More importantly, you'll learn how to write one for yourself!

Now you will beat out the competition with the new resumé we'll write together as you use this book. A better resumé is your ticket to a new job, more personal satisfaction, more money, and a better future. In today's competitive workplace your resumé cannot just be good, it must be *outstanding.*

Together we're going to create an advertisement of your skills and abilities that really causes employers to stop and want to meet *you!* This book is based on the past successes of my clients. I also conducted new research and an extensive employer survey to determine employers' needs and preferences. The advice in this book will enable you to deliver exactly what employers want.

What must you do to stand out? Must you lie? Deceive the employers? Make stuff up? Is that the way to the top? *Absolutely not!* The employer will see right through that scam, and it will surely be exposed and unravel on you during the interview. The exclusive survey I undertook for this book went to 600 hiring managers and human resource personnel to provide you with the facts on the best ways to create an outstanding resumé. In my experience reviewing over 10,000 resumés, most people are too general and devalue their experience. They lack the know-how to self-market and capture employers' attention. Ineffective or weak resumés remain in the stack and never elicit an interview. I do not want that to happen to you. I'm committed to your success. Here's the secret to writing a more powerful resumé that gets employers' attention. Create accurate assessments that use facts, statistics, and noted contributions that demonstrate your ability to perform the job. To write your winning resumé, you'll use The Goldmining Technique. This is a writing technique that I developed and used for years to help clients and seminar participants hone and advertise the very best they can offer to excel at the potential employer's job. This seven-step process is easy to use. You'll learn how my clients rose above the other candidates. How, even in a crowd of 1,200 resumés, the one using The Goldmining Technique stood out and got the interview.

In no time, we'll have a great resumé put together for you. Soon you'll be *beating the competition* when employers respond to your new resumé by saying: *"Call this one in for an interview."*

## Success Stories

Every person in this book was looking for a new job. Success eluded them until we improved their resumé. During the writing process they learned about what they had to offer an employer. Their ability to communicate their most important skills heightened. You will be able to relate to their challenges: being fired or laid off, seeking a promotion, just launching a new career, or bored at the old job and wanting something better. You'll learn how the job analysis and the dissection of their skills relates to your situation and skills. You'll see the whole process Cindy went through and how she only sent out *one* resumé and got the job. You'll discover how Gladys became a human resource manager at one of the country's top companies. Joe got a promotion and landed a bigger store to manage. Dennis found a terrific new job and really learned his true value to employers when he started with a $20,000 jump in salary. Better jobs. Bigger salaries. Happy people working, contributing, and adding meaning to their lives every day. This is what we'll be working to obtain for you. Your success is my goal. We'll define your strengths and your accomplishments to stress the very best you have to offer an employer. We'll work together to land you a great new job.

## Only One Purpose

Your resumé *must* get you an interview. It's the final test. It either works, or it doesn't. Once you get the interview, a great resumé sets the tone to elaborate on your skills and actions at past jobs. Employers want to draw conclusions by learning the results of your efforts elsewhere. You'll walk away from this book with a clearer notion about the importance of analyzing the jobs you've done and noting both the actions and the results. You'll find it's an easier task than you feared once you use The Goldmining Technique. Proven resumés and employers' insights will aid in creating a resumé that gets an interview for *you.*

**ACTIONS = RESULTS.**
*That's what employers respond to.*

# *Real Facts about Resumés and Employers*

I've spent over 20 years helping people advance their careers and find meaningful employment. I've worked in higher education and in corporations and have personally hired over 300 people. My work with thousands of clients has led to their success in landing great new jobs. Additionally, I have taught hundreds of employers how to screen out and hire the best people. I have written other books on job search: *Winning Cover Letters; What to Do with the Rest of Your Life;* and *60 Seconds & You're Hired!* These are all solid credentials to advise you on your resumé. But, that wasn't enough for me. I wanted you to know the latest, most accurate information on what makes a resumé really grab an employer's attention. Therefore, I created a survey and sent it out to 600 hiring managers and human resources people. The results of the survey gave us firsthand insights on what mistakes people make and what really impresses employers. I've laced this book with so many of their comments. Their advice will definitely help you to write a stronger resumé as well as perform better in the interview.

Exactly who participated in our hiring survey? Thirty-eight percent were human resource managers with a few executive recruiters. The other 62% held senior-level management positions. The human resource respondents worked at Fortune 500 companies—some of the most impressive organizations in the world. Others worked for medium-sized companies, nonprofit organizations, or within state or federal governments. They work in various industries from manufacturing to telecommunications, from service and retail to education and high tech. Healthcare, tourism, hospitality. The survey respondents came from all across the country offering a variety of insights but with common suggestions and advice. The human resource managers in the survey had all hired more than 200 people. One pointed out that he'd hired over 1,200 for the Fortune 500 company he worked for.

The 62% who held management positions were CEOs, vice presidents, senior managers, presidents, department heads, and program managers. They came from a broad cross section in every industry from Miami to Seattle, New York to Los Angeles, and most places in between. They have each hired an average of 80 professionals or managers (all the way up to the CEO position). Those at the largest organizations had hired more than 100 people. Their experience and insights will be eye-opening as you learn firsthand what they think and how they decide exactly who to hire.

## Market-Tested Resumés That Landed Jobs

The resumés in this book are taken from my client records. Every resumé you'll see got the person an interview; most went on to land the job. Only their names and personal information have been changed to ensure their confidentiality. Though their background and circumstances differed, there's one commonality among them all: using The Goldmining Technique to write a resumé. IT *works!* I've selected people of all ages who've been fired or laid off, new graduates, senior executives, or career changers—real people just like you with real circumstances. I've taught resumé writing seminars for over 12 years, and seminar participants and clients all used this seven-step Goldmining Technique process. They praise the technique stating that it is easy to apply. You won't find silly gimmicks, untried resumé tips, or dumb techniques that won't work here. You'll do a thorough job and skill analysis; you'll consolidate your solid accomplishments to create your new resumé. To increase your competitive advantage, you'll benefit from our employers' hiring survey and get recommendations from the horse's mouth, America's hiring managers, on what it takes to get their attention and what impresses them.

## Only 15 Seconds to Sell You

You have only a few seconds to snag the employer's attention. You must create interest in a proven, well-organized format, or the employer will simply move on to the next person. You'll soon discover that as you proceed through The Goldmining Technique, you start to clearly grasp your most important skills. You gain insight from all the advice the hiring managers have given to more succinctly list your skills. We're in a race—a race for time. You must sell the employer within *15 seconds* of looking at your resumé or you'll lose that job. No interview, no higher salary, and no new position. The competition is heated, and the use of The Goldmining Technique will enable you to develop a competitive edge.

One added benefit of this writing process is that it will let you move ahead in the interview. You'll have the facts on your actions and noted results that allow you to offer interview answers packing information and punch to convince them to hire *you.* Before your next interview, I suggest you read about the 60 Second Sell™ and other interview strategies in my book, *60 Seconds & You're Hired!* (Penquin). It will keep you performing at your optimum level.

## *You're Now in the Advertising Business*

Your resumé is a succinct advertisement of you: your abilities, skills, talents, and experiences to do the job. Using The Goldmining Technique, you'll learn to create an accomplishments approach resumé. You will note the ACTIONS = RESULTS that you have achieved. ACTIONS = RESULTS—a powerful combination that is impressive to employers.

Step aside for one moment, and you will realize that you now have undertaken the job of an advertising executive—to create an interesting ad, or resumé in your case, that gets noticed. Your advertisement must be the very best you have to offer (your top skills, strongest abilities, talents, and credentials). Just as any company plans its marketing strategy, designs its ad, and sells the most moving benefits to the buyer, you must do the same. This time, the product is you. This is a critical piece of advertising. This self-marketing piece or resumé announces to the world that *you* are the *one* for the job.

What you'll learn from this book will enable you to improve the effectiveness of your resumé. It will open the door to more job interviews for some of the better jobs out there. We've got some important work to do to help you reach your goal and land a new job. Let's get started.

# BIG MISTAKES HIRING MANAGERS SAY TO AVOID

The resumé errors described in this chapter are a result of the national hiring manager survey conducted for this book. In decision makers' own words, you'll learn what employers consider to be fatal errors, so you'll understand how to avoid making any yourself. Additionally, I've included solutions and ways to avoid these problems. You will find this chapter enlightening and useful.

## *Common Resumé Errors*

 **1 Lying Can Ruin Your Career**

*Pulitzer Prize Winner. Notre Dame Head Football Coach. Senator. Congressman. Washington Post Reporter. Television Evangelist. Presidential Advisor. These highly accomplished people destroyed their careers because they lied on their resumés. For many, the lies were so much a part of their career background that they may have begun to believe the lies.*

Notre Dame, the most revered of the Catholic colleges, stood by its strong values and fired its new head football coach, George O'Leary, after only five days on the job when it was revealed he'd lied in his resumé about winning three college football letters. (Truth was, he'd never played, due to illness and injury.) He also "added" that he'd been awarded a Master's Degree from New York University, which he never earned. Oregon Congressman Wes Cooley claimed a war record that was simply made up.

*Washington Post* reporter Janet Cooke inflated her academic record to get hired at the *Post.* She sneaked by for a while, but years later Cooke won a Pulitzer Prize for writing a story that chronicled the life of a young heroin addict. But the youth was only an imaginary character, and when it was exposed that no real person existed, the *Post* was stripped of the coveted Pulitzer and Cooke's reporting career was over. TV evangelists are often not the most reputable people, but Pat Robertson's reputation was respected until it was discovered he'd altered his marriage date and claimed graduate study abroad in his credentials when in reality he'd only taken an arts course for tourists. The list of people who have suffered public embarrassment, professional humiliation, and had their careers left in ruins because they lied goes on and on.

And it isn't just a few notable faces. *USA Today* surveyed 7,000 executives and learned that misrepresentation—or lying—on resumés is now rampant in epidemic proportions. The survey's figures show that more people lie now than did five years ago. And even then, 33% of the people who claimed completed degrees hadn't earned them.

Many employers commented that this was a serious problem in many of the resumés they saw. "Overselling is a red flag," Karen Martin, a National Sales Manager wrote, "typically used by someone whose qualifications are thin." Lisa O'Toole, an attorney who's hired close to 200 lawyers, adds: "You would think lawyers would be *exact* in their qualifications, but it's not true. I've found so much exaggerated experience—overstating and intentional misrepresentation. The applicant tries to make their tasks or work sound much more important than it was. I know the field and this industry. Their lies are so evident to me—it's very annoying that people actually think they'll get away with it."

This current survey stated that 52% of applicants lie about completing education. Why? *Why* do they do this? "People often lie or misrepresent themselves because of their own insecurities. They feel they need to bolster their self esteem by claiming education, military, professional, or sports achievements," noted Charles Ford, college professor and author of *Lies! Lies! Lies! The Psychology of Deceit.* "Unconsciously, these people see themselves as inadequate and

**EXECUTIVES PAD RESUMÉS**
*Seven thousand resumés surveyed reveal many job seekers misrepresent themselves. Here are the top offenses and the percentage of time they are misrepresented:*

*Number of years in job 71%*
*Accomplishments exaggerated 64%*
*Size of organization managed exaggerated 60%*
*Partial degree indicated as full 52%*
*Compensation exaggerated 48%*
    *Source: **USA Today***

feel they have to enhance their resumés, then they'll get positive feed-back from others."

In many cases, the lies were trivial but the act of lying nevertheless was fatal for the person's career. They got fired! Helen, an executive recruiter inside a prominent company, said this, "One person I hired (and later fired) lied about having a college degree when they did not have one." Employers are well aware of this kind of misrepresentation. They now check on degrees and professional claims (some do this in the first few months of employment) and have been known to fire people after lies are revealed. Other employers have gone so far as to demand transcripts and copies of awards and diplomas.

It's not only employers that you have to worry about exposing your lies. I recently was called by a major radio station to comment about a city employee who had landed a prominent position as director of the arts by lying about her education. She listed two master's degrees that she was close to finishing, her undergraduate major, and a specialty certificate. It seemed a jealous colleague hired a private investigator when he didn't get the job. That investigation disclosed that both master's endeavors were fictitious and the noted college did not even offer the specialty certificate stated on the resumé. Not only was this woman fired; she was publicly humiliated on the front page of the city newspaper. The moral here is *never lie.* Eventually, you will get caught, and, as happened here, get fired.

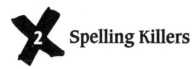 **Spelling Killers**

Hands down, this was "numero uno" with every manager and HR person in our survey. Many said: "I stop reading when I find spelling mistakes." Employers believe that your resumé reflects your very best ability. Karma Reavis, HR Manager at Dean Foods, says: "Spelling errors are the worst mistake people can make, especially when they are applying for a position that requires being detail-oriented. Too often they say they pay attention to details and then make lots of mistakes on their resumé and cover letter that prove otherwise." Make sure your message can pass the spelling test. Spell-check, use a dictionary, and proofread! Proofread! PROOFREAD! Don't be eliminated by something you have total control over.

*Spellcheckers don't think.* The advances of technology were most welcomed by many of us who find spelling a lifelong challenge. The spellchecker was almost like winning the lottery (well, almost, in a work sense). Unfortunately, it doesn't think about word usage, it simply corrects misspellings. Words such as "no" are correct, but they are the wrong choice if you meant to type "not." Similarly, "see" is *not* a body of water (i.e., sea). Reading your resumé out loud, and asking a friend to read it word-for-word, will help pick up wrong usage or inappropriate words.

*Typos scream.* "Don't hire me!" is the message most managers get when they see typos. Above all else, employers felt typos forecast the poor quality of work they can expect from you. I recommend that you always read your letter out loud and let one or two other people read it. Perfection is a necessity to remain competitive.

**3 Being General Just Won't Cut It**

"Job applicants fail miserably when they do not address their resumé to the position posted," points out Tom Wermerskirchen, HR Manager at Mustang Manufacturing. "When it's too general, it sends the message that 'I'll take any job,' and that's not what we hire for." Most employers we surveyed noted this same thought—*generic resumés were heavily criticized as a worthless effort.* "Not tailoring the resumé to a particular job is a major mistake," noted Kirk Beyer, a HR Director, who also identified this problem: "Individuals send out resumés with no job in mind, not knowing at all what they want. Their skills are incongruent with the job they are applying for, which leads us to quickly disregard them as a candidate. Employers will not use their time to figure out where a person might fit into their organization. That's a career counseling issue the candidate needs to handle *before* starting to mail out resumés. Unfortunately, though, we get hundreds who mail in worthless generic resumés every month."

Allen, a CEO for a manufacturing company, expressed his sincere dislike at receiving "form letter resumés" not targeted to his specific job opening or company. This "mass mailing" approach rarely works anymore, though many people do it. "Targeted resumés are necessary to match you to an employer's needs. A resumé that really shows skills, how they were used, and what was achieved is the only way to impress me," Allen concludes. Most of the other employers polled wholeheartedly agreed.

Too many candidates try to write all their skills down, and their resumé looks like a repetitive job description but not a summary of what the person has accomplished and would likely achieve if the employer were to hire them. I've found that many people probably qualify for more than one type of job. Some self-assessment and career decision making is essential to succeed in landing a new job. When you can pursue numerous avenues, take the time to hone in exactly on what it is you want to do. Then create a resumé for each job title you want to pursue. For example, an engineer might have two different resumés, one targeting a Program Manager position, the other for an Engineer's job. This targeted approach allows you to create a more effective resumé directing your skills to meet the employer's specific job opportunity. It's important to keep in mind when writing your resumé that employers hire people who "get results," so you must show you can do just that. If you are having trouble deciding what to focus on, seek out a qualified career counselor to help narrow your options and pursuits.

"Job hunters should customize their resumé to point out the specific skills and experience requested in our job advertisement," suggested Cathy Parham, a Director of Human Resources, reiterating a key point. "Tailor the resumé specifically for the job," echoed Connie Ley, a Department Head at Illinois State University. Noting skills, actions, and results are what's needed and warranted to target the specific needs to perform the job. Be specific and offer facts on both your accomplishments and skills to do the job that your are applying for. That's the only way to get noticed.

"Rambling, long resumés are a mistake," says Michael, a Senior Vice President. Ken, an Athletic Director, found too little information equally annoying. "Clarify about 'successful work'—dates and employers alone don't tell me much," he added. "In today's fast-paced world," one HR Manager stated, "you have only seconds to get my attention. Clear information with 'action' descriptions are what is most impressive. Stay clear of generic or broad phrases like 'hard worker,' or 'team player,' or 'excellent communication skills.' It's specific accomplishments and skills that impress me."

Avoid the cookie cutter approach. Using the Goldmining Technique™ I'll teach you in this book, you'll learn the ACTIONS = RESULTS formula necessary to succinctly elaborate on the actions and results you've accomplished to be successful. It's the most effective way to make your resumé noticeable.

**Employers Scan, Not Read**

According to our survey, even the most thorough managers say they spend only about one minute glancing over a resumé and cover letter. Notice I said *glance*; you cannot read an entire resumé word-for-word (and comprehend it) in 60 seconds. I asked Melinda, a human resource manager who's hired hundreds of professionals, how the process works in her office. She said: "We sort through them initially spending 15 to 20 seconds to determine if we should take a closer look or decline. That will eliminate 70 to 80%. Then we go back and review a little more closely those we've pulled out. Now we spend about a minute to select really good ones who closely match our needs to call in for an interview."

Most employers go through this same process. It's a two- or three-stage screening system. I know I do that for every person I've ever hired. Our survey found that 20% spent 60 seconds, 24% spent 30 seconds, 29% spent under 15 seconds, and 26% spent 20 seconds. The bottom line is that, on average, 79% of the employers spent less than 30 *seconds* reviewing a resumé. Many employers stated it was much less if they did not *immediately* see the skills or background to perform the job.

Therefore, success is dependent on a quick and easily readable format—communicating your previous actions, results, and abilities. The Goldmining Technique will aid you immensely in doing just that.

**5 You Just Haven't Got It or You Forgot to Mention It**

Lauren Thomas, a nonprofit executive, points out that "many applicants simply lack the qualifications for the positions." Over 80% of the surveyed employers agreed. Today's competitive job market often attracts 200 or more applicants per opening. With that kind of potential competition, your qualifications need to be a close fit or you'll surely get passed over. An HR Manager at a popular company told us, "We had an opening for a middle manager and had nearly 500 applicants, but 60% did not even meet the minimal qualifications." If you haven't got the basics, it's usually best to look elsewhere.

On the other side of the coin are those who do have the qualifications but leave off important credentials. "It's a colossal mistake not to clearly emphasize special credentials," offers Executive Director Ed Lincoln. Designations such as: MBA, Ph.D., CPA, or PE are vital ingredients in your package of skills. Major titles such as these need to be placed in the letterhead, after your name, at the very top of your resumé, so they won't be missed. So instead of writing "Mary Stephens," it's more powerful to have your top line read "Mary Stephens, MBA."

Too often candidates don't even mention important skills they possess. "A significant mistake many job hunters make is not mentioning their computer skills," said Linda, Director of Human Resources for a Fortune 500 company. This is especially important for administrative and office personnel, and most management positions. I've found clients, especially engineers who "assume" everyone knows they possess these skills, often don't write them down. A recent employer survey selected computer skills as the top skill sought from employees. If you don't state specific skills on your resumé, employers assume you don't have them. I recommend you state your computer abilities by incorporating them into a description (i.e., "Created a sophisticated EXCEL computerized tracking system") or by using a general statement such as: "Proficient on database systems utilizing MS WORD and EXCEL software." Computer, IT, and systems people should list specific hardware and platforms they've acquired expertise in, as well as software applications they are knowledgeable about and programming languages they can use.

"Where is their education?" asked Anita, Director of HR for a Fortune 100 company. "A serious mistake I regularly see is when individuals offer no Education or Training section and the job clearly requires it," she said. "We immediately screen applicants out if the Educational Summary is not on the resumé." Don't assume or forget—include these important credentials.

 ## 6 Too Much Is Too Much

Sandy DeHan, an HR Representative at Airborne Express, has reviewed thousands of resumés. A major mistake, from her perspective, is offering "too much information, 50% of which is useless." She further states, "Do I care if you are the president of the local pansy club?" When I went on to ask her how people can be more effective, she said, "I want to see their skills and how they match what I'm looking for. I don't want to wade through thousands of words to find out." Writing short sentences that link actions and results illustrate the "match" Sandy and other hiring managers seek. Everything included in the resumé must support and relate to the title you seek or it needs to be eliminated. "An important strategy to follow is to use a one-page resumé," she noted (more on this in a later chapter). "We get thousands of resumés, and multiple pages get lost easily, especially when faxed," she said.

Hannah, a frustrated HR Manager for a Fortune 500 company, told me she just didn't understand some job hunters' actions. "We just got this woman's resumé with 11 pages of references—11! On top of that, she faxed it, tying up our overly used fax machine. Why do people do this? I often wonder exactly what applicants are thinking—no HR manager will wade through that much info on one person; time would never allow for it. Actions like this also send us a clear message about you as a worker—that you are disorganized, focus on trivia, and can't prioritize necessary tasks." This job hunter got noticed all right—negatively. She did not get an interview, nor did she get the job.

HR people make snap judgments. Keep your presentations concise to hold their attention. References are generally provided in interviews. A very good reference (and I do mean just *one*) can go with a resumé if it's truly outstanding. Less often carries more impact.

**Drop Useless Stuff**

Large organizations often use cryptic job titles, such as "Tech I," "Tech II," and "Tech III," all of which have no relevance to the outside world as to what the job entails. It's wise to change the actual title "Tech II" to a more appropriate (and accurate) reflection of duties held, such as "Systems Analyst" when you list the title on your resumé. Many hiring managers said that in order to quickly comprehend the job you performed they need a descriptive title that means something.

Janice, a Director of Human Resources for one of the largest 10 employers in the United States, pointed out, "I see too many people using 'I's on resumés—it's a HUGE mistake." Albert, a CEO, told me, "Job hunters would benefit by sticking to short, powerful phrases that are directed to the right aspects of the available position. These should be supported by specific examples of personal accomplishments." Starting every sentence with an action verb will allow you to create "short, powerful phrases" and continue to include the results of your actions, which meet the exact formula most employers desire. You'll get more details on exactly how to achieve the actions = results formula as you look through the resumé samples in this book.

"Forget the overused phrases," John Brown, Director of Catering at Hilton Hotels, advised job hunters. "Stay clear of generic or broad phrases like 'hard worker,' or 'good customer service skills.' Offer the specific accomplishments and skills to impress me," he noted.

Your resumé is not the place to include any information on past salaries. One HR manager said, "Sometimes people actually list their former salary in their resumé. Seems like a big mistake on their part as it makes it very easy to screen them out." Another hiring manager told me, "I was surprised to see some professionals list their former salary. I got the immediate impression money was all that mattered to them and I suspected that they were not an exemplary employee either. Seeing it there just left a bad taste in my mouth about the candidate." The best time to mention salary is *after* you have been offered the job. That's when you'll have the most power to negotiate and get the employer to pay the highest salary possible.

A hiring manager sent along some resumes to highlight mistakes. He particularly noted one that listed the applicant's reason for leaving at the end of each job description. This left no need to talk to the candidate, especially when one departure stated "fired." I suggest you simply stick to offering skills and results. Save the tricky issues—salary and reasons for leaving—until the interview.

One resumé sent to me by a company president had an extensive list of traveling and sport activities under a heading called "Interests." The applicant may have thought it would show he was well-rounded, but the response the employer gave me was, "When does this guy ever find the time to come to work?" noting work obviously wasn't the only thing on his mind. Never list interests on a resumé unless they are vitally related to the job. For example, for a client seeking an international marketing position dealing with South America, I wrote, "*Numerous trips to South America, with fluent Spanish conversational skills.*" In most cases, interests are seen as unnecessary, unappreciated fillers.

Other useless items of information that hiring managers said you should leave off your resumé include: "References upon request," a tag line that is a fact known to all employers. The words "Resumé" or "Profile of" at the top of a resumé are also unnecessary and should not be used. Where you went to high school, or noting your football or other sports achievements are irrelevant and not the information employers seek. Technical training and college degrees are all that belong under the "Education" heading.

Old-fashioned resumé styles included personal statistics on health, marital status, gender, and age. But with current discrimination laws in today's market it's unwise to offer such information—so don't include it. One recruiter told us, "We still see people using too much filler and not enough substance. I just saw this one yesterday that said, 'Married. Four children, ages: 8-Mary, 6-Janis, 4-Thomas, and 1-Susan. Owner of golden retriever.' All irrelevant. This is a mistake that particularly older executives continue to make. It's a sign they are behind the times, probably in everything they do," he concluded. Offer the solid skills the employer needs and wants to know about. That's how you'll get attention.

One final caution: more than one HR Director said that movie stars and models need photographs, job seekers don't. Employers don't want or need your picture, so it's best not to add one.

# 8 Not Paying Attention to How It All Looks

"Overall appearance is the one of the most important things," Oris Barber, a Director of Human Resources said regarding the key elements of resumés. "If it's poorly presented you do tremendous damage that's challenging to undo," noted Mike Hurst, Vice President at Baxa Corporation. "As I review dozens and dozens of candidates, I use numerous systems to eliminate the pile. A terrific presentation will catch my eye much faster. I'll often draw comparisons between the candidates. If an applicant can't write a good resumé, it seems to me they may be less than stellar at the job too."

A strong, easy-to-read, professional format is truly essential. WHY? *Because employers don't read resumés, they scan them.*

"I have to question why anyone would select a microscopic typeface that makes reading the resumé quite difficult," wrote one human resource manager. Too often, seminar participants hear me say they need to have a one-page resumé. They go home, turn on the computer, select the entire document and shrink it down so small that you need a magnifying glass to see it. They are actually proud they got it all onto "one page."

One Recruiting Supervisor wrote, "So many resumés I see are simply too wordy. The applicant uses a smaller typeface, making the entire page packed with information and then too difficult to read." Edit the text, but leave the font size at 12 or 13 so it's easily readable. To consolidate your resumé, eliminate fillers, irrelevant information, or much of the detailed experience on work that's more than 10 years old.

"I glance over the resumé for an overall impression first. Does it seem professional, crisp, with a good format? That tells me a lot about the person," said Jim, a VP of HR at a Fortune 100 manufacturer. "I look at the professionalism of the format and style as a good predictor of the person's initiative and competence on the job—or a key indicator of a mediocre worker," he added. The message is that plain, crammed, or boring won't make it. The resumé must be easy to read, with qualified accomplishments and headings that clearly stand out.

Jennifer Lynch, a partner in one of Boston's top recruiting firms, pointed out another very common problem that she sees. "The content is fine," she says, "but organization and formatting are incorrect so that nonessential items are highlighted, or worse, nothing stands out at all. Why emphasize dates of employment?" she went on to say. A popular resumé style that lines up the resumé with employment dates in one column and duties in a separate column was highly criticized by employers. It looks like this:

3/95–6/98   Manager, Federal Express. Served as manager in this Fortune 500 company's distribution center overseeing staff, scheduling and workflow. Was involved in the total quality management process. Good team player, work well with most employees, and handle many projects simultaneously.

When you see a whole page of this you know what catches the eye first? Right—the dates of employment. The important stuff, the "what you did," is minimized or "shrunk down" to fit all the information on the page. I talked to a lot of managers and human resources people and they all agreed this was a poor layout choice. The most effective layouts—*Chronological* and *Combination*—are taught in this book. They illuminate strong points and emphasize what's important by using proper formatting that allows significant elements to stand out.

Another strong criticism involved resumés that leave off job history in favor of just accomplishments. Kelly Bachman, Director of Finance, and several other personnel reps agree with HR Consultant Martha Steinborn—they all wanted to see "dates, job titles, and employers." These are important elements people should never exclude. "What are they hiding?" Steinborn wrote. Suspicion is not a good way to start an interview (if you even get to that stage.) Melanie Prinsen, a Vice President of Human Resources, warns, "Resumés that have NO WORK HISTORY listed, only qualifications, get put in the 'no' stack." Always include the proper employment record—we do one in every one of our examples. If you wish to downplay who the employers were, or the job titles you held, then use the *Functional* resumé style. It is designed to emphasize the skills you've acquired, not where you performed them.

A key to formatting and polishing your resume is to forget English 101. Perfect grammar and long flowing sentences weigh down a resumé. "The best way to impress me is to offer clear information with brief 'action' descriptions of previous experience," says Laurie Hamre, dean at a prominent college. Sound bytes—short catchy phrases—and even fragments are quite effective, as the employer glances over the resumé. "Managed $14 million budget." "Wrote employee manual." "Taught four computer software courses." All short, but more effective statements because they start with all-important ACTION VERBS. You'll see what a difference using action verbs makes in later chapters and throughout all our resumé examples. To consolidate and improve the readability, especially when you are trying to effectively summarize long careers on one piece of paper, eliminate EVERYTHING that does not succinctly tell us how you can perform the job.

Employers noted they dislike what many called lazy job hunters. "I hate it when people send in an 'old' resumé that doesn't even have their current and most recent experience on it," says Molly, an HR Director. "Usually a person hasn't gotten around to updating it yet or is too afraid the current employer will be notified that they are job hunting. They are the first people we screen out." A Fortune 500 human resource representative told us that job hunters frequently cross out their old telephone number or email address and write in a new one. It is not acceptable under any circumstances to cross out and handwrite in a correction on your resumé. Retype—or the employer will disqualify you for shabby work, assuming you are not the type of employee they want to hire.

"I really hate cutesy resumés—they are almost always from women who use a graphic font like Old Gothic or Calligraphy and are almost impossible to read. Most of the time, I *don't* read it," said an HR Manager at a Fortune 500 company. Another HR Supervisor said, "Cutesy graphics make the person look childish." Stick with simple fonts—like Arial—and acceptable symbols, like bullets. They're easy on the eyes and proven to be an effective formatting approach. Distracting designs are just that— distracting. Always use a computer laser-printed resumé with a clear font (if copied, it must be a perfectly dark, clear copy) that sends this message: "I'm a pro in everything I do."

## 9 Missing Important Parts

"Having no career objective," said Melanie Prinsen, a VP for Human Resources, "is the worst mistake I see applicants make. They must indicate *what* job they are applying for, and have the rest of the resumé supporting the position applied for with stated accomplishments to back it up."

"I dislike those long flowing mission statements people use as a career objective. The 'I want to use my management skills and communications abilities, as well as strong organizational skills as I seek advancement opportunities within your organization' kind of stuff. Just state the desired position and leave the flowery, puff statements off," advised one HR Rep. Employers all seem to agree—your resumé must be directed toward performing a specific job to get their attention. Therefore, I advise you to have a clearly stated job title as the career objective you want.

One of the sections employers liked best from our samples were the SUMMARY OF QUALIFICATIONS sections. I never write a resumé without it. These few sentences are powerful, as they illustrate the top selling points you bring to perform the job. Your resumé must include this section. An added benefit to you is that 90% of other job hunters don't include it. Don, a CFO and former client, wrote to say, "I found the 'SUMMARY OF QUALIFICATIONS' a new and especially effective technique. It was a powerful introduction and worked very well." Don's new resumé, using the "accomplishment-oriented" approach, attracted several interviews. He got two offers and accepted one with an impressive, up-and-coming organization. You'll learn how to write your own and incorporate it into your resumé.

One HR Recruiter told us, "I've done a lot of corporate and on-campus recruiting. Too often I see people who spent years getting an MBA or Bachelor's Degree and think that that *alone* will impress me. I'd like to see what else they've learned. Specifically, projects completed in a group or team, research, or writing ability. Candidates would do well to draw comparisons between their experiences and the job they hope to do. Volunteer work (or unpaid jobs) often require valuable skills and should be mentioned." His final advice was sage. "We don't hire a degree, we hire the person who has used or can use the education to perform the job better," he said.

"They left off their phone number," laughed one HR Manager. "So exactly, who ya gonna call—ghostbusters?" Several people mentioned similar oversights. One even said a resumé came in with no name, address, or phone number. It's amazing how people can overlook the obvious or the essential. Always list your name, address, and home phone number on any and all pages you send.

 ## Not Targeting the Right Position

Often, seminar participants say the entire job market is such a challenge if you're over 50. They keep hearing, "You're overqualified." Applicants quickly learn hiring managers get very nervous interviewing people who have the qualifications to hold the interviewer's job. There are two solutions to this problem. First, apply for positions more in sync with your abilities. I find most seasoned job hunters are applying for jobs well under their abilities because "they need a job." Hiring managers want enthusiastic employees, not competitors to be the boss.

At higher levels or in specialty areas, you may need to consider relocating. In today's market, most of us must go wherever the jobs are. I remember one client, Bill, who had a very prominent position as VP of Finance for a real estate developer. A merger devoured his job. For two years he looked in his local city, not wanting to move for family reasons. There just were no real estate developers who needed him at the time. After 27 months, he came to see me. Three months later, he was employed with a wonderful salary in a new city 1,200 miles away. Since he couldn't retire, he moved because he had to.

Of course, there is an alternative—to downsize the specific position you want (and the potential salary), targeting a lower-level job. To do that, you may need to "reduce" the levels of documented accomplishments on your resumé. After all, employers know what you tell them. Many a Ph.D. has left that credential off their resumé so as to not scare off nonacademic employers.

Be careful when offering an explanation why you want a "lesser" job. Employers often worry that the person is "burned out," and simply wants to "coast to retirement." You may have been the office manager before, but eliminating the phrase, "supervised department and nine people" from your resumé and playing up organizational and computer proficiencies will be more effective in landing you an administrative assistant job. Just be sure that truly is the job you want to perform once you get hired, or you may find you have a lot of new problems if your boss feels threatened by your "ambitious" attitude. Also, employers might translate you saying that you want something "less stressful" into you saying that you don't wish to work too hard. Even at a lower-level job, employers still want to see evidence of your enthusiasm and productivity. The bottom-line requires you to target the resumé to meet the actual needs of the job.

Many employers commented that the other side of this was also a serious concern and mistake. Karen, a national sales manager for one of the country's largest pharmaceutical companies, wrote, "Overshooting is such a common mistake, typically used by someone whose qualifications are thin but thinks they can be the BIG BOSS. I don't think so," she wrote, noting that "it's best to not reach for a position three levels above anything you've done before."

One healthcare administrator said he was amazed that so many people claim they can do jobs, without providing any evidence that they have held similar positions. They often seem to be quite naive about how challenging jobs are to do and do well, he said.

## 11 Job-Hopping Is Still a Bugaboo

Laurie Hutcherson, senior VP for an insurance company, said, "Believing that many different jobs equates to diverse experience and therefore a more desirable employee is a large mistake." Several other hiring managers pointed out that "loyalty to a company is still an asset." Unfortunately, downsizing and limited opportunities with small employers often do not lend themselves to the longevity at an employer, the factor our VP highly valued. The solution to this tricky situation is to use the *Functional* format resumé style, which quickly stresses skills but does not address the actual work history until the end of the resumé. On rare occasions, I'll advise a client who had a job that lasted only a few months to drop it completely (especially if it was a very negative experience) and not mention it all. I also recommend you be more selective in the next job you take. Seek to stay a few years or you may continue to endanger your long-term future. Sometimes a long career history just goes back too far and makes you look unstable, so 15 years is about all you need to mention in most cases, to condense it.

Dr. Steven Thomas reported something that many other employers also noted—having too many different jobs is a key tip-off that an employee isn't going to work out. Many times, though, the candidate has separately listed every job they have ever held—many with the same employer. Best to consolidate and state the entire dates of employment, then list your most current position with the employer, followed by the phrase *"promoted from."* Many employers want long-term employees, as numerous tech people found out when, finally, no one wanted to hire them after years of running off all the time to the highest bidder.

## 12 Relying on Technology

Computers with fax capability are a wonderful invention. Unless, of course, you need to fax a "perfect document." Employers alerted us to the fact that computer faxes are often reformatted as they are being transmitted, and sometimes sections of text are deleted. I've seen several come through our system where the client swore it was "perfect" on their computer screen and was shocked at how distorted it was at the receiving end. I recommend using a "real" fax machine, and for good measure, *always* mail a copy too, with a note that says "this was faxed" and list the date. "Fax machines don't guarantee a perfect reception at the other end," pointed out an HR manager at a governmental agency. "So many come in with half the page erased or smudged so badly we cannot read them," he noted.

One head of HR let out this little-publicized secret. "Emailing a resumé is not as efficient as many believe. People are using those awful resumé blaster services or just sending their resumé to a zillion employers themselves, thinking this will get them noticed. So many of my colleagues tell me that anywhere from 40 to 60% of all electronic resumés are not even readable once they arrive. I'm not sure exactly what happens to them but the are often empty or full of code. Worthless efforts, and God forbid, don't expect us to tell you to send another," she lamented. You'll see my solution to this problem when you read the chapter on electronic resumés later in the book.

"Here's the thing that drives me crazy," wrote one HR manager. "No one answers the phone—no machine, nothing. It rings and rings and it rings!" Today, way too many people are on the Internet, tying up their only phone line. It's frustrating, and some hiring managers may just forget to ever call you back after a couple of times. It's essential to have either voice mail or an answering machine to get important messages from employers, particularly one that answers when you are on the phone or line.

Another problem I often hear about is that young children, rude teenagers, and risqué recorded greetings don't create positive impressions with potential hiring managers. One HR manager wrote in to say she became very unenthused about an applicant when she called and got a bizarre message that said something about "beaming me up Scotty, Captain Kirk needs to save the day since the Klingons have attacked. Bring a phaser or simply encrypt a message." Seems this decision maker wasn't a *Star Trek* fan and found this influenced her to NOT leave a message. Be sure to be professional, and by all means don't allow *anyone* to answer the phone who cannot politely and correctly take down a name and phone number.

One complaint I've heard too often in my hiring seminars is about employees who job hunt using their company's equipment. This is particularly troublesome with small employers. One company president pointed out that the message given to the employer when people did this was. "So if I hire you, you'll waste *my* money too." That is not the right image you want to project. It's best to fax off of a home system or use a local vendor like Mailboxes, Etc., or Kinko's. When listing an e-mail address, use the one on your home computer.

## 13  No Cover Letter

"Huge mistake," according to almost everyone in our survey. "We want to see evidence of their writing ability," says Deanna, an human resource manager. "I know resumés can be bought, but a good, well-written cover letter that the person probably wrote themselves can really impress me." George, another human resource manager, states: "The worst mistake job hunters make is not including a cover letter that relates their qualifications to the opening sought." "Give me a good, strong cover letter addressing strengths deliverable to the position and I eagerly move on to more closely review that candidate's resumé," states senior executive Lawrence Tomon. "Too long of a cover letter is a 'killer,' " said one Fortune 500 human resource representative. Cover letters are an essential part of your application package. I recommend you read my book, *Winning Cover Letters.* It will enable you to easily write highly effective letters by using The Power Impact Technique.™ A good cover letter teamed with your resumé creates a strong introduction and enables you to stand out from the competition. Always use one.

## 14 Fancy Designs Don't Always Impress

I've seen some printers who found a great way to make money—offer fancy resumés. Not the content mind you, which is the more important part, but they spruce up the overall design. Frank Gibbs, district manager at Medtronic, Inc., said he dislikes too glitzy resumés. He continued to say: "I recently got one that looked like a brochure." This was a significant mistake to Frank, and most of the other managers also agreed. "Too often job hunters use 'designer resumés' simply trying to hide a weak set of skills or a mediocre job history," said one human resource manager. Many employers told us that designer paper, borders, and graphics were a *negative influence.* The exception was from graphic artists. Plain, easy-to-read formats on white or cream paper were what employers told us they wanted from everyone else.

 ## 15 References Can Sink Your Ship Fast

All references are not created equal. Employers want to talk to former supervisors and others who have worked with you and can attest to your performance on the job. I've written an entire section in Chapter 7 on selecting references. Here's an important reply to our survey to keep in mind: Liz, a CEO, told us, "I'd been looking for a while and was pretty excited about the applicant and wanted to offer her the job. As standard policy, I asked her for references. She gave me a list and, as I called each one, I found that none of them had been her boss but seemed more like a friend. I called and asked for the listed company's department head and told her I was calling to inquire about my applicant. The department head seemed quite surprised that I had gotten her name, as this boss had fired my candidate for being incompetent on the job. She went on to offer some specific performance details that convinced me to keep looking further."

## 16 Gimmicks

"Clever gimmicks people try are usually to hide a lack of true substance," a senior vice president wrote. "People will do anything for attention—most of it never works," said one news director at a prominent TV station. "Every day someone tries a new trick: flowers, candy, even a box of cookies wrapped in their resumé. I might have eaten the cookies, but it didn't get them the job." We had numerous comments from our hiring managers that gimmicks, designer papers, oversized envelopes, or Federal Express did not improve your chances of getting an interview. They often proved to be a negative. Nothing will replace solid facts focused on how you can excel at performing the job. It's the *meat* of your resumé—proven experience, skills, and accomplishments—that keeps the employer's interest long enough to call you in for an interview.

# *The Formula for the Perfect Resumé*

Content! Content! Content! That's what matters. Your resumé must have strong powerful sentences that pique an employer's attention.

✔ Strong ACTIONS = RESULTS content

✔ One page

✔ Professional layout

✔ Easy to read

✔ Quantify skills and accomplishments

That is the formula for the perfect resumé. Read on. I'll show you just how to write it so you will stand out in a crowd and get called in for an interview on the job you want.

# VITAL RESUMÉ COMPONENTS AND FORMAT STYLES

How your resumé is developed, the format and style, is vital to its success. In *Winning Resumés,* you will find market-tested resumés that have a proven track record of obtaining job interviews. Based on research, my clients' successes, our employer survey, plus my own hiring experience, I've concluded that there are *only three* widely accepted resumé styles. Those three are the only ones I use with my clients. That's what I recommend you use. The employers we surveyed prefer good content and traditional, easy-to-read formats. No gimmicks. Only what's been truly effective in the marketplace is included. Every resumé in this book got people a job interview, and, in most cases, they went on to land the job. My recommendations are based on what has worked (and worked well) in the marketplace.

These three resumé formats have been in existence for a long while. Most human resource people, employment specialists, and career counselors recommend them. The three accepted format styles are:

1. Chronological
2. Functional
3. Combination

Additionally, there are specific components that need to be included in your resumé to be competitive in today's marketplace.

CAREER OBJECTIVE

EDUCATION

SUMMARY OF QUALIFICATIONS

PROFESSIONAL EXPERIENCE

WORK HISTORY

***Optional Headings***

COMPUTER SKILLS

HONORS/AWARDS

COMMUNITY ACTIVITIES

RELATED TRAINING

Let's examine what each resumé style looks like and then discuss the individual pieces important in selecting which style is the best one for you to use.

# Resumé Formats

## Chronological

This is the oldest and most traditional resumé style. It's organized by dates of employment. You begin with your most recent job, working backwards to include all your other jobs as well. The major emphasis of this style is on the job title you've held and the company in which you performed the job. This style illustrates your progressive career path and is easy to follow. I recommend you use it in the following situations.

✔ You have a clear job target.

✔ Your next job is in a direct line or logical progression up from your past experience.

✔ Both your job title and company are impressive.

✔ Your current job is in healthcare, science, engineering, finance, or top senior management.

Individuals with a spotty work history, with unknown employers, who are changing careers or fields, or who have work gaps are better served by using either the Functional or Combination styles. Let's take a closer look at the Chronological resumé.

**CHRONOLOGICAL**

# Dorothy Adams
1 Main Street
City, NY 11111
(201) 555-0111

CAREER OBJECTIVE: **Computer Programmer**

## SUMMARY OF QUALIFICATIONS

Ten years computer programming experience within the business engineering and finance divisions for a manufacturer. Strengths lie in project management, technical support, systems/process analysis, and communications skills. Proven track record of troubleshooting, enhancing systems, reengineering processes to increase efficiency while providing substantial cost savings. Received three special recognition awards in the last four years.

## PROFESSIONAL EXPERIENCE

*Computer Programmer,* Ford Computer Services, Detroit, MI, 1990–Present

- Programmed both business engineering and finance computing systems in a mainframe environment including enhancing code, troubleshooting, modifying systems, testing processes and procedures, and documentation.
- Key team member on a complete mainframe system overhaul streamlining thirteen corporate finance/accounting systems into one system. Two year conversion resulted in $12 million dollars in savings, eliminated twelve positions, increased efficiency and eliminated 80% of previous system problems.
- Served as technical troubleshooter/system programmer support to interdepartmental technical personnel. Resolved data complications, user errors, and miscoding.
- Responsible for database downloads and system backups. Ensured maximum productivity and efficiency.
- Created new graphs, charts, data flow illustrations and policy/procedural documentation plus comprehensive reports used in business analysis, and long term strategic planning.

## COMPUTER AND TECHNICAL SKILLS

Programming Languages: COBOL/COBOL II, JCL, Mark IV, C
Platforms: Mainframe, LAN, PCs and Macintosh
Machines: IBM 3390/MVS (JES2/JES3)
Software: TSO/ISPF, Syncsort, Librarian, Rumba, Maestro, Word, Windows, PageMaker

## AWARDS

*Special Recognition Award,* Finance Department, 1998
*Appreciation Certificate,* Finance Department, 1999
*Special Recognition Award,* Computer Programming Department, 2001

## EDUCATION

Bachelor Degree, Michigan State University, East Lansing, 1988
Programming Certificate, Ford Computer Training, 1990

Notice that Dorothy's looking for another computer programming position. We've detailed her important accomplishments at this prominent employer under PROFESSIONAL EXPERIENCE. Prospective employers who glance only at her SUMMARY OF QUALIFICATIONS clearly realize that this is a strong programmer with a proven track record of success. Her technical skills are outlined in their own section. We elected to mention key service awards that are impressive as important evidence of her skills and level of contribution to a company. Finally, since she's been out of college over 10 years, the degree is placed at the end of the resumé. (*Note:* Individuals with less than five years' work experience have the option to place the EDUCATION section after the SUMMARY OF QUALIFICATIONS section if they prefer.)

Dorothy's resumé got her several interviews allowing her the luxury of selecting from two very good offers.


## Functional

This option allows you to focus on what you did (paid, volunteer, and community experience) but not on where you did it. I don't use the style much with clients. I recommend you use this style in the following instances.

✔ You want to downplay work gaps. This can often be accomplished by also noting the years worked, e.g., 1997–2000 instead of months with years (5/97–1/00). Then, if your next position started in November of 2000, using years to date your employment actually covers up the gap of time spent job hunting.

✔ You held jobs where the title was not very reflective of all that you did.

✔ You are changing careers, allowing you to focus on your transferable skills and not the old job title.

✔ You have acquired a lot of experience and skills through volunteer activities and professional associations.

✔ You are reentering the workforce after being away more than two years.

✔ New college graduates with limited experience can create more attention by better illustrating academic experiences and internships in this format.

There have been critics of this resumé style. Human resource people recognize it's often used to hide something that's lacking. Kathy, an HR supervisor for a major employer, says she reviews nearly 500 resumés every week. She told me that in her experience the Functional style was criticized because many people completely left off their work history, never listing the company or employer and job title held. This is a *major no-no.* (*Note:* All of our resumés include a work history.) Remember, a main function of the human resource job is to eliminate people. Therefore, this style will garner closer scrutiny by personnel. That is offset when you offer strong skills and accomplishments. This format compared with the Chronological style makes it harder to dismiss someone without an interview or telephone screening, which is an important plus.

Let's examine a Functional resumé. This appeared as a one-page document when employers saw it.*

*Because of typesetting restrictions, some resumés in this book have continued onto a second page. However, in virtually all instances, these resumés were submitted to employers in a single-page format.

# John Buckman
1 Main Street
City, NY 11111
(201) 555-0111

CAREER OBJECTIVE: **International Sales Manager**

## SUMMARY OF QUALIFICATIONS

Proven expertise in international market development and joint ventures to establish markets, governmental relations and international distribution. Ten years in retail management. Developed new store that achieved 20% record sales increases each year over a five year period. Strong financial management, auditing and computer systems experience that focus on increasing profitability. International sales experience dealing with Japan, Korea, former Soviet Union, Norway, Denmark and Canada.

## PROFESSIONAL EXPERIENCE

### New Business Development
- Established joint venture with Russia, one of the first and largest to be established under new government.
- Managed day-to-day operations of start-up fishing joint venture including: joint venture negotiation, marketing, international regulations/banking/distribution/shipping, budgets, legal trade agreements, sales, governmental relations, customs, computer systems, economic forecasting, and accounting.
- Developed Private Placement Offering with Paine Webber brokerage which was successful in attracting two investor groups totaling $36 million.

### Retail
- Established new retail store including layout, construction buildout, hired/trained employees, buying, advertising, merchandise display, marketing, operations, financial management. Profitable in 90 days.
- Achieved aggressive market penetration of 20% each year of five year period, ranked in the top 10% of 5000 stores nationally for expansive growth.

### Accounting
- Implemented computerized financial and inventory systems for retail store.
- Audited cash, accounts payable, accounts receivable for Marriott Hotel. Prepared financial reports.
- Streamlined procedures, increased internal controls, trained financial staff. Received performance award.
- Established and handled ongoing international banking relations, lines of credit, currency conversions.
- Developed plans for product expansions, start-up ventures, profit ratio, budgets, and sales projections.

### Computer Skills
- Expert proficiency on IBM, Macintosh, mainframe and networks using Excel, Lotus, Word, WordPerfect, databases, spreadsheets, and customized accounting software.
- Converted retail store from manual to automated inventory system.
- Automated entire financial operations for international company.

### JAPANESE

Four month language study in Tokyo. Wrote 2 theses on Japanese Markets.

### WORK HISTORY

*International Operations Manager,* International Fishing Investment Corp., Anchorage, AK, 1999–Present
*Store Manager,* Reva's Hallmark, Nashua, NH, 1993–1999
*Auditor,* Accounts Payable/Receivable, Marriott Hotels, Boston, MA, 1997–1998
*International Relations/Trade Specialist,* State of Maine, Augusta, ME, 1997

### EDUCATION

B.A., Economics with emphasis on International Trade, Colby College, Waterville, ME, 1997
Semester Abroad, School for International Training, Tokyo, Japan

John had been involved with a venture capital group. He gained a lot of experience and tremendous understanding of overseas markets, customs, and buying trends. But he had begun to dislike the three owners who feuded constantly and were each pulling the company in different directions. He feared that it would break apart under all the tension, so he decided he'd move on. During our coaching session, he repeatedly brought up his desire to return to the retail world, ideally as an international sales manager. His retail experience was more than five years old and was for a small franchise store. Therefore, we chose the Functional style to emphasize both the international market expertise and retail background. You can see how we accomplished this when reading his SUMMARY OF QUALIFICATIONS that brings both experiences into the forefront.

John knew that he was stretching to try to go into international sales management, but we were able to emphasize important strengths: finance, marketing, capitalization, strong computer, and bottom line experience. Notice that we brought particular attention to his Japanese language, writing, and business marketing abilities.

WORK HISTORY came just before the end, as the joint venture company he worked for was in fishing and seafood sales.

John got interviews. One of his first was with a top U.S. retailer who was beginning an international catalog sales division. The depth of the job and the challenge really got John's juices flowing. He wanted this job; he knew he could do it. Like many other career changers find out, employers are often reluctant to take the chance on a "might be." This employer needed a person with a proven international retail sales track record already and would not hire anyone without it.

John was disappointed that he wasn't given the job. A lot of his energy was tied up in his passion to do something bigger than he had done before. When we met again, we analyzed the interview, and I told John that he'd done well to at least be invited for an interview. We plotted out his action plan: prospective employers and the steps to contact them. We used referrals, targeted letters, and direct phone calls. We also looked more exclusively at the Japanese market since he really had an edge there.

It took a couple of months, but he did indeed find a dream job with a U.S. company who wanted to move into Japan. This was his chance, and I heard he's done very well in this new position. I spoke to him recently, and he offered this advice: "Go after your dreams. Be enthusiastic. Believe in yourself until you convince an employer to hire you. Then work your tail off to prove yourself, which will also position yourself for your next job." I agree. If John had *given up,* he'd never be enjoying the success and terrific job he holds today.

## Combination

This resumé style is my personal favorite. It combines the employer information while also emphasizing the candidate's skills. I often use it with my clients. Employers really react well to this style. For people with a lot of experience, particularly with one employer, you can emphasize your most recent experience while downplaying duties that are less important from years ago. If you have more than three years at your current (or last) job, consider this option.

I recommend you use this format as follows.

✔ You have four or more years at your current/last employer.

✔ You have substantial accomplishments to emphasize.

✔ Anyone in middle or senior management.

Now, let's see why I like the Combination style so much.

**COMBINATION**

# Karen Fitzpatrick
1 Main Street
City, NY 11111
(201) 555-0111

CAREER OBJECTIVE: **Hospital/Managed Care Administration**

## SUMMARY OF QUALIFICATIONS

Eight years in hospital contract administration, negotiating 50+ insurance and managed care contracts for the Midwest's premiere hospital. Proven track record in negotiating profitable contracts and serving as liaison between hospital and insurers. Excellent financial analysis skills. Bring strong strategic analysis to identify issues and find workable solutions.

## PROFESSIONAL EXPERIENCE

*Contract Analyst,* University Medical Center, Kansas City, MO, 1994–Present
*(Promoted from Utilization Manager.)*

### Contract Negotiations
- Eight years negotiating more than 50 PPO, HMO, and insurance provider contracts including: Blue Cross, Blue Shield, First Choice, and Regional Health.
- Served as liaison between the hospital and the provider on the terms, policies, procedures, and implementation of the contract.
- Prepared 60+ third-party contract proposals including multipage applications, services definitions, contract terms, and financial rates.
- Negotiated and added 38 new contracts over eight-year period. Renegotiated 80+ contract renewals with a 92% renewing track record.

### Financial Analysis
- Prepared comprehensive financial analyses of provider demands and hospital's requirements, maintaining Midwest area hospitals' smallest discount to providers, maximizing hospital's profitability.
- Utilized sophisticated computerized system to analyze medical services utilization and financial data to provide accurate model activity for proposed reimbursements and to ensure hospital profitability.

### Administration
- Coordinated extensive overhaul of interdepartmental policies and procedures to adhere to the demands of insurance contracts.
- Coordinated contract implementation, integrating admitting, utilization review, and billing departments to meet contract terms and to ensure payment.
- Established communication procedures with multiple departments to process problems, legal issues and contract terms, resulting in effective solutions.
- Developed computerized systems to create customized software applications to enhance productivity and to increase data accessibility and financial capabilities.

*Project Analyst,* Blue Cross, Kansas City, MO, 1991–1994

## EDUCATION

Master of Health Administration, University of Missouri, 1994
Bachelor of Arts, University of Kansas, 1981

Karen had worked eight years for her current employer. Her job had evolved a lot as healthcare was changing radically. She probably would never have thought of leaving until the day she came to work and the hospital had fired all its senior department managers including her boss. With more major layoffs looming, Karen felt shell shocked about this loss of job security. She came to see me. Our career analysis revealed that Karen had developed herself into a new breed, the managed care administrator. I pointed out that this was where she should look. We created her resumé. Notice under her PROFESSIONAL EXPERIENCE we listed her current title and on the next line stated "Promoted from Utilization Manager." This was to point out an earlier job she'd also held at the hospital. Karen had mountains of expertise. We spent a lot of our time going through the Goldmining process (detailed in the next chapter) to extract her most relevant and important accomplishments.

You'll note we elected to include one of her other employers, Blue Cross, but simply added it on as the last item in her PROFESSIONAL EXPERIENCE section. I felt it wasn't necessary to go back further than that with the specific job duties or details. Most employers are really only interested in work you've done in the last five to seven years. Our global economy changes so fast, experience from 10 years ago is deemed to be so out of touch that it holds little, if any, weight with an employer.

So what happened to Karen? She discreetly made inquiries, as the healthcare world is small in most major cities. She wanted to move on before she was laid off and feared that if top management knew she was actively looking, she'd be the first to go. I reassured her that the bloody layoff that axed 55 top managers in one day created an environment where everyone who worked at the hospital was now job hunting (or at least should be).

Her contacts told her of a new managed care group that was just getting off the ground. She accepted their offer and negotiated a significant raise, too. She felt triumphant the day she resigned, and a week later 200 more people lost their jobs at her old hospital. She called me to say, "It could have been me. It wasn't, but it sure could have been!" She certainly was glad that she got out of there when she did. Karen went on to say her new job was a good fit, and she felt confident and happy with her choice.

# Resumé Components

"A well-thought-out resumé with a clear objective and summary statement that matches the position available in my company is impressive. Couple this with well-stated accomplishments or work experiences that highlight the person's strengths and abilities, and now you've got a resumé that will stand out," offers Josh, a personnel director for a prominent, national retail chain. The Goldmining Technique will create just that—the perfect resumé that touts the very best you have to offer that specific job. The technique will help you focus on creating concise but solid evidence that you can do the job well.

Every resumé has specific components that are all essential parts of your resumé. The top, or letterhead, must begin with your name, address, and home phone number. You can elect to also include your private e-mail address, as long as it's located on your home computer and not your company's system.

The next section lists your CAREER OBJECTIVE. This simply points out the job title you currently seek. Tina, a VP of human resources, stated: "I hate these long, flowing career objectives that are wordy and totally irrelevant. Just tell us the job title you're going after and forget the 'want to grow and blossom within your organization' nonsense." Many other employers agreed.

Simply use the job title alone as your career objective. You'll want to create a different resumé for each different job target. Many mid-career and senior professionals could qualify in numerous different areas. Soul search, select, and then concentrate on one or two. The career object should be concise, such as Events Planner, Brand Manager, or Nurse. At the very minimum, use "Position in Telecommunications Management" if you prefer not to declare a specific manager's area or title.

To many hiring managers the most important part of your resumé is your SUMMARY OF QUALIFICATIONS section. Adding this *triples* your impact. Employers reported that this was one of the very first areas they read. It's the highly influential summation of what you bring to the job. This section usually consists of four to six sentences that present an overview of your experience, talents, work habits, and skills. I never write a resumé without this section—it's much too valuable. You'll read about numerous examples later in this book to teach you how to create this critical section.

EDUCATION or PROFESSIONAL EXPERIENCE can follow. A general rule of thumb to follow is if your degree is less than five years old or you have an important credential (law degree, Ph.D.), then Education may follow the SUMMARY OF QUALIFICATIONS section. In all other cases, put it at the very bottom of the resumé.

PROFESSIONAL EXPERIENCE is the meat: your duties and accomplishments are all illustrated here. A major function of the seven-step Goldmining Technique I've developed is to allow you to pull out the most important aspects that matter to employers. WORK HISTORY might follow if you are using the Functional style.

COMPUTER SKILLS is one of the top skills employers want. We often give it its own heading.

I use the HONORS/AWARDS heading sparingly. I will only include those that specifically relate to the job target and are required skills. "Everything I ever won" can cloud out the biggies that matter to employers. "Treasurer of your school's PTA" has relevance if you seek an accounting position or one within a school, otherwise don't waste the space. Club and association memberships mean you've paid your dues. Unless you've been an officer or chaired an important committee in your profession, leave these memberships off.

Other possible headings include the following list.

RELATED TRAINING.   This may include volunteer or nondegree work (e.g., "Seminar on Preventing Sexual Harassment in the Workplace").

RELOCATION.   Be sure to state where or use "Willing to relocate as needed."

FOREIGN LANGUAGES.   For example, state "Fluent in French and German."

You can add a new section like this by just repeating the format style already used and outlined in the resumé. Place a new section closer to the bottom unless it is an essential asset to the job. For bilingual and international jobs, we will often add a FOREIGN LANGUAGE heading right before the PROFESSIONAL EXPERIENCE section.

# THE GOLDMINING TECHNIQUE

## 4

Thi*his is it!* The *big* Kahuna! This is the technique that will differenti-
ate you from the competition. You're about to learn an easy,
seven-step process that beefs up your resumé's content. We'll
probe for your most important accomplishments and skills. You'll uncover
hidden talents that you never realized you had. This technique will allow
you to document the important skills and on-the-job results that are so
influential in obtaining an interview. We know that this technique is
effective based on the success of hundreds of my clients *and* on what
employers told us they want to see on a resumé.

Colleen Kill, senior executive at Searle, said: "The best way to
impress me is to create a clear, easy-to-read resumé—generally on one
page. Accomplishments must be clearly stated which are applicable to
the job they are applying for." Helen, a department head at a large
insurance company, pointed out: "I want to see major accomplishments,
not just a list of skills. I want to know *exactly* what has the person
done with the skills he/she has." An executive recruiter added: "Easy to
read with *quantified* accomplishments clearly stated, that's what I want
to know."

The Goldmining Technique is used to achieve the goal of writing a
resumé that employers want to see and hire from. I originally developed
this technique to teach resumé writing in my seminars. I've received end-
less feedback on how this technique made the resumé writing process so
much easier and produced effective results. One participant told us: "Prior
to your resumé class, I never got an interview. You taught me how to pull
out many accomplishments I'd just generalized or never mentioned at all.

As a result of your seminar, I quickly got interviews and shortly there-after accepted a prominent new position." These resumés worked for thousands of clients and seminar participants. The Goldmining Technique was the key to creating the resumé.

This seven-step process is much easier to do than you'd expect. Here's all you need to get started: an old resumé or job description, or simply write out the jobs and duties you've held.

Now let's begin the Goldmining process.

## Step One

Define the job title. This goes under CAREER OBJECTIVE. For example,

Career Objective: Accountant

Career Objective: Assistant Store Manager

Career Objective: Sales Representative

Career Objective: Engineer

## Step Two

Write out your EDUCATION in the format that follows: degree first, the major can follow (but only if it's related to the job you wish to do), then college name, college city and state, and finally the year the degree was conferred. Always list your most advanced degree first.

Here are the five writing style options to choose from:

### Option #1: Abbreviation Style

J.D., Patent law, University of California, Berkeley 1994

M.S., Chemistry, University of Washington, Seattle 1989

B.A., Chemistry, University of Washington, Seattle 1988

### Option #2: Full Style

Bachelor of Science Degree, Seton Hall University, South Orange, NJ 2001

### Option #3: No Degree Style

There are two options: Eliminate an education section *or*

College coursework, Tampa Community College in Business Accounting with several computer classes

### Option #4: Enrolled in Classes Style

Either of these will work:

Master's Degree, Education, University of Nebraska, Omaha, presently attending

Bachelor's Degree, Psychology, Creighton University, Omaha, Nebraska, anticipated graduation, June 2003

### Option #5: Some Graduate Work and No Longer Enrolled Style

Graduate studies in Business Administration, Boston College, including human resource management and organizational development courses

## Step Three

Proceed to the PROFESSIONAL EXPERIENCE area.

From your old resumé or job description <u>underline</u> the important duties you've had that *specifically* relate to accomplishing the job duties in the career objective job title. Do this for all the jobs you've held, but be most thorough on your last five to seven years of employment.

## Step Four

We are still working on PROFESSIONAL EXPERIENCE.

Look at each underlined point in your professional experience. Ask yourself these questions: what did I do (ACTION) and what was the RESULT? ACTIONS = RESULTS. Big concept. ACTIONS = RESULTS—a very important concept when applied to your resume. Let's consider an example for a corporate controller. Suppose the controller has written down that he has strong computer skills. First, I'll define them: Excel, Lotus, databases, and Word. Then I asked him, "*What did you do with these soft-ware programs?*" His answer: "converted manual system to an auto-mated one." *What was saved—time or money?* This question is seeking to find the result. The response was "saved time and the conversion also allowed for the elimination of one staff position." Both ACTIONS had important RESULTS: a significant accomplishment the employer will surely notice. Go through this step for all your major points.

## Step Five

Now we need to write these points as they'll appear in the resumé. We incorporate both the ACTION and the RESULT to write the power statement. Here's our controller's:

- Converted general ledger from a manual to an automated system. Results eliminated one staff job, increased accuracy significantly.

## Step Six

Repeat steps three through five. Process all the points you've highlighted from your job or volunteer experiences. Now, incorporate the most impor-tant ones into your resumé.

## Step Seven

Review all the points you've written out. We need to have a clear idea of the important contributions and strengths you are bringing to the employer's job. We're ready to write your SUMMARY OF QUALIFICATIONS section.

Make a note now of what you believe to be the most important points needed to do the employer's job. This job analysis is a vital part of the process. Ask colleagues and hiring managers to provide you extra insight if it is not clear to you. Draw from your experience per-forming that job, your market research, and any inside information you may have obtained from your contacts. Let's continue with our controller example. We identified the following list as his biggest selling points.

Ten years experience

Computer skills

Public and private accounting

Negotiation skills

Strategic planning

Now write these points out in a few sentences and use no more than five or six. That's all the space you have to tell an employer about your skills. Nothing more. It's a brief summary that we want to create, one that will capture the employer's attention at first glance and get him to keep reading the entire resumé.

For our controller we wrote the following.

Ten years in senior financial management with proven expertise in strategic planning to lead companies into higher levels of profitability. Strong computer systems background having automated entire financial operations. Excel in vendor and bank negotiations with fluctuating, cyclical cash flow cycles. Able to develop cohesive and productive work teams.

*Here's an Important Tip.* Everything written in the resumé offers evidence that the candidate *can* do the job. The *focus* is always on filling the employer's needs and selling the skills to do just that.

To illustrate exactly how this process works, read on. In the next chapter, I've selected some client case studies that used the seven-step Goldmining process to write resumés that got them the interviews they wanted.

# SELLING YOU

## 5

T o help you see how this whole process works, I want you to pretend that you are a fly on the wall overhearing my coaching sessions. You'll experience how I work with clients just like yourself when we are writing their resumé together. One of the first things I tell a client is that we need to analyze the job you want to do. Next, we select your most marketable skills to do that job. "The best way to impress me," says Oris Barber, director of HR, "is to show that the time has been made to research our institution and its needs. Demonstrate that you will be an asset." Mary, an HR recruiter, added: "People must take the time to spell out the specific accomplishments. Don't gloss over your background, or you'll never stand out." I've selected six case studies from my clients which cover a wide range of circumstances and offer some important insights into the resumé writing process. You'll see exactly how The Goldmining Technique uncovers the influential facts and accomplishments that employers want to see and notice.

## *Goldmining Technique Resumés*

### Scott Purchaser's Success Story

Scott was ambitious and had sacrificed a great deal to earn his MBA by taking classes at night and on weekends. When he completed his degree, he experienced a very neutral and anticlimactic response from his current employer. As so often happens when you are working at a job while attending college, the performance improvements are gradual, and thus the employer doesn't leap to promote you the day you are conferred with the new degree. In fact, the employer is often happy with you doing the job you currently have. In Scott's case, he grew distressed when his current employer failed to advance him during the two years after he completed his MBA. His discouragement, though, led to a new determination to move on.

Scott started to job hunt. He'd answered over 100 newspaper ads over a one-year period but never got an interview. The problem was that Scott's old resumé was a very poor representation of himself. He came to see me and once we rewrote it, Scott's talents and accomplishments were immediately apparent to employers resulting in interviews from prominent companies including Microsoft and B.F. Goodrich. I've included Scott's old resumé and outlined the problems it contained. This will allow you to compare the two. I've also repeated some of my counseling session with Scott. You'll be able to overhear that session and to see exactly what the Goldmining process accomplished for him. His new, more appealing, resumé was the end result of our session and the advertisement that finally got employers to stand up and notice him.

**OLD**

# SCOTT PURCHASER
126 Southeast 95th Street
St. Louis, Missouri 63111
Home: 555-0111 • Work: 555-2777

## EDUCATION

MASTER BUSINESS ADMINISTRATION • Washington University, St. Louis, Missouri • 1997

BACHELOR OF ARTS • Economics • University of Missouri • Columbia, Missouri • 1988

## WORK EXPERIENCE

SENIOR BUYER • MCDONNELL DOUGLAS AEROSPACE • 1993 - PRESENT
Manage $25 million in contracts. Responsible for supplier quality, schedule and cost compliance. Negotiate terms, conditions and pricing. Manage foreign supplier base in England, France, and Russia. Duties include overseas travel, supplier evaluation, import and export restrictions, foreign exchange, banking and payment terms. APICS training, statistical process control familiarization as well as exposure and utilization of McDonnell Douglas' Total Quality Management techniques. Extensive use of both mainframe and personal computer systems.

INDUSTRIAL ENGINEER • MCDONNELL DOUGLAS AEROSPACE • 1990 - 1993
Experience included production control, scheduling, factory capacity and load analysis, manpower forecasting, floor layout, work measurement, capital asset planning, budgeting, and variance analysis.

INSURANCE SALES REPRESENTATIVE • GUARANTEE MUTUAL LIFE •
1989 - 1990

## PROFESSIONAL STRENGTHS

Strong project management and organizational skills. Ability to communicate effectively with broad range of business functions in an advanced procurement process: engineering, operations, manufacturing, contract management, finance, and business systems. Self starter and highly motivated.

## ACTIVITIES

Golf • Hunting • Fishing • Tennis • Weight Lifting • University of Missouri's Football Team
1984 - 1987

## REFERENCES

Available upon request.

The following list highlights some problems with Scott's *old* resumé.

✔ *No career objective.*   The degree alone suggests entry-level work, and Scott had progressed way beyond that.

✔ *Needs a summary of qualifications.*   His professional strengths were too weak and buried under his insurance experience.

✔ *Lacked substance.*   He mostly gave just a laundry list of the job duties he'd handled, probably taken directly off his personnel records. He had only one fact, "manage $25 million in contracts," for substance.

✔ *Activities were worthless.*   They didn't demonstrate he could do the job. He hadn't played college football for more than 10 years—it had no relevance whatsoever. In fact, since his resumé was so short, it almost seemed like he was more interested in free time than work contributions. This was far from the truth. Scott's a hard worker, but this activity emphasis and light content gave the employer a different idea.

✔ *References available.*   All employers know this, making that line outdated and unnecessary.

✔ *Did not emphasize his advanced degree.*   Scott's MBA was pointed out only in his education section. A strong credential, we added it to his name for a powerful emphasis on his new resumé.

✔ *Work phone number and no area code.*   Not every employer is in your own backyard, so always use your area code. It's also not wise to have potential employers call you at your current job. You might not get the message, others could learn of your job hunting, and it advertises that you'll waste work time on personal stuff. List only your home phone number. And do be sure that the answering machine has a professional message on it that is suitable for employers to hear.

✔ *Forgot his email.*

Here's how the Goldmining process helped Scott create a far superior resumé to the one he started out with. I've italicized the important questions that got Scott to offer the necessary details and proof that the Goldmining process is meant to uncover.

Not far into our coaching session, Scott began to understand all the weaknesses in his old resumé. He realized that he had failed to show actions that produce measurable or important results. I encouraged him to *talk about what he did.* He brought up the contract negotiations he handled. So I asked him, *"Exactly what did you do?"* He replied that he "had developed a team on a $50 million contract for a new international supplier." *"What happened as a result of that?"* He responded by saying that he "had negotiated the final new contracts."

I continued to ask, *"Did you save any money?"* He came back with a quick *yes! "How much?"* I asked. Scott wasn't too sure, so I told him we needed to figure it out. We did a calculation or two, and he later checked his work records to verify that the action saved $7.5 million. *"Were there any more results from your efforts?"* I asked. "Yeah, we improved the service and quality as well." This was then written into his third bulleted point under the Operation Management/Program Management title:

- Developed a team to deal with a $50 million contract with a new international supplier including all engineering, manufacturing, delivery, and pricing requirements. Resulted in improved quality, more efficient service and reduced costs. Negotiated final contract with total savings of $7.5 million.

Continuing, I asked Scott in exact dollar terms, *how much had he purchased for his company.* "$100 million in parts," he replied. *"From whom?"* I said. "Twenty domestic and international suppliers." I then asked if he *ever got the company a better deal.* "All the time," he replied. When I asked *"How?"* he answered, "I negotiated." *"What exactly?"* I asked. He replied, "terms, delivery, and better distribution." *"Did this result in saving anything or improving anything?"* Now Scott got very excited. He now began to realize his true value to employers! "Yes!" he exclaimed. "I figure I saved $4 million plus improved cycle time and lowered inventory." Then we documented these points.

- Purchased $100 million in parts from over 20 domestic and international suppliers. Negotiated better prices, improved quality, improved delivery, better terms, faster distribution, and volume discounts. Results yielded $4 million in savings, reduced inventory 15%, and improved cycle time 25%.

We also found some important skills missing from the *old* resumé. Computer skills, vital on his job, were not even mentioned in his old version. When I asked if he had any computer experience, I found that Scott indeed had excellent computer abilities. He assumed everybody did, so he didn't bother to include them on the old resumé. What he learned from me was that computer skills are tops with employers, so we emphasized an entire section to point his out. Here's what we wrote.

### Computer Skills

Proficient abilities on LAN, mainframe, and PC Network environments. Experience using Windows, Excel, Lotus, Word, Internet/World Wide Web, customized accounting, and project management software. Converted manual systems to computerized spreadsheets. Established an electronic data transfer system between company and international suppliers.

Now let's look at the *new* resumé. You'll see an amazing difference, and so did employers, because this new resumé instantaneously got him an interview.

**COMBINATION**
# NEW

## Scott Purchaser, MBA

126 Southeast 95th Street
St. Louis, Missouri 63111
(314) 555-0111
scottmoneyguy@msn.com

CAREER OBJECTIVE: **Purchasing Manager**

### SUMMARY OF QUALIFICATIONS

Extensive operations and purchasing management experience for international manufacturer with proven expertise in re-engineering processes and productivity enhancements, with implemented cost savings that directly impact the bottomline.

### EDUCATION

*Masters, Business Administration,* Washington University, 1997

*Bachelor of Arts,* Economics, University of Missouri, 1988

### PROFESSIONAL EXPERIENCE

*International Contract Administrator,* McDonnell Douglas Aerospace, 1990–Present
*(Promoted from Buyer. Promoted from Industrial Engineer.)*

### Operations Management/Program Management

- Purchasing department's representative on pilot Manufacturing Business Unit program implementing Just-In-Time manufacturing.
- Managed the daily operations dealing with two international suppliers including: delivery, cost analysis, quality assurance, contract negotiations, policies and procedures compliance, training, logistical coordination, financial accounting management and liaison support.
- Developed a team to deal with a $50 million contract with a new international supplier including all engineering, manufacturing, delivery and pricing requirements. Resulted in improved quality, more efficient service and reduced costs. Negotiated final contract with total savings of $7.5 million.
- Team contributor on the re-engineering process implementing total quality management.
- Analyzed part rejection process. Developed and implemented new system that reduced part rejection rate by $250,000 annually.

### Purchasing/Contract Negotiations

- Purchased $100 million in parts from over 20 domestic and international suppliers. Negotiated better prices, improved quality, improved delivery, better terms, faster distribution and volume discounts. Results yielded $4 million in savings, reduced inventory 15% and improved cycle time 25%.
- Implemented new purchasing system: staff training on contract negotiations, policies and procedures.
- Key team contributor with finance, MIS, and quality assurance organizations creating a cost-of-procurement model to more efficiently screen suppliers and gross margins. Implemented this process within the purchasing department to more accurately predict overall costs.

### COMPUTER SKILLS

Proficient abilities on LAN, mainframe, and PC Network environments. Experience using Windows, Excel, Lotus, Word, World Wide Web, Internet and customized accounting and project management software. Converted manual systems to computerized spreadsheets. Established an electronic data transfer system between company and international suppliers.

It's important to ask yourself questions to clarify your results. By asking Scott probing questions, we were able to compile a better resumé. Definitive questions (e.g., how much?, how many?) are the effective process by which to apply The Goldmining Technique and write your significant points. You can see an amazing difference if you backtrack now and look at Scott's old resumé (p. 77) and his new one (p. 81). You can clearly see *why* employers started to notice Scott once he'd applied The Goldmining Technique. Not only did he get interviews, but he also got a top-notch job offer from one of the top U.S. companies! Additionally, he had passed around his new resumé at his current employer. Word leaked out that he'd gotten a job offer, and *Scott found himself being offered two very good jobs* right inside his own company. What a difference a good resumé makes!

## Cindy Pharmacist's Success Story

Cindy had spent almost 20 years at one hospital. As the '90s began to rock the healthcare industry, the changes at Cindy's job became intolerable with lots of weekends and rotating shifts, even nights. Cindy was downright terrified to look for a job since working at this hospital was all she'd ever known. After I helped her husband find a better job, she convinced herself that there just might be something better out there for her. A big concern to Cindy, though, was still wanting a part-time position, since she was a working mother.

Cindy began talking to her colleagues and heard about a potential opening. She wanted my help to prepare a better resumé to apply for a specific part-time job that sounded very appealing. That's when we wrote her new resumé. It worked! The very first resumé she submitted got her an interview for what she deemed would be the perfect job. It was part-time, day hours, with just an occasional Saturday morning. It even offered a higher salary than her current position. She prepared for the interview incorporating the major points we'd added to her resumé, and *yes indeed, she did get that job!* Think about it, *Cindy only sent out that one resumé and landed the position!* That is substantiated proof that this process really works.

Now let's examine her old resumé, the Goldmining process, and the new resumé that helped win her that new job.

**OLD**

**PROFILE**
**CINDY PHARMACIST**
7722 120th Place S.E.
San Francisco, California
Telephone: (510) 555-4332
cindyp@earthlink.net

## EDUCATION

1985    Bachelor of Science in Pharmacy Degree, High Honors
Medical College of Virginia
Richmond, Virginia

## EMPLOYMENT HISTORY

1995-Present                              Children's Hospital Medical Center

**Position:** Staff Pharmacist practicing in the following areas of this 671 bed Medical Center: bone marrow transplant inpatient and outpatient satellite pharmacies, Central outpatient and take-home pharmacy, and Tumor Institute satellite pharmacy.

**Responsibilities:** Serves as the unofficial lead pharmacist of the bone marrow transplant outpatient pharmacy; assuring its smooth operation and relationship with the University Cancer Research Center Outpatient Department.

**Overall:** "Distinguished Performance" in every annual evaluation; received numerous merit raises as a result.

1991 - 1995                              Children's Hospital Medical Center

**Position:** Investigational Drug Coordinator/Staff Pharmacist

**Responsibilities:** Established and managed all Investigational Drug Service activities of the Hospital and the California Oncology Group, with duties including: Institutional Review Board Membership, drug acquisition, drug dispersal, and maintenance of investigational drug patient profiles.

## SPECIAL PROJECTS

*** Serves on the BMT Discharge Planning Committee, an interdisciplinary board responsible for developing policies and procedures for discharging BMT patients from inpatient units and monitoring their outpatient care.
*** Obtained Board of Pharmacy approval for Pharmacist Refill Prescriptive Authority for pharmacists staffing the BMT outpatient satellite pharmacy.
*** Implemented the "just in time" inventory control system for all bone marrow transplant satellite pharmacies.
*** Developed and published the I.V. drug/total parenteral nutrition compatibility manual for Children's Hospital.

## OTHER STAFF PHARMACIST POSITION

1985-1991 Medical College of Virginia Hospital, Richmond, Virginia

Problems with Cindy's *old* version follow.

✔ *Style was old-fashioned and dated.* This resumé looked like it was done on a typewriter, though it wasn't. Just changing the format added a lot to the projection of Cindy as a candidate. Putting the word *Profile* or *Resumé* at the top also projected a very dated look. These words simply are not necessary.

✔ *Needed a career objective.* By adding *Pharmacist* to the resumé, it easily told people the exact job she wanted.

✔ *No summary of qualifications made her background weak.* She didn't exploit the fact that she's worked in numerous department areas, which is a big benefit to most hospitals who need part-timers to fill in. The *distinguished performance* would catch a manager's eye, but it needed to be written up front in the summary, not buried in the middle of her resumé.

✔ *Other staff pharmacist position.* This was so long ago (1979) that we didn't need to even mention it.

✔ *Distracting to break up the jobs she had over her 20 years at the hospital.* In fact, it looked like she'd been at two jobs and that the special projects were a part of the 1981–1985 experience. That would be too long ago to hold much weight with a prospective employer. This wasn't accurate, as it was experience acquired over her entire tenure.

**WHAT THE GOLDMINING PROCESS UNCOVERED FOR CINDY**

We incorporated the job tasks and special projects together. At the start, Cindy insisted that she had *no accomplishments* she was just *a pharmacist.* It was a challenge for her to see anything of value. So, my first question was *to get a simple laundry list* to show an employer the range of experience she's had. Since many hospitals now hire part-time professionals to fill in where there are work overloads, the diversity she'd acquired would be a big selling point. We wrote the following when I asked her to *list everywhere she'd worked in the hospital.*

• Performed pharmacist duties for one of the region's leading hospitals with experience in ambulatory/outpatient, bone marrow transplant, investigational drugs, I.V. therapy, inpatient, and oncology.

I told Cindy that we should just include her special projects into the body of the experience. She agreed. I then asked her: "After filling prescriptions, *what is the most important thing you've done?*" She said, "writing policy and procedures and training other pharmacists." We then highlighted her policy work with four specific bulleted points. These came to light when she answered the following questions.

1. Give me a specific, important example.

2. Can you think of another?

3. Any more?

When I asked about *the training she had done,* she quickly said, "I wasn't in the training department." I replied, "*Does the training department teach the new pharmacists?*" "No," she said, "I do." "*So how many people have you taught over the years?*" Cindy wasn't sure exactly how many she had helped over the years. So I asked *whether there was one a week.* "No." "*Did you teach one a month?*" "More like every other month." So we calculated out the number of years and determined that she had trained at least 75. We illustrated this in the following bulleted point.

- Trained 75+ pharmacists and pharmacy technicians in operational and clinical policies and procedures.

Finally, *I questioned her computer ability.* "Oh yes," she replied. "I do use the computer a great deal on my job." We made special note of her computer skills, as an extensive part of her job involves so much data entry and retrieval. It was so important that we created a special section to highlight these abilities to employers.

### Computer Skills

Proficient skills with personal, mini and mainframe computers, using many programs that include customized pharmacy software, ASTRA third party billing, Micromedex, Word, Excel, plus others. Daily use of computer systems to process prescription orders, unit-dose orders, I.V. orders, access drug information data banks, acquire drugs, and maintain patient records.

Note how the Goldmining process has created major improvements in Cindy's *new* resumé, because the first employer she sent it to called her in for an interview and then offered her the job.

# Cindy Pharmacist

7722 120th Place S.E.
San Francisco, CA 94105
(510) 555-4332
cindyp@earthlink.net

CAREER OBJECTIVE: **Pharmacist**

## SUMMARY OF QUALIFICATIONS

Twenty years working as an efficient, well organized hospital pharmacist in numerous areas including: ambulatory/outpatient, bone marrow transplant, investigational drugs, I.V. therapy, oncology and inpatient. Established pharmacy policies, procedures, and protocols while setting up new services. Excellent interpersonal skills dealing with both patients and medical staff. Repeatedly recognized in annual evaluations for *distinguished performance.*

## PROFESSIONAL EXPERIENCE

*Pharmacist,* Children's Medical Center, San Francisco, CA, 1991–Present

- Performed pharmacist duties for one of the region's leading hospitals with experience in ambulatory/outpatient, bone marrow transplant, investigational drugs, I.V. therapy, inpatient, and oncology.
- Established the Hospital's Investigational Drug Service; responsible for assessing, evaluating and writing policies and procedures; developed drug tracking system; served on Institutional Review Board for five years.
- Served on the bone marrow transplant discharge planning committee that established policies and procedures to efficiently discharge patients from inpatient to outpatient.
- Trained 75+ pharmacists and pharmacy technicians in operational and clinical policies and procedures.
- Wrote and implemented California State Board of Pharmacy Pharmacist Refill Prescriptive Authority Protocol for bone marrow transplant outpatient satellite pharmacy.
- Published I.V. Drug/Total Parenteral Nutrition Compatibility charts for nursing and pharmacy staff.

## COMPUTER SKILLS

Proficient skills with personal, mini and mainframe computers, using many programs that include customized pharmacy software, ASTRA third party billing, Micromedex, Word, Excel plus others. Daily use of computer systems to process prescription orders, unit-dose orders, I.V. orders, access drug information data banks, acquire drugs, and maintain patient records.

## EDUCATION

Bachelor of Science, Pharmacy Degree, *High Honors,* 1985
Medical College of Virginia, Richmond Virginia

## Evelyn Counselor's Success Story

Evelyn had stopped working when she had her family nearly 16 years ago. At 40, she had just finished a master's program. Armed with mostly intern and volunteer experience, she began to job hunt. The college had passed out a sheet on writing resumés so Evelyn created the old resumé. It got her no interviews. That's when she came to see me. The Goldmining Technique helped her obtain interviews, including one that landed her a plum counseling position.

**OLD**

## EVELYN COUNSELOR
21135 32nd Avenue South
Columbus, Ohio 66666
(201) 555-0111

EDUCATION:      M.A., Psychology: Antioch University, 2002
                          B.A., Psychology, University of Ohio, 1998

FIELD EXPERIENCE:

**Neighborhood Clinic, Columbus (March 2002-Present)**
- Counseled diverse population at free clinic.
- Referred clients to community resources.

**Catholic Community Services, Columbus (September 2001-August 2002)**
- Counseled diverse population in Counseling and Consultation Program.
- Treated clients with issues including depression, personality disorders, anger, PTSD, adjustment disorders, sexual abuse, physical abuse, emotional abuse, domestic violence, eating disorders, marital difficulties, phobias, identity, and suicide issues.
- Presented cases in bi-monthly case consultation groups with Psychiatrist and Psychologist.

**Literacy Tutor (November 2000-August 2002)**
- Participated in 12 hours of training for work with adult nonfunctional readers/writers.
- Taught reading/writing skills weekly, using non-shame based methods.
- Assisted in empowerment process of individuals by focusing on students' strengths and empathetically working on areas of difficulty.

**Mental Health Institute (July 1999)**
- Assisted with Older Adult Services support groups.
- Listened/cooked/traveled in outings with older adults seeking treatment for a variety of disorders, including major depression, phobias, manic-depression, and schizophrenia.

**Angeline's Day Center for Women (July 1999)**
- Monitored multicultural homeless population with high potential for violence.
- Actively listened to consumers with personal issues or conflicts.
- Diffused violent outbursts negotiated conflicts. Modeled social skills.
- Educated and referred consumers to available social services.

**Rape Relief - Crisis Line Counselor (1998)**
- Participated in 80 hours of training.
- Counseled persons in crisis due to sexual violence.
- Clients consisted of teenagers, adults, senior citizens, gay/lesbians.
- Implemented supportive, caring relationships.
- Honored individual healing processes.
- Listened to client concerns, encouraged disclosure through comfortable relationships.
- Validated client feelings.
- Supported client in synthesizing thoughts into action plan. Guided toward healthy solutions.
- Educated friends/partners of victim, case workers for developmentally disabled.

RELATED LIFE EXPERIENCE

- Death/dying.
- Divorce/remarriage/step-parenting.
- Recovery through intensive physical therapy.
- Understand value of counseling through personal experience.
- One year of travel, including third world countries: US/Central-South America/Europe.
- Life experience is integrated: no overidentification with client.

Note the main problems with Evelyn's *old* version.

✔ *Related life experience: poor substitute for work experience.* Evelyn's life section incorporated potential counseling issues, but would have been better used in context within a cover letter applying the particular background to the employer's group and needs. And when I read the *Death/dying* bullet I stopped to think, does this mean she's dead or dying? Obviously not, but it sure looked that way to me.

✔ *Lacked both the summary of qualifications and career objective.* These are vital and mandatory to really bring out your experience and talents. Notice the impact they make on Evelyn's new resumé.

✔ *Too many short jobs.* Evelyn originally used the Chronological format but it had six jobs, and two with only one month of experience. This would have really been a negative to employers. Switching to the functional format achieved a great deal in building a more solid experience picture. We were able to focus on skills and experience to allow her to look like a stronger candidate and not announce that she was an amateur in her new field.

### WHAT THE GOLDMINING PROCESS DID FOR EVELYN

First, I switched formats to the Functional style. This allowed me the latitude to draw off what experience she had acquired to better demonstrate her solid training and ability as a counselor.

My first questions to Evelyn were: "*What kind of counseling do you do?*" "*Who is the population you work with?*" "*What counseling issues have you dealt with?*"

Evelyn's answers allowed us to write her first two bullets.

• Good exposure dealing one-on-one with a diverse population and wide range of clientele from teenagers to older adults.

• Maintained a caseload of clients, effectively assisting individuals with depression, anger, loss, marital problems, suicide, domestic violence, chemical abuse, child abuse, personality disorders. Very low no-show rates.

Since most of Evelyn's work was with community clinics, I asked her *to be more specific about what she actually did at her internships.* "I counseled," she said. "*Two people?*" I asked. "Oh no," she said, "I worked with over 100 at the Rape Center." "*How many hours of counseling was it?*" After a minute she said, "225." This was important because it showed that Evelyn had a lot of experience dealing with acute trauma problems.

I told her that looking at her old resumé, I saw two areas: *counseling* and *outreach.* She agreed. Her illiteracy work, child protective services experience, and her office administration skills came out when I repeatedly asked: *"Tell me what you did . . . as a literacy tutor, . . . as an office administrator."*

I also asked Evelyn *if she'd done any record keeping.* Employers and every other counselor know that paperwork is an important part of the job. Indeed she had, so we incorporated it into a bulleted statement that added to her depth as a counselor.

- Coordinated office administration, budgeting, organized work flow and schedules, supervised staff, trained employees on computer system usage for governmental agency over five year period.

Finally, Evelyn needed a SUMMARY OF QUALIFICATIONS. When we were all done with her PROFESSIONAL EXPERIENCE, we reviewed what we had written.
We selected her top selling points.

✔ Experience with diverse clientele

✔ Broad exposure to counseling issues

✔ Able to counsel others using eclectic approach

✔ Ability to make assessments and diagnoses

✔ Committed to helping people improve their lives

Goldmining really helped Evelyn understand her skills and abilities as they relate to a prospective employer. From all the self-discovery during this process, she became much clearer in her thinking about exactly what she had to sell an employer. Her *new* resumé impressed employers and helped *Evelyn land a terrific job.*

**FUNCTIONAL**
**NEW**

# Evelyn Counselor
21135 32nd Avenue South
Columbus, Ohio 66666
(201) 555-0111

CAREER OBJECTIVE: **Case Manager**

### SUMMARY OF QUALIFICATIONS

Broad exposure to numerous counseling issues working with diverse clientele. Able to make accurate diagnoses and assessments and provide comfortable environment where individuals make changes. Use eclectic therapeutic approach plus outreach and community referrals to aid individuals either in therapy or in crisis environments. Committed to helping individuals change and improve the quality of their lives.

### PROFESSIONAL EXPERIENCE

## Counseling
- Good exposure dealing one-on-one with a diverse population and wide range of clientele from teenagers to older adults.
- Maintained a case load of clients, effectively assisting individuals with depression, anger, loss, marital problems, suicide, domestic violence, chemical abuse, child abuse, personality disorders. Very low no-show rates.
- Counseled, 225 hours, individuals calling rape crisis line, providing acute intervention.
- Manned drop-in medical clinic for DSHS, homeless, welfare, low income individuals offering counseling, referrals, interventions and outreach.
- Provided anger management counseling for men involved in domestic violence.

## Outreach
- Worked with Child Protective Services issuing child abuse reports on clients.
- Taught illiterate adults basic reading and writing skills over two year period.
- Coordinated office administration, budgeting, organized work flow and schedules, supervised staff, trained employees on computer system usage for governmental agency over five year period.

### WORK HISTORY

*Counselor Volunteer,* Neighborhood Clinic, Columbus, March, 2002–Present

*Intern,* Catholic Community Services, Columbus, September, 2001–August 2002

*Literacy Tutor,* County Multiservice Center, Nov. 2000–Dec. 2002

*Counselor Volunteer,* Mental Health Institute, Angeline's Day Center for Women, Rape Relief, October, 1997–August, 1999

*Office Administrator,* Metro, Columbus, OH, September, 1990–September, 1996

### EDUCATION

Master of Arts, Psychology, Antioch University, 2002
Bachelor of Arts, Psychology, University of Ohio, Columbus, 1998

## Tracy Program Manager's Success Story

Tracy had spent 10 years working for a professional association. She excelled at her job and brought her department into major prominence within the association. Tracy enjoyed her position, and although she'd discussed writing a resumé, she never seemed to get around to doing it. In fact, she didn't have one and, without a burning need, was a little overwhelmed at the thought of writing a resumé. Then one day she had a call from a colleague telling her about a position. He encouraged her to apply. Tracy was about to dismiss it because she had no resumé, until she learned it paid nearly $20,000 more than her current job. The new position was similar in scope to her current one, so she decided to go for it. She called me. Tracy had no resumé to work from; prior to our meeting, she wrote a brief job description of her duties.

She handed me the following list to begin our session.

### CPE Director

- Manage the CPE (Continuing Professional Education) Department
- Supervised CPE staff
- Coordinated all classes, contract with instructors
- Coordinate state and regional conferences
- Active in NYSAE and Convention Management Association

It wasn't much to start with. I've included her case to clearly illustrate exactly how powerful The Goldmining Technique is.

I gave Tracy the Skill Area list (see Chapter 8), and together we identified three areas that her job comprised: event planning, program development, and administration. The choice for formatting style was easy; all 10 years she'd been at one job, so Combination was the clear one to use. To begin any resumé, I usually start out with my first bullet providing a good overview on the depth of the job and its responsibilities. You can ask yourself exactly what I asked Tracy: "*Describe what you do for the organization.*" "Manage the professional continuing education department." "*How big is it?*" I asked. "8,700 members." "*How much revenue do you bring in?*" Here's where Tracy had really underestimated her value. She replied, "You mean today or when I first started?" "Both," I answered. "Well let's see," she went on, "it was about $1 million when I joined; now we're at $2.4 million." This was significant information. My next question allowed us to create her opening bullets. I asked, "*What did you do to generate that major increase?*" The answers to the above questions formulated these three bulleted statements.

- Managed the entire professional continuing education program for state association serving 8,700 members with annual revenues of $2.4 million.

- Doubled program revenues from $1.2 to $2.4 million by implementing new training programs; new marketing options; satellite programs; developed curriculum, adding self-study programs, corporate needs-based classes, and joint partnerships; plus new marketing/sales campaigns and sales programs to other state associations.

- Tripled course offerings from 120 to a current selection of 400+ classes. Expanded the professional and business operation classes to more adequately meet members' needs with educational options that included breakfast roundtables, technical forums, conferences, full-day, mini sessions, staff training, and extended classes.

Continuing, I asked Tracy: "*How big was her staff?*" "*How large were her budgets?*" "*Who did all the annual schedules and planning?*"

She mentioned that she handled all the vendors, hotel, and speaker contracts. I asked, "*Who negotiated them?*" "I do," she replied. So I asked, "*How many contracts have you handled?*" "A lot," she replied. When I prompted her to *give me a figure,* she said over 500, and I made a note of it. I praised her on the terrific job she had done and told her that she would be a very impressive and qualified candidate with her new resumé.

We continued to discuss all the event planning she had done. Again, she had made impressive contributions. I was about to end our session (because I had all the major bullets done), when I asked one final question: "*Have you won any major awards, or are you involved in any professional associations in a leadership role?*" Was I in for a pleasant surprise! Tracy had been one busy lady. She was president of two leading associations in her field and had won a national award of Meeting Planner of the Year. Wow! Not only did we add an AWARDS AND HONORS section, but also Tracy had just given me the opening lead for her SUMMARY OF QUALIFICATIONS:

Award winning state continuing education director . . .

That certainly would prompt attention. And it did. Let's see the results.

> **Editorial Note: Original resumé all appeared on one page**

# Tracy Program Manager
1 Main Street
City, NY 11111
(201) 555-0111
tracypm@aol.com

CAREER OBJECTIVE: **Director of Continuing Legal Education**

## SUMMARY OF QUALIFICATIONS

Award winning state continuing professional education director that doubled profitability while increasing annual revenues from $1.2 to $2.4 million. Recognized for innovative programming, curriculum development and marketing expertise.

## PROFESSIONAL EXPERIENCE

*Director of Continuing Professional Education,* New York Society of CPAs,
New York, 1993–Present

### Program Development
- Managed the entire professional continuing education program for state association serving 8,700 members with annual revenues of $2.4 million.
- Doubled program revenues from $1.2 to $2.4 million by implementing new training programs, new marketing options, satellite programs, developed curriculum, adding self-study programs, corporate needs-based classes, and joint partnerships, plus new marketing/sales campaigns and sales programs to other state associations.
- Tripled course offerings from 120 to current selection of 400 classes. Expanded professional and business operation classes to more adequately meet members needs with options that included breakfast roundtables, technical forums, conferences, full day, mini sessions, staff training, extended classes.

### Administration
- Supervised staff of 7, plus 150 professional committee members including training and team building.
- Managed $2.4 M budget. Negotiated 500 major conference facility contracts, vendor/speaker contracts.
- Developed annual strategic plans and marketing plans.
- Coordinated expansive computer systems upgrades that improved both productivity and accuracy on continuing professional education records, sales and registration areas.

### Event Planning
- Planned and coordinated 30+ national and multi-state regional conferences plus 220 state conferences including: facilities negotiations, speaker selection and fee negotiation, marketing, advertising, promotions, manual/classroom material reproduction, registration, on-site program coordination, volunteer staffing, site selection, catering, lodging, travel, and program evaluations.
- Scrutinized all classes/programs evaluations, implemented changes to maximize member satisfaction. Achieved national recognition as one of the country's top five state continuing education program.

### AWARDS AND HONORS

*President,* New York Society of Association Executives, 1998
*President,* Chapter of Professional Convention Management Association, 2000–2001
*President's Award,* New York Society of Association Executives, 2000
*Meeting Planner of the Year,* National Speaker's Association, 1999–2000
*Chairman,* National American Institute of CPAs Conference on Education, 1998

### EDUCATION

Bachelor's Degree, Regents College, Albany, New York, presently attending
Associate Degree, Business, City Community College, New York, 1993
Certified Meeting Professional, 1999
American Society of Association Executives Education Certificate Program, 1992
Institute for Organizational Management Certificate, 2002

Tracy was called for a screening telephone interview with the association's director days after her resumé arrived.* They were impressed, and she was asked in for an interview. She did well. They called for a final interview; just two candidates remained. And as interested as they were in Tracy, that interview put serious doubts in her mind about them. The director repeatedly said that they didn't care about member service, it wasn't an important priority to them, but it was to Tracy. He also didn't really want any innovation. He didn't want to change their program and felt it was good the way it was. Tracy felt strongly that new ideas were one of her major contributions. She was shocked and unsettled. She couldn't really believe what she was hearing. Tracy knew that innovation and change are the only way to keep these educational programs attracting new members and satisfying the needs of the old. After all, there's tremendous competition for available seminars out there.

We discussed this in detail to put Tracy's feelings, values, and true desires in perspective. She came to realize that she already had the perfect job, and that she'd come to appreciate it in a new light. In her words, "Money isn't everything. When the price tag means giving up what you value and think is important, it's not worth it. I couldn't do it. I would have had to leave a job I loved to go to a place that would have been structured, rigid, and with limited creativity." So she called the director

*Because of typesetting restrictions, some resumés in this book have continued onto a second page. However, in virtually all instances, these resumés were submitted to employers in a single-page format.

she'd interviewed with and declined the final interview saying, "I'm very happy where I am."

Tracy reported that the whole experience rejuvenated her and her interest in her current job. It brought out new creativity, and she began to think that there was a lot of opportunity for growth in the job she had and realized that she had the power to create it. With renewed interest, she plowed happily forward. A few months later, *she got a promotion and a raise.*

## Craig Educator's Success Story

Craig came to see me because a back injury had endangered his job. He was a lieutenant who joined the Fire Department and spent almost his whole career there. When he'd hurt his back two years ago, the department had him serve in an administrative role. He recovered, but Craig's injury would forever prevent him from a 100% recovery, thus making him ineligible to be a fireman on active duty according to the Fire Department's personnel policy. He was thus told he would get a disability rating and lose his job.

Craig had taught a lot of education courses for the Fire Department and, faced with a career change, wanted to be a trainer. He loved the experience of teaching others. He had conducted numerous training programs and really wanted to move into education, since he was being forced out of his Fire Department job. He came to see me and asked me to look over his resumé.

**OLD**

# CRAIG EDUCATOR
1 Main Street
City, NY 11111
(201) 555-0111
ceducator@yahoo.com

## SUMMARY OF QUALIFICATIONS

### TEACHING EXPERIENCES

Bayside Community College Emergency Communication/Operations Support Program; Instructor, program development, and course developer.

Bayside Community College Fire Command Administration Program; Instructor, On-line Classes.

Records Management System component of DADECOM's CAD/RMS computer system; Instructor, course developer, and co-author of local user's manual.

Training department members in use of the CAD/RMS system and IBM PC software.

Post-hurricane Evaluation of Buildings instructor.

Certified CPR and First Aid Instructor.

Developing, preparing and conducting a wide range of training classes.

Certified as Hazardous Materials Awareness Level and Hazardous Materials Operations Level instructor.

Vocational - Technical Education Certificate, Bayside Community College.

### FIRE DEPARTMENT MANAGEMENT

Planning, coordinating, and directing the activities of the Operations Division as Acting Assistant Chief of Operations.

Preparing management reports and studies for the Fire Chief.

Preparing policies and standard operating guidelines for the Fire Chief.

Purchasing major and minor items of firefighting equipment and general supplies.

Serving as department Duty Chief at night and on weekends.

Participation in several labor contract negotiations.

### FIRE PREVENTION

Directing, monitoring, and coordinating the department's company-based commercial inspection program.

Performing company fire prevention inspections and re-inspections.

Conducting and coordinating department wide sprinkler system inspection program.

Directing department-wide pre-fire planning program.

Working with and assisting the Maps officer including work on converting the map program to a computer-based system.

### FISCAL MANAGEMENT

Performing budget preparation, analysis, and monitoring for the department.

Prepared general and individual specific wage and benefit comparisons.

Familiar with the use of purchase requisitions and purchase orders.

Preparing Fire Department's Capital Improvement Program proposal for facility contruction and vehicle purchases.

## SERVICE TO OTHER CITY DEPARTMENTS

Bloodborne Pathogen Exposure Control Plan, development and teaching of exposure control material to Police, Public Works, Parks and Aquatics staff.
Hazardous Materials Awareness Level Training for Police Department.
Emergency Management work conducting major revision of city of Miami Emergency Operations Plan and coordinating and conducting a city-wide hurricane drill.

## BOARD AND COMMITTEE EXPERIENCE

Bayside Community College Emergency Communication/Operations Support Program Advisory Board, Member.
Bayside School District #15 Fire Science Advisory committee, Chairman.
Disaster Educators of Puget Sound, Secretary/Treasurer.
Southwest Dade Public Safety Communications Agency (DADECOM) Records Management System (RMS) Committee.
Southwest Dade County Emergency Information Plan Committee.
City of Miami Safety Committee.

## EMPLOYMENT

| 1998 to Present | Bayside Community College |
| | 2000 68th Ave. W. |
| | Miami, Florida |
| | INSTRUCTOR |
| | Teaching and course development in Emergency Communication/Operations Support and Fire command Administration Programs. Program development work in Emergency Communication/Operations Support Program. |

| 1985 to Present | City of Miami Fire Department |
| | P.O. Box 5008 |
| | Miami, Florida 33333 |
| | LIEUTENANT |
| | Recently completed seven months as the Acting Assistant Fire Chief in charge of the Operations Division. Previously served as Training Officer, Administrative Assistant to the Fire Chief and Assistant Fire Chief. Also served as Company Officer supervising a five man engine company in routine work, emergency operations, and emergency medical work. |

## EDUCATION

| Present | Final Quarter, Western Florida State College, Open Learning Fire Service Program, Bachelor of Science Program in fire Service Administration. |
| 1982 | Associate of Technical Arts Degree in Fire Science, Bayside Community College. |
| 1978 | Electronic Data Processing Diploma, College of Technology and Commerce. |
| 1978 | United States Coast Guard Academy. |

Numerous professional classes and seminars (see attached sheet).

## CLASSES AND SEMINARS

National Fire Academy
    Incident Command II
    Interpersonal Dynamics Fire Service Organizations
    Organizational Theory and Practice
    Executive Information Planning
    Western Florida State College Representative to the 2000 Executive Fire Officer
        Symposium

Emergency Management Institute
    Emergency Operations Center/Incident Command System Interface
    Professional Development Program
        Problem-Solving and Decision-Making
        Leadership and Influencing
        Exercise Design

Washington State Fire Service Training Instructor Training Courses
    Elements of Instruction
    Manipulative Skills
    Preparation of Training Aids
    Emergency Vehicle Accident Prevention Endorsement

Vocational/Technical Education
    Elements of Teaching
    Occupational Analysis
    Vocational Course Development

Miscellaneous Classes
    Emergency Medical Technician
    Fire Service first Aid and Rescue
    Operation Support
    Emergency vehicle Accident Prevention
    Fire Incident Report System
    Firefighter Role in Fire Investigation
    LPG Firefighting
    Railroad Early Response
    Leadership and Human Relations
    BARS System Budgeting
    Hazardous Materials - Awareness and Operations Levels
    Incident Command System
    Meeting the Leadership Challenge in the Fire Service

Seminars
    How to Supervise People
    Strategy and Tactics
    Firefighter Survival
    Command School, 1994, 1995, 1996

The following list points out significant problems with Craig's *old* resumé.

✔ *Too long!*   Craig's resumé was three pages and not at all succinct to target the community college teaching job he wanted. This is a common mistake with long careers. Craig had listed *everything* he'd ever done plus every class he'd ever attended. It read more like a laundry list checking off the job duties than a powerful advertisement of his skills.

✔ *No results are listed.*   Craig's SUMMARY OF QUALIFICATIONS simply segmented all his job duties, and then he made a laundry list under each one. It lacked actions, results, and failed to identify any accomplishments. By selecting the Combination format, we greatly improved both the clarity and readability of his resumé.

✔ *No clear job focus.*   It was very unclear exactly what kind of job Craig wanted. Assuming the employer will take the time to decipher all his skills and figure out how they would apply to the employer's company is a big mistake. Craig needed to select a job objective and streamline the related data to support how he could do that job.

✔ *He took a zillion classes and seminars—so what?*   A full page of classes he's taken does not provide any substance to doing the job and performing the work. In the new resumé, we incorporate a statement under his EDUCATION to point out how Craig stays current in the field (which is the rationale for taking so many seminars and classes).

### THE GOLDMINING PROCESS FOR CRAIG EDUCATOR

What's important to remember is the need to eliminate the clutter of a lifetime career and draw attention to the skills vital to performing the desired job. I selected the Combination style since it would be easier to condense his experience. In Craig's case, we needed to stress his teaching abilities. He felt that he was perfect for the community college's new job in fire administration, but he faced stiff competition. One big obstacle was that he lacked his bachelor's degree, though he would finish it within the next few months. My first step with Craig was to evaluate the job duties that needed to be done. We came up with three major requirements.

• Teach fire and emergency management courses

• Advise students

• Develop curriculum

In essence, that was the entire job. So that's how we came up with the skill areas: *Instruction, Curriculum Development* and *Program/ Department Management.*

The education issue had to be addressed, as degrees are quite important in college teaching positions. I felt that we could best define his education by stating the following.

B.S. Fire Services Administration, Western Florida State College, June, 2001

This gave the resumé more weight, even though June was over two months off at that time.

He was skeptical that we could get all of his information onto one page. We discussed it, and he agreed that one page was the strategic preference. We went to work. Here are the key questions I asked him to allow us to create a better resumé on just one page: *"How many courses had you taught at the college?"* "Eleven," was his answer. *"Name them."* He did. Next, I asked about the job training of other firefighters that he'd done. *"How many classes did you teach?"* "A lot." *"I need a number,"* I continued. *"Count up the number in a month, then over the entire year. Now how many years and multiply the two numbers together."* The answer was over 200.

I then asked: *"Have you advised any students?"* *"How many?"* *"On what issues?"* With that topic covered, I went on to ask: *"Have you developed any new course curriculums?"* Indeed he had. Those specifics led to the content of our curriculum development section. Here's what Craig's *new* resumé looks like. *He beat out over 230 others to land the job!*

# Craig Educator
1 Main Street
City, NY 11111
(201) 555-0111
ceducator@yahoo.com

CAREER OBJECTIVE: **Instructor/Program Coordinator**

## SUMMARY OF QUALIFICATIONS

Extensive professional background in Fire Command, Administration, and Emergency Management. Developed curriculum, coordinated program and taught numerous college courses. Consistently received high teaching evaluations from all students and seminar participants. Advised hundreds of students on curriculum and course selection.

## PROFESSIONAL EXPERIENCE

*Instructor,* Bayside Community College, Miami, FL, 1998–Present
*Assistant Fire Chief/Lieutenant,* City of Miami Fire Department, 1985–2001

### Instruction
- Taught eleven community college courses for the Fire Command Administration and Emergency Communications programs including: Introduction to the Fire Service, Medical Terminology for Dispatchers, Emergency Communications Internship, Fire Protection Systems, and Building Construction.
- Taught 200+ classes for Fire, Police, City Staff, and Community Participants. Topics included: Hazardous Materials Awareness, Bloodborne Pathogens, Firefighting Training, Emergency Preparedness, CPR/First Aid, and various computer software programs.
- Coordinated the Emergency Communications internship program including development and supervision of placements.
- Served as an academic advisor for the Emergency Communications program.

### Curriculum Development
- Developed six new community college Fire Command Administration and Emergency Communications courses including new on-line delivery system as well as establishment of new Emergency Communications program.
- Created new Fire Department Administration training program.

### Program/Department Management
- Planned, coordinated, and directed the operations and administration for a local Fire Department.

## EDUCATION

B.S., Fire Services Administration, Western Florida State College, June, 2002
A.T.A., Fire Science, Bayside Community College, 1982
50+ classes of Technical Training on Fire Command from the National Fire Academy, Emergency Management Institute and others

# *Summary*

You can easily understand how employers *reacted* to these clients' new resumés. They are clear and offer specific details that truly address the needed duties of the job. The probing question and job analysis is very important to uncover your forgotten or unstated achievements. My clients all discovered how to analyze their jobs looking for both ACTIONS and RESULTS. Each one landed a better job, except Tracy who turned down the option to move on. Still her new vitality at her old job quickly turned into a promotion. Goldmining is an exciting self-discovery process.

Another benefit of this process is that you become clearer on what to tell employers in your interviews. By illustrating how your actions achieved specific (and positive) results you are persuading the employer that *you* are the one they must hire.

As you read through the next chapter, you'll continue to note how we identified specific accomplishments and wrote out the powerful statements that employers notice. Then we'll get to work writing your new resumé that will cause employers to call *you.* Soon you will also enjoy a great new job.

# PROVEN RESUMÉ SUCCESSES

## 6

These resumés work!!! They landed my clients the interviews that got them the jobs they really wanted. You realize how influential this document is; your resumé must sell you quickly and concisely with eye-catching skills to garner an employer's attention.

I've selected a wide range of professions, fields, and circumstances to assist you in meeting your particular needs when writing your resumé. I've broken this area into 10 groups. The first covers people looking for the same job (Similar Jobs). Then, those who want Promotions, one internal and the other external. Next we cover those sticky issues where you have Employment Gaps likely from illness, child rearing, pregnancy, or lengthy unemployment. After that, I've covered the necessities and strategies to develop a great resumé when you are Changing Careers. We also have women reentering the workplace (Volunteer/Reentry), one with only volunteer and no paid experience. Relocatees will profit from the Relocation section that has both job hunting tips and a resumé that got the client a terrific job in less than a month in the new city. Those who want to use the Internet will find important guidelines in our Internet section. The Consultants section includes the resumé for the professional who wants consulting jobs. The second example is for a consultant who wants to close up shop and go to work as a full-time employee again. I didn't want to leave out Doctors and Ph.D.'s, so a special section on Curriculum Vitaes (CVs) is next, to better accommodate their particular needs. Finally, I conclude with the New College Graduates plus offer some successful job hunting techniques grads can use to get hired for a good job, fast!

All these resumés (in fact every one of the 1,000 or more I've worked on) have one factor that proves to be the reason they are successful; it's the foundation of the entire Goldmining process: ACTIONS = RESULTS. That's the key!

I want you to be able to *apply* my principles. These sections are real-life situations that will make it much easier for you to create your own resumé. All these resumés worked, but they did so because they were created and customized to the person's unique background. You, too, are unique and special, so use these samples as tools and guides. But do your own goldmining in Chapter 7 to put forth the particular strengths and the unique talents that you have to offer an employer.

## Similar Jobs

Many professionals have achieved a high level of success and want to move on within their field. Stressing accomplishments and demonstrating skills are essential. We want your resumé to put your accomplishments in their best possible light, without exaggerations or falsehoods. You must be able to defend your claims during the interview. Be accurate, but don't devalue your accomplishments, either. The use of statistics always captures the employer's eye. Numbers, percentages, things increased or decreased, and cost or time savings each demonstrate both your actions and the results you have achieved.

Everyone in this section went through the Goldmining process. They knew it would take time to create powerful sentences, but using our seven-step formula, with the ACTIONS = RESULTS concept, made it easier. Notice that most of them summarize their position and responsibilities in their first bullet or sentence under their PROFESSIONAL EXPERIENCE. Many employers in our survey repeated what Colleen Kill, a senior executive, said: "The best way to impress me is with an easy-to-read, one-page resumé, where accomplishments are clearly stated and applicable to the job they are applying for." Study these resumés to see exactly what employers mean. Every one of these people got an interview, and most got the job. As you read over their resumés, you want to observe how we wrote their SUMMARY OF QUALIFICATIONS and PROFESSIONAL EXPERIENCE.

Gladys' human resource manager experience became stronger and more impressive when she added bullets that told about the number of stores and employees she oversaw. She landed a great new job with one of the country's fastest growing retailers.

Doug, a credit manager, faced strong competition for the few jobs out there. So did Gayle, a real estate property manager. Both got interviews and new jobs once they'd added specific accomplishments, such as those listed in the following.

- Collected $160,000+ in NSF checks over a ten-month period

- Created new computerized spreadsheet and tracking systems reducing past due accounts from 32% to 12%

- Achieved up to 18% sales growth for prominent urban shopping center for each year over seven years of center's existence

- Organized more than 300 large-scale merchandising and special events

As you can see, these actions demonstrated quite clearly the candidate's ability to do the job. Dennis, our engineer, originally had a very technical resumé that was impossible to read. With Goldmining, we emphasized the quality assurance program he implemented that caught the attention of his new employer after his old resumé had been ignored by that very same employer two months earlier.

Anne had a three-page resumé full of her old company's phraseology and internal language. She wrote lengthy descriptions on every job she held over her 20-year history. The Combination format allowed us to key into the experience and skills as we focused on meeting another employer's needs. Both she and Dennis added a COMPUTER SKILLS section listing skills basic to their job but that had not been included on their original versions.

Both Doug and Andrew were in their middle 50s and quite worried about age discrimination. So we left off the year of their college graduation when we listed their degrees and institutions where they were earned. Both did indeed land great new jobs, and age was never an issue once they began to effectively self-market themselves.

Every one of these resumés worked. As you look through this section, actually read the bullets and summaries, and you'll quickly see that it's these ACTIONS = RESULTS statements that give the resumé the meat that makes employers salivate.

Because of typesetting restrictions, some of the following resumés in this chapter have continued onto a second page. However, in all instances, these resumés were submitted to employers in a single-page format.

# Gladys Dunbar, PHR
1 Main Street
City, NY 11111
(201) 555-0111
gdunbar@yahoo.com

CAREER OBJECTIVE: **Human Resource Manager**

## SUMMARY OF QUALIFICATIONS

Nine years management experience in human resources dealing with fast paced, rapidly expanding companies. Expertise includes employment law, recruiting, employee and labor relations and affirmative action. Analytical decision maker with excellent problem-solving skills. Recognized for ability to develop employee's professional growth and increase their productivity.

## PROFESSIONAL EXPERIENCE

*Human Resource Manager,* Software Stores, San Jose, CA, 1997–Present

- Managed employee relations for high growth, rapidly changing high tech sales and retailer with 251 stores, 150 sales offices, 2 distribution centers, 5500 employees in 40 states and Canada.
- Brought all affirmative action reporting to comply with government contracts in-house eliminating outside consultant.
- Designed and implemented three new training programs for management and employees dealing with sex harassment ADA, and cultural diversity.
- Expert on employment law.
- Investigated and responded to discrimination complaints. Company was never found liable.
- Analyzed, revised and developed human resources policies and procedures.
- Developed innovative computer tracking and department performance system.

*Human Resources Consultant,* HR Services, San Francisco, CA, 1996–97

- Recruited new employees including exempt/non-exempt staff for Macy's and Apple.

*Personnel Manager,* Family Stores, San Francisco, CA, 1992–96

- HR Administrator for 79 retail stores in 8 states, 2500 employees (all sites unionized).
- Recruited and trained new employees to man 26 new stores.
- Established complete personnel record/employee hiring tracking systems for entire organization.
- Facilitated training programs for managers and staff.
- Updated orientation, affirmative action and store cash terminal procedures and manuals.

*Assistant Division Personnel Manager,* Pay 'n Save Corp, San Francisco, CA, 1990–92

- Investigated and responded to all complaints of discrimination for all divisions (9) of the corporation, (20,000) employees.
- Conducted management recruiting and management training.

## EDUCATION

B.A., Speech Communications, University of Southern California, Los Angeles, CA, 1987

**FUNCTIONAL**

# Douglas Mullet
1 Main Street
City, NY 11111
(201) 555-0111
dmulle@aol.com

CAREER OBJECTIVE: **Credit Manager**

### SUMMARY OF QUALIFICATIONS

Fifteen years in Credit Management with a proven track record of establishing credit departments, policies, procedures, terms, and administering collections. Excellent customer negotiation skills and securing firm payment commitments while employing a high level of customer service.

### WORK EXPERIENCE

## Credit Management

- Established credit departments for five rapidly expanding companies including: establishment of credit policy/procedures, assessment all customer credit contracts, conducted credit investigation, set credit limits, and collected funds due.
- Collected $1.9M on one-year old debt previously deemed uncollectable through customized payment programs, negotiated settlements, and conversions to installment notes.
- Negotiated payments from large creditors received 90% of funds due within 90 days.
- Collected $160,000+ in NSF checks over ten month period.
- Resolved large multi-problem account, collecting $30,000 and saved customer from changing companies due to effective teamwork solutions.
- Collected full payment of $27,500 from financially troubled customer, receiving last payment one week before customer filed Chapter 11 bankruptcy.
- Created new computerized spreadsheet and tracking systems on past due accounts, reducing past dues from 32% to 12%.

## Policies and Procedures

- Wrote company's credit terms, policies and procedures including manual.
- Used innovated techniques that legally collected funds due by proposing solutions, offering financing, and providing exceptional customer service.
- Filed numerous bankruptcy claims to ensure some payment.

## Customer Service

- Built solid, long term customer relationships assisting customers with problem resolution to be the first in line to receive payment.
- Negotiated hundreds of customized payment plans to assist customers that resulted in collecting 95% of company's outstanding accounts receivables.

### CREDIT MANAGEMENT EXPERIENCE

*Credit Manager,* Sandstone, Inc., 2001–2002
*Credit Manager,* Freight Systems, Inc., 1998–2000
*Collector,* Building Materials, 1–11/1998
*District Credit Manager,* Food Services of America, Inc., 1994–1996
*National Credit Manager,* Werner Enterprises, 1988–1993

### EDUCATION

Bachelor Degree, Business Administration, Michigan State University

# Dennis Slaven, MBA

1 Main Street
City, NY 11111
(201) 555-0111
denniss@aol.com

CAREER OBJECTIVE: **Manufacturing Engineer**

## SUMMARY OF QUALIFICATIONS

Twelve years proven expertise in manufacturing engineering, quality assurance and design engineering within a manufacturing environment. Demonstrated technical problem-solving abilities utilizing superior communication skills. Successfully implemented Total Quality Management concepts within manufacturing plants and at vendor sites. Results-oriented through development of cost-efficiency modifications, productivity increases and labor cost reductions.

## PROFESSIONAL EXPERIENCE

### Quality Assurance

- Implemented new 4-year quality assurance programs to 7 manufacturing plant personnel including: training on-site applications, Failure Mode and Effect Analysis, change recommendations, Design of Experiments, extensive documentation, vendor quality requirements. Received Ford's Q-1 award at 4 plants within two years.
- Efficiently dealt with employee resistance to quality improvements through training, selling teamwork concept and personal empowerment.
- Evaluated 50 suppliers in on-site inspections to improve quality of parts received to build final product. Eliminated 8 suppliers, set requirements for 30 organizations' improvements.
- Coordinated the successful implementation of new SPC systems on steel welding to retain $6.3M vendor contract over 3 year period.

### Engineering

- Evaluated labor cost for production, redesigned production area and work flow, increased productivity and reduced labor costs by $79,000 annually.
- Analyzed work flow & production use for cost/benefit on 90 new equipment proposals: $8K–250K range.
- New product designer of gauges, fixtures, metal fasteners, transportation packaging, wood products, plastic components and equipment modifications.

### Management

- Implemented new bar code system on multi-thousand piece inventory for three plants. Resulted in 21% accuracy increase and eliminated 6 full time positions for annual savings of $300,000.
- Extensive budget experience dealing with strict financial constraints, 10% cutbacks, maintaining productivity and employee motivation.
- Audited consumer product packaging using SPC techniques. Evaluated, analyzed, achieved national consistency on products. Implemented changes, reached image goals, reduced costs $135K.

## COMPUTER SKILLS

Proficient on Mainframe, IBM, Macintosh with experience in Lotus, Quattro Pro, Word-Perfect, AutoCad, customized design/drafting software, 3-D design. Troubleshooting ability to repair hardware problems.

## WORK HISTORY

*Design Engineer,* Kids Toys, Inc., Detroit, MI, Oct., 1996–Present
*Quality Assurance Engineer,* North American Automotive, Indianapolis, IN, 1990–1996
*Manufacturing Engineer,* John Deere Parts, Milan, IL, 1985–1988
*Industrial Engineer,* Equipment Company, Detroit, MI, 1983–1985

## EDUCATION

MBA, Indiana State University, 1990
B.A., Engineering, Indiana State University, 1983

# Anne Jennings
1 Main Street
City, NY 11111
(201) 555-0111
Annejen@yahoo.com

CAREER OBJECTIVE: **Executive Assistant**

## SUMMARY OF QUALIFICATIONS

Twenty years providing secretarial support to managers and executives. Outstanding organizational planning and scheduling abilities. Superior computer and office systems skills. Highly productive and efficient problem-solver. Strong budget and spreadsheet background.

## PROFESSIONAL EXPERIENCE

*Executive Assistant,* Edison Company, Las Vegas, NV, 1995–Present

### Administration

- Served as Executive Assistant to Division Manager. Duties included: all secretarial work, mailing lists, spreadsheets, confidential reports, computer systems, budgets, risk management, ordering, scheduling, planning, organizing and facilitating meetings, coordinating outside vendors, handling customers, confidential correspondence and coordination of multi-department projects.
- Automated the entire department's filing and tracking system. Trained staff on system usage. Time saved: 60 hours week
- Provided monthly expenditure reports, trending analysis and special reports to Division Manager for Senior Management and Board of Directors.
- Monitored all financial claims, established a tracking spreadsheet for accrual and budget purposes on $5 million.
- Purchased all supplies for department.
- Organized and coordinated Division Manager's meetings, appointments and schedules.
- Processed weekly payroll requirements using the mainframe computer system.
- Devised new process for planning department work order/work flow scheduling.

### Computer Systems

- Maintained department computer information system and provided technical support to staff and managers.
- Formulated/created hundreds of sophisticated reports that contained charts, graphs, spreadsheets.
- Troubleshooted and resolved all system related problems.

*Lead Data Entry Operator,* Bally Hotels, Las Vegas, NV, 1994–1995
*Work Flow Supervisor,* Edison Company, Las Vegas, NV, 1983–1993

## EDUCATION

University of Nevada, Coursework: Computer Programming, Statistics, Business Management
Nevada Community College, Two years in Secretarial Science

## COMPUTER & OFFICE SKILLS

Proficiency on mainframe and PC computer systems. Superior software expertise using: Word, LOTUS, Excel, Freelance, databases, spreadsheets, E-mail, Internet.
Office Skills: Typing—80 wpm; excellent knowledge of shorthand, fax, dictation.

**COMBINATION**

# Joseph Zorman, CFM
1 Main Street
City, NY 11111
(201) 555-0111
joezor@msn.com

CAREER OBJECTIVE: **Facilities Management**

## SUMMARY OF QUALIFICATIONS

Fifteen years in facilities planning and construction management for a rapidly changing company. Implemented automated systems, policies and procedures that increased productivity by 15% and streamlined costs substantially with innovative, resourceful programs and systems. Built cohesive teams and solid relations with internal and external customers.

## PROFESSIONAL EXPERIENCE

*Facilities Planning Group Leader,* Signet Corporation, Chicago, Illinois, 1985–2000
*(Promoted from Senior Planner)*

### Planning and Construction

- Managed the development, design, feasibility studies, budgets, contract negotiations, site supervision and construction management for 20 buildings in multiple locations. Responsible for new construction and hundreds of alterations and additions.
- Implemented transit, land use, building code and city ordinance compliance policies. Developed excellent relationships with city, county, commute-trip-reduction and growth management groups.

### Administration/Financial/Budgets

- Managed the facilities department in the Alabama plant during a critical emergency. Redesigned the systems, streamlined operations and saved $300,000. Reduced safety priority work schedules by 50% through implementation of training of internal customers (employees) and staff. Facility included 5 buildings and a $3 million budget.
- Developed and implemented innovative commuter applications for AutoCad design, security, energy management (EMCS), Excel spreadsheets and facilities maintenance management systems. Results of automation were a 15% increase in productivity, elimination of several positions and sustainable annual savings in excess of $600,000.
- Managed the facilities budgets for projects, capital improvements and operations, approximately $15 million.
- Established/implemented a comprehensive training program on total quality and professional development for staff.

## PROFESSIONAL CERTIFICATION

Certified Facilities Manager (CFM) issued by the
International Facilities Management Association (IFMA), 2000

## EDUCATION

B.A., Pre Law, University of Kansas, 1971
Post graduate studies in Accounting, Finance, Marketing, Computer Systems
and Management, University of Chicago
Facility Management Certificate, University of Illinois, 2000

# Stanley Riceman

1 Main Street
City, NY 11111
(201) 555-0111
sricem@msn.com

CAREER OBJECTIVE: **Customer Service Manager**

## SUMMARY OF QUALIFICATIONS

Ten years in top level customer service management implementing effective reorganizations that resulted in significant increases in productivity. Well developed communication skills that build lasting client and company relationships. Proven expertise to develop productive teams, increase morale, and streamline processes with measurable effects.

## PROFESSIONAL EXPERIENCE

*Regional Manager,* Providence Insurance Group, Jersey City, NJ, 1991–Present

### Client Relations

- Managed 100+ clients' contracts that provide $160 million in healthcare benefits to clients' employees annually.
- Implemented higher standard of quality service through employee training, team development, department reorganization, job accountability, and recognition of individual performance. Results: increased quality, achieved customer retention goals, increased productivity by 50%, reduced turnover, reduced staff from 130 to 60. Annual savings of $2 million.
- Reorganization of department resulted in eliminating our 15% higher price differential, putting us in line with competitors and increasing our company's marketability.

### Administration

- Managed major departmental reorganization: unified two divisions into one, restructured work flow and job descriptions, and eliminated 70 positions, streamlined processes and procedures, and eliminated office space. End results increased profitability.
- Achieved 50% productivity increase during the downsizing process by implementing a new workplace atmosphere that recognized individual performance, accountability, and team building which resulted in a significant increase in employee morale.
- Created new performance standards and assessment tools that ranked employee performance, provided training and employee counseling to help employees meet new goals. Received national award for this achievement.
- Received top company awards for three years for division's achievements in Productivity, Quality, Service and Unit Cost.

*Regional Benefits Manager,* Life Assurance Corporation, New York, NY, 1985–1991

- Managed day-to-day operations of the benefits claim office with a staff of 45 overseeing claims of 100,000 users.
- Trained new employees regionally on the company's processing procedures.

*Industrial Relations Manager,* Tenne Systems, Morristown, NJ, 1978–1985

## EDUCATION

Three years studies in Business Administration, Rutgers University

**COMBINATION**

# Victor Welsh, MBA
1 Main Street
City, NY 11111
(201) 555-0111
vicwelsh1@aol.com

CAREER OBJECTIVE: **Management Position in Information Technology**

## SUMMARY OF QUALIFICATIONS

Strong business and information systems background with proven expertise leading an engineering/business systems department for Fortune 500 company. Excellent strategic planning, team development skills. Able to develop systems that increase productivity, contain costs and satisfy user needs.

## PROFESSIONAL EXPERIENCE

*Manager Engineering Business Systems,* Mobil Corporation, Fairfax, VA, 1991–Present
*(Promoted from Manager Scientific Systems, promoted from Programmer Analyst)*

### Computer Systems/Technical
- Five years managing computer information systems on IBM mainframes, TI Miniframes, UNIX Servers, IBM and Macintosh PC Networks.
- Computer Programming Languages: C, FORTRAN, COBOL, PASCAL.
- Software expertise includes: customized databases, Excel, Word, Freelance, and customized project manager programs.
- Converted entire system from older system to new mainframe system. Project manager over four year project. Duties included: data modeling, strategic planning, programming, train staff, resource allocation, interface with other departments, coordination installation and user training, established programming standards, quality control and team development.
- Analyzed current/future needs, researched selected and purchased hardware and software packages for mainframes, UNIX servers, PC networks, to meet long term user needs.

### Management
- Managed the daily operations of engineering business systems including: team development staff of 19, interdepartmental coordination, establishing/revising policies/procedures, $4 million budget allocations, resource scheduling and planning.
- Established new total quality improvements processes and complete work flow reengineering processes. Resulted in 20% department productivity increase.
- Contributed to department's long term strategic planning.
- Administration of the work reduction planning and implementation process.
- Coordinated human resources activities including: hiring, training, terminations, performance evaluations, compensation packages and team development.
- Created new processes and training programs on critical computer operation skills.

### Foreign Language
- Fluent Spanish: 15 years residing in Latin America.

## EDUCATION

Master of Business Administration, City University, Norfolk, VA, 1999
Bachelor of Science in Computer Science and Mathematics, Purdue University, IN, 1991

# Jack Schwartz
1 Main Street
City, NY 11111
(201) 555-0111
jacksch@msn.com

CAREER OBJECTIVE: **Public Relations/Marketing Director**

## SUMMARY OF QUALIFICATIONS

Fifteen years in marketing and public relations with a proven track record aiding organizations and manufacturers in increasing sales and product awareness. Produced tangible results that increased the bottomline. Strong national media contacts in print, television and radio. Coordinated trade shows, publication productions and new product rollouts. Able to identify and capitalize on consumer market trends quickly.

## PROFESSIONAL EXPERIENCE

*Media Relations and Marketing Director,* Worldwide Homes Association,
Los Angeles, CA 1997–2002
*(Promoted from Communications Director)*

### Marketing

- Managed all marketing and advertising operations for international association of 250 manufacturers. Duties included: advertisement planning and placement; liaison to advertising and public relations agencies; trade show events; supervised sales lead referral program; co-op advertising; educational seminars. Created award-winning publications; monthly newsletters; promotional materials; supervised promotions of four district managers. Managed budget of $2 million.
- Introduced new product industry-wide rollout including: product research, promotion, marketing campaign, and advertising. Results increased sales 122% during first year.
- Redirected marketing focus from vendors to consumers, developing new demand. Increased consumer awareness and product sales by 10%.
- Produced consumer educational video from inception through marketing and distribution.

### Media Relations

- Acquired $2 million value of free editorial and publicity space in key trade journals (Good Housekeeping, Better Homes & Gardens, Sunset Magazine, Popular Mechanics) as well as major wire services (AP) and newspapers nationwide.
- Interviewed on over 20 radio programs on products and product usage (Los Angeles, Dallas, San Francisco, Chicago, Kansas City and Seattle markets).
- Created press campaign targeting national Worldwide Homes Association affiliates, gaining television coverage and interviews in Dallas, Denver, Kansas City and Seattle markets.
- Conducted media training seminars for managers: media inquiries, handling television interviews and reporters.

### Public Relations

- Managed external and internal communications by producing monthly newsletter, annual report, product publications, manuals, international architectural awards competition, and press releases.

- Established in-house desktop publishing program, reducing outside costs by 85%.
- Developed design, themes, marketing concepts to promote association's efficiency and products.
- Lobbied state and federal legislators obtaining the industry's first-ever government funding.

*Assistant Director,* UCLA Athletic Department, Sports Info., Los Angeles, CA, 1992–1997

*Sports Information and Promotions Director,* San Francisco pro teams, 1988–1992

### EDUCATION

Bachelor of Arts, Public Relations, UCLA, 1988

# Deirdre Mattison

1 Main Street
City, NY 11111
(201) 555-0111

CAREER OBJECTIVE: **Legal Administrator/Secretary**

## SUMMARY OF QUALIFICATIONS

Ten years experience in the legal field with recent management experience. Strong organizational, planning, and financial skills. Efficient manager who is able to maximize resources while containing costs. Excellent communication and interpersonal skills dealing with partners, staff and clients.

## PROFESSIONAL EXPERIENCE

*Administrative Manager,* Graham Law Offices, Atlanta, GA, 2001–Present

*Legal Secretary,* Jefferson Toms LLP, Atlanta, GA, 1991–93 and 1994–2001

*Executive Secretary,* Simons Company, Atlanta, GA, 1993–94

## Management

- Managed the daily operations for a legal firm, duties included: accounting, work flow delegation, staff supervision, staff training, salary/employee benefit administration, purchasing, and facilities management.

- Coordinated entire relocation and tenant improvements of 20,000 sq. ft. office space. Handled construction build-out, floor/workspace layout, new equipment/ furniture purchase and office move.

- Established office policies and procedures.

- Implemented new accounting system and financial software. Trained staff.

## Legal

- Ten years in legal field with skills in various areas including: corporate, estate planning/tax, business and real estate.

- Experience with court procedures, court rules, legal documents, legal correspondence, pleadings, agreements, wills, trusts, and billing.

- Handled thousands of clients, explaining legal procedures, office policies and billing issues.

- Office Skills: Type 75 wpm, dictation, editing/grammar/proofreading.

- Computer Skills: Windows 95, WordPerfect, legal & financial software.

**COMBINATION**

# Christopher Jackseme

1 Main Street
City, NY 11111
(201) 555-0111
artman@msn.com

*He landed a job offer with the first employer he sent this to.*

CAREER OBJECTIVE: **Advertising Creative Director**

## SUMMARY OF QUALIFICATIONS

Award winning, 16 years in creative/advertising/design field with proven strengths in innovative design developing results-oriented marketing and advertising campaigns. Excel at interpretation of client needs to produce high levels of satisfaction on time and within budget hitting desired concept in first go around 95% of time. Develop efficient, highly productive teams to create responsive department to exceed corporate goals.

## AWARDS

2 Gold ADDYS, 1 Silver ADDY, 11 Regional ADDY Awards of Excellence,
Print Award for Design Excellence, 3 Strathmore Awards for Design Excellence,
3 DESI Awards for Design Excellence

## PROFESSIONAL EXPERIENCE

*Creative Director,* McKinnis Advertising Group, Chicago, IL, 1994–present

*Creative Director,* Tennison-Smith Inc., Detroit, MI, 1991–1994

*Art Director,* Dayton Brown, Detroit, MI, 1989–1991

- Managed the creative advertising & design process working with hundreds of companies from concept to completion, with proven expertise across a full spectrum of industries & products & services. Clients included: NCR, Whirlpool, Toro, Upjohn, KitchenAid, John Deere, Guardsman, American Food Products, Electro-Voice, Miles Laboratories, Heath-Zenith, Litton, Morgan Creek Film Productions.
- Established/improved hundreds of corporate identities & marketing materials plus direct mail campaigns, television spots, catalogs, magazine/newspaper/trade ads, trade show booths, package design POP materials.
- Project manager on Fortune 500 company project for new advertising campaign for multi-million dollar project launch. Direct mail campaign drew immediate break even response greatly surpassing first year sales goals.

## TECHNICAL SKILLS

- Handled all daily operational and managerial responsibilities including: client relations, project management, estimate/budget management, photo shoots-photo direction, film management, and printing coordination.
- Computer expertise utilizing: Pagemaker, Illustrator, Photoshop, Quark, Databases, Netscape. Possess advanced electronic/digital technology skills on website, prepress coordination.

## EDUCATION

Bachelor's Fine Art, Ohio University, Athens, 1986

**FUNCTIONAL**

# Jason McBride
1 Main Street
City, NY 11111
(201) 555-0111
jasonmcb@earthlink.net

CAREER OBJECTIVE: **Television Producer**

## SUMMARY OF QUALIFICATIONS

Producer of daily radio and television consumer programs for NBC affiliate with proven expertise in designing and formatting a show for maximum viewer appeal. Strengths lie in organization, guest selection, interviewing and editing.

## PROFESSIONAL EXPERIENCE

*Producer,* WJBK TV/WJBK News Radio, January 1998–Present
(NBC Affiliate—7th Market)

### Producing

- Produced 120+ television business news segments and 300+ two-hour live radio shows for NBC affiliate.
- Screened, selected and booked 50 guest experts per month (700 to-date) featuring business topics, financial experts and consumer news.
- Developed the format for new two-hour live daily radio show called "Money Hour."
- Coordinated/produced 12 live remote broadcasts from major league stadium games, trade shows, and shopping malls.
- 2 years experience of daily television editing on Beta and ¾ inch formats.

### Communication

- Wrote 360+ television scripts (daily evening news), 670+ radio morning features (morning commute), 280+ business reports (daily radio), and 280+ stock market reports (daily radio).
- Interviewed experts to extract, edit and compile 850+ on-air interviews for television and/or radio airing.

### Promotion

- Wrote daily promos to advertise topics and attract listeners.
- Selected "hot topic" spots to air throughout the day to promote the "Money Hour" show.
- Created a new quarterly newsletter to increase listenership.

## EDUCATION

B.A., Communications, Albion College, Albion, MI, 1994

**COMBINATION**

# Andrew J. Stevens

1 Main Street
City, NY 11111
(201) 555-0111
ajstevens@msn.com

CAREER OBJECTIVE: **Telecommunications Management**

## SUMMARY OF QUALIFICATIONS

Twenty years in Telecommunications Management with proven expertise in coordinating large scale company needs with state of the art communications to increase company's effectiveness and profitability. Proven track record in strategic planning, streamlining costs, reducing trouble reports plus interfacing effectively with all levels of management and field staff.

## PROFESSIONAL EXPERIENCE

*Corporate Customer Service Manager,* AT&T, New York, NY, 1983–Present
*(Promoted from Regional Project Manager, promoted from Operations Manager)*

### Strategic Planning

- Developed company-wide plan, assessed current telecommunications operations, identified reorganization of future communications and implemented plan in stages over a two year period for a $9 billion dollar client company.
- Coordinated both companies' needs and implementation of extensive network and sophisticated telecommunications products and services, interfacing between technical staffs on both sides to bring new services on-line, on-time and within budget.
- Team contributor on two 3-Year Strategic Communications Plans for a Fortune 100 company with continual adjustments, improvements and ramifications.

### Administration

- Coordinated monthly performance reports for a top 10 U.S. company. Providing on-line performance, troubleshooting, assessment of communication operations. Over four year period, decreased trouble reports by 80%.
- Interfaced between company field managers, department heads, engineers, security and marketing individuals to coordinate effective service/system upgrades from AT&T to a top 10 US company, with capacity increases over 30% in 18 months.
- Managed entire communications network and work teams, with a 5,000 terminal system.
- Consolidated telecommunications operations centers, streamlined work flow, processes and procedures. Initiated remote operations. Results: eliminated 10 manager positions and 5,000 square feet of floor space.

### Customer Service

- Pivotal role between client company and AT&T during crisis telephone interruption included organizing troubleshooting, and technical response teams.
- Expert problem-solver to correct complex technical situations involving numerous work teams and decisions to quickly and efficiently solve any communications failure.
- Managed all equipment vendor/suppliers to coordinate needs assessment, time schedules, repairs and resources to maximize on time performance. Reduced downtime by 50%.

## EDUCATION

Bachelor Degree, St. Bonaventure University, NY

Editorial Note: Original resumé all appeared on one page

# Megan Browne-Smith
1 Main Street
City, NY 11111
(201) 555-0111

CAREER OBJECTIVE: **Director of Office Administrative Services**

## SUMMARY OF QUALIFICATIONS

Ten years in administration management with proven expertise in office administration, landlord/vendor coordination, contract negotiations, financial operations, computer systems, and team development. Expertise includes assisting with office planning and administration for start-ups/expansions enhancing rapid growth. Proven track record of successful vendor and banking negotiations on 400+ contracts involving amounts up to $2 million. Project management of office layout, space planning and acquisition, construction and remodeling on office and laboratory space with the abilities to resolve conflicts quickly and amicably. Excellent communication skills dealing with a diverse and international clientele.

## PROFESSIONAL EXPERIENCE

### Administration

- Established office administration for three start-up/rapidly expanding international companies including: office layout, construction, personnel needs analysis, hiring, purchasing, computer network, telecommunications, relocation coordination, policies and procedures, budgets, forecasts.
- Corporate project manager of $2.1 million office and laboratory construction including: negotiations, construction meetings, compliance auditing, and financial review resulting in $200,000 savings.
- Negotiated contracts with vendors/bankers on negotiations up to $2 million on over 400 contracts/deals.
- Analyzed work flow needs, evaluated hardware and software options, negotiated terms, purchased complex computer network (LAN) with cost savings of $60,000.
- Established policies and procedures on human resources, purchasing, security, financial practices, office administration, and systems and procedures. Hired 50+ staff.
- Versatile manager coordinating three large office expansions including new space acquisition, planning, work space analysis and allocation, construction build out on projects up to $1.5 million.
- Built cooperation to quickly resolve issues and receive efficient service in landlord/tenant negotiations.

### Financial

- Financial management of A/P, A/R, payroll, general ledger, financial statements, fixed assets, grant management, banking relations, with annual revenues of $15 million.
- Established financial systems and internal controls for start-up companies.
- Negotiated line of credit with over 400 vendors for start-up companies.
- Evaluated and purchased property and liability insurance and bonding programs.

## COMPUTER SKILLS

Extensive knowledge of technical hardware and software capabilities. Proficient IBM computer abilities utilizing Windows, WordPerfect, Excel, E-Mail, accounting and scheduling software.

## WORK HISTORY

*Administrative Manager,* International Systems, Inc., Chicago, Ill, 1994–Present
*Business Manager,* BioLife Inc., Madison, WI, 1991–1994
*Owner/Manager,* Bayside Gifts, Bay, WI, 1985–1990
*Office Service Manager,* Enviro Inc., Milwaukee, WI, 1982–1985

## EDUCATION

B.S., Business, University of Dayton, Ohio, 1974

*Editorial Note: Original resumé all appeared on one page*

# Paul Schoffield
1 Main Street
City, NY 11111
(201) 555-0111
pauls@aol.com

CAREER OBJECTIVE: **Trainer**

## SUMMARY OF QUALIFICATIONS

Eighteen years experience in Training and Management in both manufacturing and service industries. Trainer in Total Quality Management/Continuous Quality Improvement (customer focused). Experience instructing all levels with emphasis on high retention and practical application. Hired and trained managers. Trained sales representatives twice annually on product knowledge. Designed, facilitated, developed materials for training programs on Cultural Diversity, and Effective Visual Aids for government agencies. Designed and facilitated Train-the-Trainer program for computer software training.

## PROFESSIONAL EXPERIENCE

### Training
- Extensive facilitation experience in courses and programs for Customer Service emphasizing areas such as listening, handling difficult people, managing conflict, effective communication.
- Sixteen eleven-week courses for engineers, technicians, line supervisors, line employees on Continuous Quality Improvement, public speaking. Effective with all levels of employees.

### Curriculum Development
- Course Designer in one year development project creating new quality improvement training program for corporation management. Project included needs assessment, Beta testing.
- Introduced innovative training methods and process materials which have been adopted as a current company model.
- Authored and designed training materials and education curriculum for five other programs.

### Manufacturing
- Five years as a manager in a Fortune 500 Company.
- General Manager, International Division, paper product manufacturer.
- Revamped sales structure and product mix resulting in 40% sales increase within two years.
- Developed effective, extensive inventory control program resulting in decreased inventory costs, faster delivery to customers, decreased transportation and import costs, yielding an 80% increase in profitability.
- Two years General Manager, consumer products company.
- Established new sales program, marketing strategy to infiltrate tight market. Results: 300% sales increase within eighteen month time frame.

## WORK HISTORY

*Contract Trainer/Course Designer,* 1996–Present
*Manager,* Paper Products Company, 1988–1996
*General Manager,* Liz Little Ltd., (clothing manufacturer), 1984–1986
*General Manager,* Regency Inc., (paper products company), 1981–1983
*Principal,* Gerstone, Smithstone Inc., (consumer products), 1976–1981

## EDUCATION

Master's Degree, Organizational Communication and Training, Loyola University, 1996
Bachelor's Degree, Business Administration, University of Maryland, 1974

# Steven Burnstein

1 Main Street
City, NY 11111
(201) 555-0111
steveb@central.net

CAREER OBJECTIVE: **Project Manager**

## SUMMARY OF QUALIFICATIONS

Twenty years in the construction industry with the last eight in large scale commercial project management. Proven expertise to develop accurate bids, negotiate contracts and subcontracts, streamline costs, and bring projects in on time. Strengths lie in utilizing computer systems, project scheduling knowledge, communication abilities, and requiring accountability at all levels of the construction process to meet contract goals.

## PROFESSIONAL EXPERIENCE

*Project Manager,* Murray Contractors, Newark, NJ, 1998–2002

- Established solid computerized management systems in job costing and project management as part of business expansion plan to develop into a larger general contractor. Company growth over $12 million in two year period.
- Managed seven projects, from $300,000 to $8 million including: bidding, negotiation of all subcontracts, change order pricing and negotiations, purchasing, scheduling, cost analysis, plus providing interface with architects, clients, and field personnel.
- Streamlined systems, processes, and procedures to eliminate necessity of manager level work. Annual savings of $75,000.
- Prioritized needs, reorganized project schedule, and implemented accountability to schedule in order to turn around school project that was 45 days behind. Brought project in on time saving potential liquidated damages of $45,000.
- Renegotiated contract on large project to obtain payment for additional work that was done on-site by field personnel. Resulted in $200,000 increased project revenue.
- Contributed to strategic plan of business expansion into larger general contractor organization, achieving 30% growth in two years.

*Project Manager,* DePinto Construction, Newark, NJ, 1997–1998

- Managed two renovation projects for $500,000 and $1.4 million including estimating, bid proposals, contract negotiations, subcontract negotiations, purchasing, and supervision of field personnel.
- Brought $1.4 million project in $120,000 under budget. Result: shared savings and $48,000 profit.

*Contractor,* Construction/Design, Milwaukee, WI, 1980–1997

- Redesigned and renovated commercial bank foreclosure properties.

## COMPUTER SKILLS

Expert user on multiple software programs for project scheduling, job costing, estimating, and contract management. Proficient skills using databases, spreadsheets, and word processing. Established a computerized job costing system for two companies resulting in accurate cost data to manage projects and provide data for future bids.

## EDUCATION

Master Degree, University of Wisconsin, Milwaukee, 1980
Bachelor of Science, Economics, University of California, Irvine, CA, 1978

# Kay Harrington
1 Main Street
City, NY 11111
(201) 555-0111
kayha@attbi.com

CAREER OBJECTIVE: **Loan Processor**

## SUMMARY OF QUALIFICATIONS

Six years in mortgage and loan processing. Excellent organizational skills working in high pressure, highly productive environment. Strong attention to detail. Accurately verify figures. Take pride in doing jobs correctly and in a timely manner. Excellent customer service, phone skills to problem-solve, verify information, answering questions to ensure positive rapport, referrals and repeat business. Committed to high quality service, performance and accuracy.

## PROFESSIONAL EXPERIENCE

*Loan Processing/Funding,* Manhattan Bank, Rochester, NY, 1998–Present

Executive assistant for two loan officers handling all clerical duties involved with the start to finish process of residential loans. Duties included: data entry of applications, ordering appraisal, title, setting up underwriting preparations, escrow, appraisal review, drawing up loan documents and liaison to customers. Coordinated prospecting direct mail marketing campaign. Wrote numerous letters to customers, lenders, escrow and title organizations.

*Administrative Assistant,* Eastman Kodak Company, Rochester, NY, 1996–1998

Administrative accounting support for 130 persons including computer input for electronic time card, accounts payable, verification of employee expense reports for accuracy and adherence to company policy. Data entry, payroll records, expense reports, input verification and corrections. Provide professional strong customer service skills dealing with a high volume of telephone calls.

*Loan Processor,* Downtown Savings Bank, Rochester, NY, 1991–1995

Review loan file, verifying accuracy. Prepare escrow instructions. Type loan documents. Computer input of data and balancing escrow figures before disbursing funds. Audit all files to verify correct and complete information. Verify final file and materials. Dispersed funds. Follow strict standards, policies and procedures for accuracy. Final loans had 99% accuracy rate. Created tracking system to process all materials in timely, efficient manner.

## OFFICE SKILLS

Type 70 wpm, 10 key by touch, 10 line telephone system, facsimile machine

## COMPUTER SKILLS

IBM, mainframe, LAN. Data entry customized accounting, WordPerfect, Customized loan processing software

## EDUCATION

Computer software courses, IBM Software Training
Two years general college courses, Canandiquia Community College

> **Editorial Note: Original resumé all appeared on one page**

# Eric Steadman
1 Main Street
Any City, New York 11111
(201) 555-0111
email: ericz@aol.com

CAREER OBJECTIVE: **Writer/Reporter**

### EDUCATION

Master's Degree, Print Journalism, Boston University, 1998
Bachelor's Degree, Political Science, University of Massachusetts, 1995

### SUMMARY OF QUALIFICATIONS

Proven track record of coordinating editorial needs with strengths in reporting and editing. Ability to identify good stories, interesting angles, news value plus the aptitude to clarify writing and copy to achieve a high level of reader satisfaction. Managed editorial staffs at both weekly and daily newspapers. Assigned stories, coordinated paper style, design and page/story layout. Set high personal standards on quality, truth, accuracy and excellence as well as being highly productive and calm under pressured deadlines.

### PROFESSIONAL EXPERIENCE

#### Editing

- Served as creative control over weekly newspaper—assigning stories, assisting reporters, determining depth and layout of stories for a 44-page edition, including: News, Profiles, Features, Politics, Editorials, Sports, Education, Crime, Regional Events.
- Managed the daily operation of the city desk, covering all weekend breaking news, coordinating both reporter and photographer activities, as well as editing copy and writing regular features.
- Edited copy and assisted reporters to clarify writing, accommodate articles to space layout, created headlines and coordinated interviews plus substantiating sources.
- Handled editorial/content inquiries from the general public on various stories or news-related issues.

#### Reporting

- Wrote 500+ newspaper articles covering: politics, breaking news, social issues, features, profiles, crime, health, weekly calendar and entertainment.
- Planned and developed stories and angles that were most targeted to readership demographics by selecting subjects, sources, anecdotes that personalize the story for the reader.
- Coordinated photography to enhance the stories, grab and draw the reader's attention.
- Produced needed stories, editorial content and revisions to meet short deadlines of up to 90 minutes, achieving quality stories.

## WORK HISTORY

Assistant City Editor, *The Beach Reporter,* Long Beach, CA, 3/01–present
(promoted from Reporter, *County Journal,* Newport Beach, CA *sister paper*)

Editor, *Patriot's Ledger* (Community Newspaper Company), Medford, MA, 6/98–12/00
(promoted from Reporter, *Needham Observer,* Malden, MA *sister paper*)

FREELANCE ASSIGNMENTS: Time, Business Week, LA Times

## COMPUTER SKILLS

Superior proficiency utilizing PC & Mac computer applications in WORD, Quark, NewsEdit. Sophisticated online research ability using the Internet and databases to acquire story content and information. Trained reporters and staff on new software applications. Type 70 wpm accurately.

# Anne-Marie Esterbrook

1 Main Street
Portland, OR 97000
503-555-1212
aester@msn.com

Career Objective: FINANCE MANAGER/FINANCIAL ANALYST

## SUMMARY OF QUALIFICATIONS

Ten years of proven experience managing financial operations that emphasize high productivity, efficiency, accuracy, ease-of-use and cost containment. Excel at streamlining financial processes and procedures and parts inventory processes that dramatically improved systems and saved money. Responsible for building highly productive financial teams at each job that exceeded goals. Received national award in 2000 and 2001 for superior performance in financial reporting.

## PROFESSIONAL EXPERIENCE

### Controller, Mountain Honda, Portland, OR 2000–present

- Managed the daily financial operations for a retailer with $30 million annual revenues. Duties included: financial statements, cash management, general ledger, accounts payable, accounts receivable, payroll, purchasing, taxes, bank reconciliation, communication systems, computer systems, and supervised staff of eight.
- Researched, selected and installed a complex communications system (phones, fax lines, computer modems) that improved access and efficiency while reducing costs by 50%.
- Reorganized the financial reporting process, converting numerous manual processes into computerized EXCEL systems that increased efficiency, accuracy, and reduced staff time by 15%.
- Analyzed the annual budget expenditures; reviewed/renegotiated numerous vendor contracts securing lower prices and better financing terms, reducing annual costs by $108,000 per year.
- Evaluated entire employee overtime usage and costs. Analyzed needs, developed new policies, procedures and cross training programs that reduced overtime by 75% per month. Cost savings: $14,000.

### Business Manager, South Oregon Jeep and Eagle, Portland, OR 1998–2000

- Managed all the daily financial business and accounting operations for retailer with $20 million annual revenues. Duties included: financial statements, general ledger, accounts payable, accounts receivable, payroll and taxes, cash management, bank reconciliation, computer systems and supervised staff of 4.
- Developed new annual parts inventory process including physical counting of thousands of parts with checklists, procedures, and financial computing. Results provided easier process, dramatically improved accuracy, saving tax dollars on actual inventory vs. guessed.

### Assistant Controller, Honda and Toyota of Portland, OR 1992–1998

- Coordinated the financial accounting activities for a retailer with $50 million annual revenues. Duties included: financial statements general ledger, accounts payable, accounts receivable, payroll, taxes.
- Handled all the financial operations business, equipment purchases to start up new multimillion-dollar division (Toyota).

## HONORS

National Award, Outstanding Performance in Financial Reporting, American Honda Corporation, 2001 and 2002

## EDUCATION

BA, Accounting, Seattle University, Seattle, WA 1992

# Tony Francisco

1 Main Street
Birmingham, AL 35200
205-555-1212
franctony@msn.com

## Career Objective: SALES ACCOUNT MANAGER

### SUMMARY OF QUALIFICATIONS

Proven track record of selling capital equipment and increasing sales to achieve #1 salesperson rank at two different companies. Excel at qualifying prospects, generating new business, closing, increasing repeat business, and providing superior follow-up and customer service.

### PROFESSIONAL EXPERIENCE

*Regional Sales Manager,* Flow Systems, Inc. Birmingham, AL 1996–present

(Promoted from *Director of National Sales,* promoted from *Sales Engineer.*)

*Regional Sales Manager,* Houston Inc. Mobile, AL 1994–1996

*Southwest Regional Sales Manager,* Products Co. Dallas, TX 1990–1994

### Sales/Marketing

- Achieved top national salesperson status selling capital equipment to companies through presentations, demonstrations, trade shows, cold calls and extensive follow up. Produced $1.6 million in annual sales, doubling territory's unit sales. *Townsend Engineering, 1996*
- Took one of the lowest producing territories and moved it to the #1 tops sales producer with $830,000 annual sales within 36 months by creating and implementing new sales strategies that attracted numerous quality prospects with a high level of closures. *Allen Products, 1992*
- Developed effective new sales/marketing program based on product presentations and demonstrations at over 40 national trade shows that quadrupled sales to $430,000 annually. *Houston—Fearless, 1995*

### Customer Service

- Demonstrated, installed and serviced equipment utilizing TQM and statistical analysis procedures to ensure proper equipment operation and total customer satisfaction. Achieved lower warranty expenses to company and reduced return calls by over 10%.
- Created, prepared and presented multimedia product demonstrations to educate user groups, dealer personnel and end users. Received special recognition for total customer satisfaction two consecutive years.

### Computer Skills

- Implemented ACT! database to analyze and monitor sales processes. Established laptop reporting and tracking procedures to integrate with sales processes. Excellent PC compatible computer skills.

### HONORS AND AWARDS

Top national salesperson, *Townsend Engineering, 1989*
Top national salesperson, *Products Co., 1986*

**COMBINATION**

# Lucas Ramson

1 Main Street
Long Beach, CA 90800
(310) 555-1212
luramson@hotmail.com

Career Objective: PROPERTY MANAGER

## SUMMARY OF QUALIFICATIONS

Twelve years of proven experience as a Property Manager negotiating leases, working with developers and governmental agencies, and overseeing facilities maintenance for a large multiproperty corporation. Known for containing costs plus delivering the highest levels of efficiency. Excel at developing highly productive teams that provide superior service to internal clients/customers.

## PROFESSIONAL EXPERIENCE

*Corporate Properties Manager,* Ocean Stevedoring Co., Long Beach, CA 1984–present

### Real Estate Management

- Managed the entire multistate properties and facilities for twelve years for corporation. Duties included: property management, vendor selection, developer/vendor relations, facilities management, public agency/government relations, leases, negotiations, and marketing. Oversaw tenant improvements and construction build-outs.
- Negotiated dozens of tenant and landlord leases. Secured better terms, rates, potential prime lease spots and safeguards in triple net costs. Produced financial analysis for location/vendor/developer. Consulted with attorneys on final lease documents.
- Supervised the maintenance on numerous sites, responding immediately to problems; schedule regular maintenance plus maintained high levels of safety and cleanliness while containing costs and overhead.
- Negotiated with government officials to lower property assessments and property taxes on numerous occasions with a savings of $260,000 in property taxes.

### Business Administration

- Managed the communications and customer service process to 250 clients covering finance and statistical analysis reports, industry news and market research and analysis.
- Managed the computer systems for the business operations.

### Government/Public Affairs

- Served as liaison working closely with numerous local, state, national and international (particularly Asia and Japan) governments and lobbyists to secure legislation, easements, compliance, international transportation, and US domestic intrastate transportation.
- Prepared dozens of position papers and delivered speeches on tax issues and trade and transportation issues, to benefit corporation's business interests.

## EDUCATION

Bachelor's Degree, Economics, UCLA, 1977

Editorial Note: Original resumé all appeared on one page

# Scott O'Toole

1 Main Street
Santa Clara, CA 95000
(408) 555-1212
me123@yahoo.com

Career Objective: MARKETING DIRECTOR

## SUMMARY OF QUALIFICATIONS

Over fifteen years as a Marketing leader with proven expertise in establishing brands, developing niches, launching new products, and increasing revenue streams that result in high levels of profit and firmly established market share.

## PROFESSIONAL EXPERIENCE

*New Product/New Business Developer*—Internet Trade Associations, San Jose, CA 2000–present

*Vice President Marketing,* Living Magazine, Newark, NJ 1997–2000

*Marketing Manager,* Robeck Appliances, Newark, NJ 1996–1997

*Publisher,* Kitchen & Bath quarterly, New York, NY 1989–1996

*Assistant Co-op Advertising Manager,* Patriot Ledger, Newark, NJ 8 years

### New Business Development

- Launched a new consumer magazine including securing capital investment, determined magazine concept, target audience, design, layout; established marketing/advertising/PR campaign; hired and oversaw editorial staff. Results: 92% repeat advertiser rate, profitable after 25 months; established business to business brand recognition within one year. Sold after 8 years to large national magazine publisher.
- Developed new trade show promotions that developed niche, doubled sales and raised profits by 65%.
- Created new Internet based auction for specialty trade associations that produced new clients and free advertising, while establishing highly profitable ways for clients to increase their businesses.

### Market Research

- Established several successful marketing campaigns including: product launches, brand recognition, website/online sales, promotions, trade shows, Print/Radio/TV advertising and nontraditional sales outlets, business to business strategic alliances, innovative direct mail programs.
- Developed and sold hundreds of different targeted, niche mailing lists to companies, associations and nonprofit fundraisers.
- Researched 6 major cities to determine household incomes and home values to produce highly targeted consumer mailing list that hit top 7% of homeowners in each metro area.
- Created hundreds of promotional and marketing materials including: websites, flyers, color brochures, slide shows, annual reports, ads and specialty items.
- Conducted complete, comprehensive and innovative market analysis to conserve budget and achieve targets.

### AWARDS

National Member of the Year, 1995 & 1997, National Kitchen and Bath Association
Athena Award—"One of Nation's Best 10 Advertising Ideas,"
INAE "Best New Periodical"—WPA, 1993

### EDUCATION

BA, Communications, Rutgers University, New Brunswick, NJ

## Terry Ferrier, CPA
1 Main Street
Miami, FL 33100
(305) 555-1212
moneyman@hotmail.com

Career Objective: PAYROLL MANAGER

### SUMMARY OF QUALIFICATIONS

Proven leadership in financial operations and information technology. Known for containing costs, increasing productivity, improving efficiency, and global thinking. Excel at IT system designs that meet rapid expansion handling payroll, benefits, and HR needs. Excellent accounting skills overseeing all financial operations and establishing highly productive motivated teams.

### PROFESSIONAL EXPERIENCE

*Director, Payroll/Benefits,* Labor Ready Inc., Miami, FL 2001–2002

*Accounting Manager,* South Florida Air, Miami, FL 1997–2001

*Assistant Controller,* Herman, Thomas and Associates, Miami, FL 1991–1997

### Accounting
- Managed the accounts payable and payroll functions for 3,000 employee airline, $300M annual revenues. Supervised staff of 16. Hired new supervisor and staff.
- Managed day-to-day financial operations for restaurant/retail management firm (5 companies) with $25M in annual revenues. Duties included: financial statements, A/P, A/R, general ledger, payroll, banking relations, taxes, and internal control procedures.
- Established new policy and procedures for separate companies. Improved efficiency, enhanced reporting, tightened internal controls, and increased productivity.

### IT/Computer Systems
- Headed the major new IT/Computer system handling Human Resources, Payroll, and Benefits for international service company, 800 branches, $900M annual revenues, 3,500 employees. Responsible for entire project management; planning; internal financial and IT consulting; financial system conversion; all tax issues; troubleshooting; Y2K compliance; installation and staff training. *Results: established new computer system with no bugs or downtime, designed to expand with company's rapid growth. Contained costs and maintained staffing levels through enhancements and productivity increases as company grew by 200 branches.*
- Co-team leader on two-year project installing new financial software on a UNIX Network. Analyzed corporate/business needs, selected software, oversaw conversion, trained employees. Results include eliminating 1 fulltime employee, resolved Y2K problem, achieved multiuser capability, widely expanded user functions and efficiency.
- Converted payroll functions for 1,200 employees to independent service, eliminated one staff position, plus 10 hours/week of management time.
- Trained 20 financial employees on system usage, new user orientation, and technical troubleshooting.

- Proficient IBM and mainframe skills with expert user level on customized accounting software, Excel, Oracle, Word.

*Senior Accountant,* Blue Cross, Miami, FL 1989–1991

*Accounting Positions,* CPA firms, Ft. Lauderdale, FL 1985–1989

### EDUCATION

BS, Electrical/Computer Engineering, Florida State University, 1991

# Cassandra Reigns
1 Central Park West
New York, NY 11200
(212) 555-1212
cassier@aol.com

### Career Objective: BUYER

### SUMMARY OF QUALIFICATIONS

Proven buying and merchandising skills for fashion retailers demonstrating exceptional ability to predict trends and buying patterns, then purchase clothing that results in increased sales and profitability. Strengths include: forecasting, buying, sales/business analysis, planning, and vendor negotiations.

### PROFESSIONAL EXPERIENCE

*Associate Buyer,* Bloomingdale's, New York, NY Feb 2001–Jan 2002
(E-commerce division)
*Assistant Buyer,* Lord & Taylor, New York, NY December 1999–January 2001

*Buying Intern,* Henri Bendel, Barney's New York, Liz Claiborne, Donna Karan
1998–1999

## Buying and Merchandising

- Bought Women's Contemporary Sportswear/Dresses/Coats/Special Occasion for Bloomingdale's and Lord & Taylor. Duties included: attending trade shows, selecting/buying clothing, monitoring inventory, reordering, in-store floor merchandising, sales forecasting and analysis, creating financial reports, planning sales/promotion events, determining markdowns, managing vendor relationships and negotiations, developing key items and exclusive lines plus generating numerous weekly/monthly/seasonal profitability reports.
- Established the sportswear buying process for Bloomingdale's e-commerce division. First season clothing sales exceeded projected revenues by 67%. Nearly doubled projected revenues, achieving 15% of entire business sales revenues.
- Developed and added new vendor clothing lines including consignments and exclusives that resulted in increased sales.
- Implemented new buying processes and procedures for Lord & Taylor. Tripled vendors for wider selection while negotiating better terms and prices. New buying program resulted in 65% of product lines selling at full price.
- Analyzed online customer buying and potential buying patterns, then developed new e-commerce buying program. Planned focus, determined fashion concept, and bought clothing that, through use of newly developed sales and design concepts, would sell online and minimize returns.
- Developed, along with web designers and programmers, onscreen visuals for Bloomingdale's e-commerce business. Direct involvement in layout designs, promos, and advertisement placement of high-push items.

## Business Management

- Developed tracking and projection system that analyzed sales, customer buying preferences, fashion trends to buying decisions, and exclusives of ready-made orders. Results: achieved more sales, higher profitability and less marked down inventory.

- Prepared week ending/month ending/season ending reports including Open to Buy, 6 Month Plan, vendor profitability and sales and markdown projections.
- Developed financial forecasting plans that helped determine optimum inventory, vendor selection and product mix to maximize sales and profitability.
- Developed strong partnerships with vendors and negotiated better terms, higher discounts, coop advertising deals, merchandise swaps, RTVs, consignments, exclusives and special deliveries. *Results: increased sales and profitability at both Saks and Henri Bendel.*

### FOREIGN LANGUAGES

Fluent in English and Japanese; speak conversational French

### EDUCATION

Master in Fine Arts, Fashion Design & Technology, Parsons School for Design, New York, NY 2001
BA, Tokyo University of Foreign Studies, Tokyo, Japan 1997

# Jeff Waeger, CPCU, AIC, ARM
1 Main Street
Hartford, CN 06110
(203) 555-1212
jeffwaeg@yahoo.com

Career Objective: INSURANCE CLAIMS MANAGER

## SUMMARY OF QUALIFICATIONS

Proven track record of superior leadership in Claims Management, having exceeded corporate goals over the last five years. Excel at team development, improving staff productivity, efficiency, and accountability to get results. Extensive experience handling corporate restructurings, while improving morale, containing costs, and streamlining processes and procedures. Strong global understanding of entire Insurance Claim process to achieve both corporate and client satisfaction.

## PROFESSIONAL EXPERIENCE

Personal Insurance Regional Claims Manager
Blue Cross Insurance Regional Claims Center, Hartford, CN 1984–present
*(promoted from Branch Claims Manager, promoted from Senior Supervisor, promoted from Senior Property Adjuster).*

- Directed the personal insurance claims area covering a four state region with 45,000 claims per year, for the last five years. Responsibilities include: claims management; customer service; strategic planning; financial analysis; budgeting; staff supervision; processes and procedures improvement; agency relations; staff training and development.

- Beat the industry average for First Party Claims Severity by 4% each of the last four years by implementing new programs, policies and procedures.

- Established new rental car cost control program that achieved the lowest average payment on Rental severity in the nine national claims regions.

- Set up new training program to more effectively process recovery claims. *Results: achieved additional recovery revenue of approximately $1,000,000.*

- Handled extensive interstate reorganizations and downsizings, streamlining productivity and finishing projects under budget.

- Wrote several important staff training manuals outlining procedures and techniques to improve claims handling effectiveness, service, and controlling costs.

## AWARDS

President's Award of Excellence (national recipient 1998)

## EDUCATION

Insurance Designations and Certifications: CPCU 1999, ARM 1993, AIC 1988

# *Promotions*

Moving up the ranks to more challenging and prestigious positions is the goal for many of you. These examples of my clients illustrate both Dan's and Lauren's desire to rise internally (though both said they would consider outside jobs, too). Dan's dream was to manage one of the company's top stores with his eyes set on eventually moving to headquarters to become a key part of the entire chain's management structure. Dan waited months before the job he wanted opened. Competition among internal store managers was steep. A big salary was the lure that brought hundreds of other managers into the competition. Dan's resumé stood out because he emphasized the accomplishments he achieved. Needless to say, Dan got the job!

In Lauren's case, she liked challenges and enjoyed learning new things. She created this resumé to look for other jobs, but I also encouraged her to pass it on to the company's top financial people and personnel. She liked her company but was bored with her current position. I told her to be sure that her employer knew exactly all she had done and achieved for them at that position. A new resumé did the trick. Her employer took notice. She was promoted *twice* during the next year.

Walter's situation was entirely different. He'd attended my seminars and came to see me when he received a 60-day notice that he'd lose his job. He called himself a computer programmer, but during our Goldmining process it became quite clear to me that indeed he had acquired so many on-the-job skills that he exceeded his old job and was in actuality a software engineer. This was quite a realization to him. Software engineers were in serious demand. I coached him to bypass personnel, as eight months of mailing to human resource departments (prior to our meeting) had gotten him no interviews. He followed my advice, dug up some old college friends and alumni, and passed his resumé along to them. Within two weeks he got a call from Hewlett-Packard. *Not only did they offer him the job of his dreams, but it also came with a $20,000 salary increase!* When his old employer found out, they came back with a promotion and matched the salary increase. Walter told me that, hands down, it was the most amazing experience of his life. He'd uncovered his true market value and two top companies wanted him; Hewlett-Packard won out. Walter said: "They really listened to my ideas; they wanted to hear my suggestions and improvements. I met some other engineers who worked in similar teams, and they all said HP valued input." That convinced him. He sold his house and moved to California. Incidentally, he still raves about Hewlett-Packard and his terrific job there.

# Daniel Carter

1 Main Street
City, NY 11111
(201) 555-0111
danc@aol.com

CAREER OBJECTIVE: **Store Manager**

## SUMMARY OF QUALIFICATIONS

Three years of Home Depot store management experience with strengths in staff development, increasing both inside and outside sales, and reducing overhead expenses. 50+ sales presentations to potential commercial accounts resulting in an increase in new business. Strong computer systems experience in EXCEL, Word, and customized database systems.

## PROFESSIONAL EXPERIENCE

*Store Manager,* Home Depot, Reno, Nevada, Desert Store, 1998–present

- Managed retail store with annual sales of $1,250,000 in an extremely competitive market.
- 7% sales increase through active prospecting for new commercial accounts through cold calls, networking, referral leads, and industry vertical marketing.
- 70% increase in operating profit through thorough analysis of all controllable expenses, trimming excess and unnecessary costs, implementing tighter inventory control based on buying demands.
- Trained staff on product lines to increase staff's ability to provide higher quality customer service resulting in noticeable increases in monthly sales and bottomline profits.
- Hired "good fit" new staff. Reduced staff turnover significantly.

*Assistant Store Manager,* Sherwin-Williams Company, Sacramento, CA, West Street Store, 1991–1995

- Assisted manager in all store operations including inside and outside sales, paperwork, inventory, staff training, and purchasing.
- Managed trial balance of all commercial accounts keeping bad debts within corporate goals.
- Managed $80,000 inventory implementing improved purchasing control based on demands of product lines.
- Maintained commercial credit accounts and corresponding collection follow-up activities.

## RELATED EXPERIENCE

*Consulting Project,* Corporate Client, San Jose, CA, 9/97–12/97
Part of an organizational development team evaluating company's employee performance appraisal process to uncover reasons for lateness in supervisor's conducting performance evaluation duties. Developed survey used in focus groups of 30 people from various levels of management. Thorough analysis of process revealed problem areas, necessary training required to correct problems uncovered. Recommendations for improvement to achieve corporate goals were made.

## EDUCATION

Master of Business Administration, University of Nevada, Reno, 1997
Bachelor of Science, School of Management, Arizona State University, Tempe, 1991

**COMBINATION**

# Lauren Nemmies
1 Main Street
City, NY 11111
(201) 555-0111
lnemmies@attbi.com

CAREER OBJECTIVE: **Accounting Supervisor**

## EDUCATION

B.A., Business Administration/Accounting, University of Illinois, 1998
Passed Certified Public Accounting Exam, 2000

## SUMMARY OF QUALIFICATIONS

Five years of comprehensive accounting experience, cross trained in numerous accounting functions, dealing with largest US insurance company. Well developed analytical skills, research abilities with proven problem-solving capabilities. Extensive computer expertise in converting manual systems into streamlined computerized spreadsheets and databases.

## PROFESSIONAL EXPERIENCE

*Senior Accountant, promoted from Internal Auditor,* State Farm Insurance, Bloomington, IL, 1998–Present

### Accounting

- Created new flow charts as internal controls to track work flow in real estate, mortgage loans, claims, cash management, cash receipts, auditing procedures.
- Prepared 32 state tax returns, plus entire federal tax return on $425M revenues.
- Oversee financial and legal compliance on 32 different, variable state regulator laws.
- Prepared, analyzed financial statements including: A/P, bond/stock investments, short-term cash management, reconciliations, G/L, subsidiary ledgers.
- Analyzed $45M budget for variances against actual expenses.
- Coordinated GAAP, statutory, investments, budget areas, financial data into comprehensive financial report.
- Bank liaison over investment of short term cash, ranged from $10M–$30M daily.
- Performed internal audits on operations, payroll, income.

### Computer

- Proficient IBM experience on customized accounting software, databases, LOTUS, Symphony, Flow Chart.
- Created 50 new spreadsheets in various financial areas on PC, converting from manual systems.
- Demonstrated expertise on complicated spreadsheets at macro level.
- Established new database to track municipal taxes on 100 cities. New system saved 16 man-hours.
- Converted monthly accrual procedures of 60 line items onto spreadsheet, used quarterly.
- Trained staff and accountant on customized accounting software and spreadsheets.

# Walter Calvert
1 Main Street
City, NY 11111
(201) 555-0111
walcalvert@central.net

CAREER OBJECTIVE: **Software Engineer**

## SUMMARY OF QUALIFICATIONS

Ten years experience designing, developing, and implementing innovative solutions for engineering/scientific software on work station, mainframe, and PC platforms. Software engineering strengths lie in productivity enhancements, technical troubleshooting, engineer/programmer training, software reverse engineering and redesign, and the modeling of business processes/system designs, and data.

## PROGRAMMING LANGUAGES

| | |
|---|---|
| C (5 yrs), C++ (2 yrs) | FORTRAN (8 yrs) |
| JCL (2 yrs) | Pascal (6 yrs) |

## PLATFORMS AND OPERATING SYSTEMS

| | |
|---|---|
| Silicon Graphics/IRIX (3 yrs) | Hewlett-Packard/HP-UX (1 yr) |
| IBM PC/MS-DOS; Windows (2 yrs) | IBM RS6000/AIX (1 yr) |
| CRAY-YMP/UNICOS (1 yr) | Apple Macintosh (3 yrs) |
| IBM 3090 Mainframe/MVS-TSO (3 yrs) | Apollo/DOMAIN (6 yrs) |

## PROFESSIONAL EXPERIENCE

### Software Engineering and Training

- Use CASE tools to analyze user and business requirements, then redesign and apply software solutions to improve productivity.
- Defined, designed, implemented and trained developers in the use of source code version control and configuration management processes on three major projects.
- Wrote the training materials on operations of a CAD/CAM communication application between UNIX work stations and IBM mainframes for engineering staff.
- Developed curriculum and training materials and instructed a four-day class on using CASE tool and associated Structured Methods for programmers and software engineers.
- Featured speaker lecturing on using CASE tools at a national Apollo DOMAIN User Society Conference.

### Programming

- Created new and restructured existing engineering/scientific software utilizing C, FORTRAN, UNIX scripting, JCL, and MVS-TSO.
- Directed a team to redesign and enhance the user interface, reliability, and functionality of an interactive, 3-D graphics application used by the Computational Fluid Dynamics Laboratory Engineers.
- Developed innovative communication link between two major CAD/CAM packages, one hosted on several different UNIX work stations, and one hosted on IBM mainframes. Included design, programming, testing, integration, and both user and developer training.

WORK HISTORY

*Software Engineer,* The Boeing Corporation, 1993–Present

EDUCATION

B.S., Computer Science, University of California, Berkeley, 1993

**Editorial Note: Original resumé all appeared on one page**

# Maria Antonio
1 Main Street
San Diego, CA 92000
(619) 555-1212
mantonio@earthlink.net

CAREER OBJECTIVE: DIRECTOR OF MANAGED HEALTHCARE

## SUMMARY OF QUALIFICATIONS

Proven leadership ability with unique background as senior executive for major healthcare insurance company, as well as many years in clinical nursing. Strong global experience of national healthcare market having managed utilization review and national case management programs. Demonstrated expertise in containing costs, streamlining operations, and developing efficient policies/procedures/processes/systems. Excel at building highly efficient and productive teams.

## PROFESSIONAL EXPERIENCE

*Director of Care Management,* Kaiser, San Diego, CA 1995–present
(promoted from *Manager of Physician/Provider Education,* promoted from
*Utilization Review Specialist*)
*Surgical Nurse,* various hospitals 1980–1995

### Program Management

- Managed two large-scale programs for medical insurance provider coordinating the national case management program and national utilization review program for nine years.
- Responsibilities as national case management program director included: established national program; developed policies/procedures/processes and systems; set up cost analysis system; provided clinical interpretations on appropriate medical care; interpreted and tracked the hundreds of contracts and various benefits stipulated; conducted financial analysis and quality of care outcomes; implemented new system coordinating pharmacy and case management; served as liaison to medical directors and senior executives; contributed to corporate strategic planning; implemented case management of managed Medicare risk program; coordinated with governmental regulatory agencies—HFCA/HCA/OIC/L&I, etc.; supervised, trained and developed staff.
- Implemented numerous cost savings and cost containment activities and programs that maintained quality of care while saving the company $30 million over the last 4 years.
- Assisted the IT department with the development of highly sophisticated cutting edge computer systems that resulted in providing enhanced reporting, more decision-making data, claims and utilization analysis, medical disease analysis, dissecting clinical outcomes and costing to improve case management, benefits, and lower company's overall costs.
- Managed thousands of providers (doctors, hospitals) and hundreds of employer group accounts to improve quality of care and increase customer service.

Utilization Review
- Managed medical utilization review of providers (doctors, hospitals, clinics), pre-authorizations, approvals, etc., coordinating internal nurse and doctor review staff in providing coverage decisions.
- Developed policies and procedures handling requirements of numerous regulatory agencies and contract benefits.
- Wrote several important staff training manuals outlining procedures and techniques to improve claims handling effectiveness, service, and controlling costs.

## EDUCATION

MS, Health Care Administration, St. Mary's College, Los Angeles, CA
*(currently attending)*
BS, Health Care Administration, St. Mary's College, Los Angeles, CA 1993
RN, Orange Community College, San Diego, CA 1980

# SPECIAL CIRCUMSTANCES:
## NO COLLEGE DEGREE, EMPLOYMENT GAPS, CHANGING CAREERS, MILITARY TO CIVILIAN, VOLUNTEERS, REENTRY, RELOCATION, CONSULTANTS, CV (CURRICULUM VITAE)

## 7

U nique circumstances require special solutions. In this chapter, I've broken down many different situations you might be facing, then discussed and shown examples of resumés that clients in these situations have actually used to land jobs.

## No College Degree

There are many talented people who have great work experience but do not have a college degree. If you look throughout the book, you'll notice some. In many cases their work experience is strong, so we actually leave the "Education" heading off the resumé and just don't mention the lack of a degree. This keeps the emphasis on what you *have* accomplished.

"Employers want people who can hit the ground running," says John Murphy, author of *Success without a College Degree* (www.thisismychance .com). "Your practical or industry experience is much more valuable than a diploma. Focus most of your energy on describing your strengths and characteristics, i.e., being very organized, meeting deadlines, or good with people. Don't think everyone has this skill; recognize that you possess individual talents employers want and hire for."

Murphy confirmed, "Employers do not see a degree as a must, they hire the person they think can do the job. Demonstrating your skills, getting the job done quickly and efficiently, that's a more appealing package."

Richard is a good example because he's in the technology field—an industry notorious for talented, nondegreed people. Merit and accomplishment are the yardsticks in the high tech field. Richard wanted to relocate to be near his wife's family in Tulsa. He went there for a two-week job search, interviewed with a couple of companies, and secured a much better job than the one he was voluntarily quitting.

**COMBINATION**

# Richard J. Montgomery

1 Main Street
Shawnee Mission, KS 66000
(613) 555-1212
richmont@nextlink.com

CAREER OBJECTIVE: **Director of Technology**

## SUMMARY OF QUALIFICATIONS

Proven track record managing the ever-changing technology needs for midsize, multi-state organization. Have extensive experience managing systems, upgrades, installation of new servers and business applications. Develop high quality systems that achieve both capacity and reliability goals. Purchasing and negotiating skills to successfully obtain lowest prices on top quality equipment and products. Excel at working with managers and department heads to meet their needs and train staff.

## PROFESSIONAL EXPERIENCE

*Manager of Partnering/Client Relations,* Systems Technologies,
Overland Park, KS 1999–present
*Systems Administrator,* Brown, Thomas and Smith, Kansas City, MO 1993–1999
(promoted from *Business Manager* 1997)

### Systems and Operations

- Managed the Information Systems and technical staff for 300+ employee company overseeing four West Coast offices; administration of company wide computer network; hardware/software selection; daily systems operations; 1.5 million dollar annual budget plus all technology upgrades, enhancements, and troubleshooting.
- Set up technology for new offices in different states including establishment of the network, communication lines to main office, hired staff, and oversaw operations and troubleshooting.
- Implemented larger server which doubled capacity for entire interstate system; resulted in increased speed and reliability without any losses or delays.
- Purchased and installed all servers, hardware, software applications for entire organization. Researched suppliers and negotiated better delays, resulting in better prices and higher quality.

### Business Development

- Developed and supervised products and services for new technology company from inception to $10 million in annual revenues. Duties included: product development, marketing and sales, strategic planning, financial management/budgeting, systems operations, client relationship management, contract negotiations and product launches.

### Client Management

- Developed and managed 300+ clients on a continuous basis dealing with both IT and senior executives. Duties included: marketing new services, sales of products, troubleshooting, problem resolution, coordinating technology needs, and maintaining relationships.

## TECHNOLOGY EXPERTISE AND COMPETENCIES

Lotus Notes/Domino, Microsoft NT and Windows, Novell Netware, OS2, Word, Excel, PowerPoint, Pagemaker, databases, spreadsheets, email, Internet browsers.

# *Employment Gaps*

Employment gaps present a challenge when you're seeking to find a job. Our survey results found that 80% of employers find work gaps worrisome. Several employers elaborated as Larry Tomon, regional sales director, did to say: "I would require a reasonable explanation." Al, a CEO in healthcare added: "I will ask a candidate in an interview to fill in the gaps for us." Susan Carroll, executive VP at Westar Insurance Managers, stated: "I find work gaps worrisome; however, I'm actually more concerned if they've held *too many* jobs."

Employment gaps are worrisome, but not deadly. If these employers are talking about your work history, then you'll need to create a resumé that draws importance to the skills and not the time worked. It's reassuring to note that only three hiring managers (from the 600 we surveyed) said they would completely dismiss candidates who've been unemployed more than one year. The vast majority (virtually all) wanted an explanation. I've found that the very best place to give that explanation is in the interview. Many women are faced with years of unemployment. Raising children, caring for an ill family member, and pregnancy all contribute. In the examples of clients who have faced this situation, you'll see in Denise's case that it took a lengthy period of time to relocate the family when her husband accepted a new job. Nearly two years went by as she found a house and got her family settled into their new community. She was very worried about the employment gap when she came to see me. Denise's previous experience and past employers were impressive. Because it was obvious that she relocated, we selected the traditional, chronological style. She sought a higher level finance position, and that field most often requires the Chronological or Combination resumé. By Goldmining, we were able to uncover important accomplishments and pare her original three-page resumé into a highly effective one-page version. Denise needed job leads. She was uncomfortable with networking since she really knew no one in the new city. I encouraged her to attend both the local banking and CPA association meetings, where she heard of a great job in the real estate division of a major bank. Her new resumé got her the interview. Denise took advantage of the opportunity, and she was well prepared. They immediately offered her the job. The two-year gap did not stop this employer from hiring her for nearly a six-figure salary.

Both Fran and Jennifer had several-year employment gaps. Jennifer had had a baby. Fran moved with her husband to a new city, leaving behind her coveted job in Paris. Shortly thereafter, she went through a long painful divorce, then finally returned to the United States. Both women faced and dealt with a great deal of rejection and fear. Today, they are happily employed. The work gaps didn't prevent them from getting hired, either, once they created strong resumés.

I recommend that you never explain work gaps on your resumé. See how all three women emphasized their skills. When they were called in for interviews, they explained their situations. In Denise's case, she mentioned the relocation in her cover letter.

Bruce, an internal corporate recruiter at a Fortune 100 company, says: "It's hard to find good people. As long as people have kept up-to-date, we often hire them even if there's been a multiyear gap. We find they have a higher desire to prove themselves again and almost always do." So be tenacious and enthusiastic. Polish your interview skills. Someone like Bruce is out there waiting for you to come through the door so he can hire you.

# Denise Stroud, MBA
1 Main Street
City, NY 11111
(201) 555-0111
dstroud@aol.com

CAREER OBJECTIVE: **Finance Manager**

## SUMMARY OF QUALIFICATIONS

Nine years in high levels of financial analysis, project management, forecasting, and financial modeling. Expertise in reducing risk, obtaining investors, determining accurate feasibility of potential projects. Global thinker with strong strategic planning ability.

## PROFESSIONAL EXPERIENCE

*Finance Project Manager,* Developers Corporation, New York, NY, 1997–1999

- Primarily responsible for putting together a partnership between the company and investors. Developed detailed budget, forecasts, cash flow and tax projections. Secured financing and obtained $2.1 million in federal tax credits for investors.
- Developed computerized financial models that project revenues, equity returns, tax options, and cash flow to establish the viability of the project.
- Redesigned and implemented new vendor payment system on a multi-million dollar project that increased the speed of payments by 120 days.

*Vice President,* Real Estate Dept., Chase Manhattan Bank, New York, NY, 1990–1997

- Managed commercial real estate loan team advancing secured loans on a portfolio which grew from $200 million to $500 million through market research, partnership building, customer service, and financial analysis while lowering risk assessment.
- Developed a new loan monitoring system which was used for internal control on bank's entire $1.5 billion real estate loan portfolio.
- Produced new marketing concept selling financial packages to commercial accounts. Created financial presentations, financial analysis, projections, and risk management incentives. Sold $300 million of these products in 18 months.
- Analyzed all financial data and developed financial projection models to determine feasibility of over fifty projects, some with retail sell out value over $180 million.
- Wrote training manual for top financial executives containing the underwriting guidelines for commercial residential development lending. Received a special corporate award for this achievement.

## EDUCATION

M.B.A., Harvard University, Boston, MA, 1990
B.A., Urban Studies, Vassar College, 1985

# Fran Gibson
1 Main Street
City, NY 11111
(201) 555-0111
fgibson@msn.com

CAREER OBJECTIVE: **Health Club Management**

## SUMMARY OF QUALIFICATIONS

Eleven years in club management, having successfully opened and operated two new start-up recreational clubs. Proven ability to design innovative programs, recruit and maintain members, operate profitable facilities, and build a service-oriented, highly productive team. Excellent financial management skills in overseeing the construction and renovation of six facilities while keeping the club open. Ability to interact effectively with members, staff and managers to provide the highest level of member satisfaction possible.

## PROFESSIONAL EXPERIENCE

*General Manager,* City Club, Paris, 6/94–11/99

- Opened new social/athletic international club, obtaining 11,000+ members and $4.5 million in annual revenues within 30 months.
- Managed day-to-day club operations including: facilities, financial operations, marketing, food and beverage, programming, personnel and membership.
- Established marketing and promotion campaign to sell twenty-seven hundred $3,200 memberships, using print advertisement, television, and direct mail.
- Conducted feasibility studies, forecast projections budgeting and demographics as basis for facilities expansion into other regions, with new facility built and opened in summer of 1998.
- Maximized productivity level of seven department managers and staff of 115, while maintaining a high level of member service.
- Developed innovative programming that attracted new members, plus maintained 95% retention of current membership.

*Athletic Director,* Oceanside Athletic Club, LaJolla, CA, 7/84–5/94

- Provided management in the establishment and ongoing operations of new start-up 160,000 square feet multi-purpose club with current membership at 3400, $1.15 million annual athletic revenues.
- Coordinated the athletic facilities expansion, construction renovations of six projects with budgets of $500,000.
- Reorganized the athletic division to streamline staff and overhead to increase profitability.
- Developed innovative programming that satisfied current members and became a magnet for new memberships.

## HONORS

*President,* National Association of Club Athletic Directors, 1993

## EDUCATION

Bachelor of Science Degree, University of San Diego, CA

# Jennifer Roberts

1 Main Street
City, NY 11111
(201) 555-0111
jroberts211@aol.com

CAREER OBJECTIVE: **Flight Attendant**

## SUMMARY OF QUALIFICATIONS

Eleven years in aviation customer service with the last four years as a Flight Attendant for major air carrier on both domestic and international flight. Served for three years as the Flight Attendant-in-charge. Excel on promoting safety as well as improving customer satisfaction aboard flights. Flexible, easily adapt to new time zones, diverse cultures and varied schedules. *Willing to relocate as needed.*

## PROFESSIONAL EXPERIENCE

*Flight Attendant,* Delta Airlines, 12/96–7/00

- Spent four years as flight attendant serving on both domestic and international flights. Flown over 700 hours.
- Achieved Flight Attendant-in-charge status within one year. Responsible for the entire cabin crew of up to 12 flight attendants as well as all communication between the cabin and cockpit.

*Flight Attendant,* Spectrum Air, Van Nuys, CA, 10/96–3/00

- Worked as part-time contract Flight Attendant for corporate plane on international flights to Europe, Asia, and South America. Flew over 500 international hours, Challenger 601 was our primary aircraft as well as Gulfstreams 2, 3, and 4.
- Responsible for handling all safety and FAA policies to ensure a safe trip.
- Prepared complete food service including ordering with catering company.
- Provided customer service and personal assistance to passengers dealing with customs requirements, purchase declarations and destination logistics.

*Customer Service Representative, Charter Sales Travel,* Houston, TX, 7/89–12/96

- Aided pilots and passengers by arranging ground transportation and hotel accommodations working exclusively with corporate accounts.

## TRAINING

Delta Airlines Intensive Training, one month program qualified to fly on entire fleet
of aircraft: DC9, MD80, 727, 737, 757, 767, and L1011 September 1996
Recurrent classes January, 1997, 1998, and 1999
Airline Emergency Training, Dallas, Texas, 2002

# *Changing Careers*

Starting over (for in many cases that is indeed what you are doing) can be rewarding or frustrating depending on your situation. Be sure you *hate the work,* and not just *hate the company* or *hate the boss.* A similar job with another company that has a more compatible environment could be the answer. The resumés at the end of this section resulted in successful career changes for my clients.

Jonathan made nearly $80,000 a year as an auto body repairer and painter. Great money, yet he was very unhappy. He was tired of the heavy work, and his body was older and ached all the time as a result. We got together and wrote the only resumé he ever had. It got him two job offers, but he took the sales rep position in which he'd sell and demonstrate car paint. He makes less money (always a serious possibility when changing fields), but the new job's worked out very well for him.

Kathryn got lots of job offers, but all in fundraising. She was determined to follow her passion and change her career leaving fundraising behind. That led to numerous challenges convincing employers, but finally she got a job in child and family advocacy. She told me: "It's not like work at all; I love it so much." Her new job was part-time to start (a hard adjustment since she was a single mother) but within several months, they put her on full-time. Following her dream and passion led her to obtaining a much desired goal that she finds fulfilling and rewarding in ways that extra money could never do.

Amy wanted a new field. Her experience was strongly related to the desired new field and transferable, as it's often referred to by career counselors. Amy wanted to leave television (she'd been fired one too many times). Playing up her transfer skills (developed during Goldmining), this client got a new, better-paying job than the one she left in public relations.

Changing from the military and finding a satisfying and meaningful job in the civilian world is a very difficult undertaking. Too many get lost in the process of simply seeking a job. Success does not often follow, nor does satisfaction. One hiring manager wrote to say: "Military transitions are tough. We get a lot here who apply for a job that they have no experience or background in. Usually their resumés are way too long. They just give useless descriptions that we find hard to interpret. We tend to toss out most that we receive."

I can personally attest to this. I worked at a military base as a director of a college. I helped a lot of officers make a move into the civilian world. I remember one man who had a 28-page resumé—28 pages! He got very put out with me when I told him *no one* would read it. Indeed, two months later he was back after several others gave him the same interpretation. I find most military folks have a difficult time because they only have one frame of reference, the military. Significant career exploration and job targeting are an essential part of this type of career transition.

Roger faced military retirement after 20 years of service. The navy was all he knew. Although he was interested in many things, after a few coaching sessions and extensive job market research, he decided to focus on the emergency management area. This was a significant step: he identified the job he wanted. Goldmining uncovered the related experience which was significant, but Roger faced a huge obstacle. There were very few civilian jobs in this area. He networked endlessly and even volunteered for almost six months before he finally got a paid job. He stayed at this part-time job for nearly a year before securing a full-time position heading services for the county. It was a long road—dreams don't always come easy—but they are achievable if you have a burning desire and the diligence to keep working toward your goal.

Robert had spent the last six years of his career in two large school districts working on technology programs and as a computer lab teacher. Prior to that, he'd worked as a film/video producer and consultant, and before that as an elementary school teacher.

He enjoyed the innovation of blending education and technology. But when a budget crunch came along, a new administrator told Robert his only options were to return to the classroom as a full-time teacher (with a pay cut) or be laid off. He was quite upset when we met, because he knew his was one of the few jobs on the leading edge of education and technology anywhere in the country. He'd job hunted to no avail and was depressed and distressed about his situation. We both agreed landing a similar job was a difficult goal—but he needed to try before ruling it impossible. We created a resumé that really characterized his skills, and he kept looking. Within two months, he'd found his dream job—at a university—mixing technology and education curricula to increase learning for elementary school students. Very innovative, very cutting edge. *Very cool,* he said. He sent in his resumé and landed the Educational Technology Project Director position. He's since amassed millions of dollars in grants for developing school programs. He feels it's the best job in the world, that he's truly making an important difference. The job, he later said, was far better than anything he could have imagined, and it paid $20,000 more per year than his previous position.

Nathan was an engineer, and a very ambitious one. He'd gone to grad school at night, while employed with a power company, and earned an MBA. He wanted to do more and advance—but to do so would require a big career change, taking him out of the engineering field. When you're earning $60,000 per year and have a family to support, you think long and hard about career changes.

We worked together to analyze his better career options. He decided to try to move into a marketing position within the power industry. Still it is very rare that engineers make moves like this—most remain in engineering and/or consulting throughout their entire career. The new resumé we created for him really opened doors, whereas the three-page one he'd been using had generated no responses. The old resumé was repetitive, long, boring, and read like an extensive job description. It had no actions = results in it. The transformation was almost miraculous. The new resumé got Nathan Myers four job offers! Each one was significantly better-paying than his current job, and he accepted a position that paid $20,000 more than the one he had. This career change put him on the fast track—three years after his move, he was earning $120,000 per year. Just goes to show how, with proper planning and good self-marketing, you can change fields and prosper. Nathan is living proof.

# Jonathan Prentice
1 Main Street
City, NY 11111
(201) 555-0111
jpnt@yahoo.com

CAREER OBJECTIVE: **Claims Adjuster/Appraiser**

## SUMMARY OF QUALIFICATIONS

Excellent understanding of entire auto repair process developed with 18 years in the auto repair field. Hands-on experience includes estimates, body repair, and customer relations while emphasizing cost containment and high quality repair. Ability to work independently as well as in a team. Highly productive with accurate eye for details and auto damage inspections and estimation.

## PROFESSIONAL EXPERIENCE

*Automotive Refinisher and Painter,* Pete's Body Shop, Lenexa, KS, 1983–2001

### Automotive Repair

- 18 years in the automotive repair business including: estimates, body repair, auto painting, parts inventory, customer service, vendor relations, purchasing. Worked on thousands of cars, all makes and models.
- Wrote repair estimates using the Mitchell manuals preparing accurate estimates.
- Provided hundreds of repair explanations to customers, adjusters and appraisers outlining repair procedures, cost options and time schedules.
- Painted thousands of repaired cars including: masking, sanding, priming, blocking, refinishing and polishing.

### Training

- Trained apprentice painters and body men technicians on auto painting and plastic auto repair.
- Provided one-on-one guidance and hands-on training of auto repair process.

### Administration

- Utilized computerized paint selection software to achieve accurate paint mixing. Used daily. Updated software monthly.
- Created charts/graphs and implemented equipment maintenance tracking system to decrease any downtime due to equipment failure.
- Implemented numerous cost containment ideas that saved $15,000+.
- Coordinated all materials inventory and purchasing over 15 year period.

## PROFESSIONAL CERTIFICATIONS

I-CAR Program, Overland Park Technical College, Kansas, 3/98 and 4/98
PPG Painting Training Center, Kansas City, MO, 3/98
IMACA, International Mobile Air Conditioning Association, 3/98

# Kathryn Franklin
1 Main Street
City, NY 11111
(201) 555-0111
katefran@msn.com

CAREER OBJECTIVE: **Position in Child & Family Advocacy**

### SUMMARY OF QUALIFICATIONS

Passionate commitment to ensuring child advocacy rights. Experienced with juvenile justice system, parental and child rights, and investigative procedures. Excellent communication and project management skills.

### PROFESSIONAL EXPERIENCE

#### Social Services
- Six years experience as Guardian Ad Litem/Court Appointed Special Advocate for abused and neglected children.
- Investigated family situations to gather relevant information and report appropriate facts to court.
- Facilitator and negotiator between families, courts and children to ensure social services fulfill obligations to the child.
- Extensive legal knowledge of juvenile justice system and parental and child rights.
- Presentations on parenting issues to associations, colleges and social service groups.
- Handled on-air interviews for WPVI TV, WPHL TV and WHYY Radio on parenting issues.

#### Fundraising
- Twelve years experience in all aspects of fundraising including: major donor solicitation, direct mail, special events, annual giving, and corporate and foundation grants.
- Build strong major donor relationships easily acquiring large contributions, highly visible volunteers and community leaders to make events and campaigns successful.
- Established new first-time major gifts campaign. Recruited 80 high profile volunteers, trained them for effective personal solicitations. $450,000 raised.

#### Events Management
- Planned, coordinated and managed hundreds of special events: conferences, educational programs, auctions, phonathons, dinners, lunches, and receptions.
- Recruited, selected, and trained 400+ volunteers obtaining high levels of work effort, commitment and financial support.

### WORK HISTORY

*Director of Development,* Community Centers, Philadelphia, PA, 1997–present
*Director of Development,* Pennsylvania Cancer Society, 1993–1997
*Program Manager,* Philadelphia Medical, 1990–1992
*Events Coordinator,* New York Medical, 1980–1990

### EDUCATION
B.A., Communications, Villanova University, PA, 1994

# Amy Vanderwell
1 Main Street
City, NY 11111
(201) 555-0111
avanderw@msn.com

CAREER OBJECTIVE: **Public Relations Account Executive**

## SUMMARY OF QUALIFICATIONS

Fourteen years in print and broadcast media. Proven expertise in producing television shows, radio features and sales videos; newspaper reporting; features writing; coordinating large scale special events and corporate sponsorships. Extensive media contacts at national networks and talk shows plus affiliates, independent stations and large regional newspapers. Able to create media pitch that results in generous positive publicity. Noted for outstanding organization and project management skills.

## PROFESSIONAL EXPERIENCE

### Writing
- Created thousands of story ideas and wrote features for local and national television broadcasts.
- Won regional Emmy award for writing. National Emmy finalist for PBS feature.
- Developed community service campaign by creating PSAs, promotional spots, sales videos and special programming for children and families. Campaign achieved 92% public awareness.
- Wrote daily news under deadline pressure for newspapers and television.
- Generated hundreds of press releases to obtain newspaper and radio coverage.

### Television and Video Production
- Produced hundreds of television talk shows with live audiences, satellite interviews and viewer calls.
- Developed story ideas, talk show topics, and news reports. Booked over 1,000 guests.
- Produced video news release securing coverage in 80% of target stations in national campaign.
- Coached corporate executives for broadcast appearances.
- Received numerous national awards for outstanding video production.

### Event Management
- Managed staff, talent appearances, transportation, site construction and creation of display booths for company co-sponsorship of annual Fourth of July event. Attendance: 175,000+
- Organized Summer Arts annual event for 200 disabled children and families. Event is 100% donation, including food, entertainment, facilities, toys, printing and volunteer coordination.
- Coordinated annual network telethon including 32-hour broadcast schedule, feature interviews, talent negotiations and production set-up. DC telethon ranked #1 nationally in income received.

## Presentations

- Delivered comprehensive media campaign presentations to advertising agencies, corporations and non-profits, including videos, written proposals and speeches.
- Established sponsorships with numerous companies including Du Pont, USA Today, Diamond Parking, Dairy Queen, American Bank, Target, Newsweek, and Time Warner.

### WORK HISTORY

*Magazine and Talk Show Producer,* WJLA-TV (ABC), Washington, DC, 1997–Present
*Video Producer and Media Consultant,* WCTS-TV (PBS), Washington, DC, 1996–1997
*Program Producer, Reporter,* WUSP-TV (CBS), Washington, DC, 1994–1996
*Segment Producer, Reporter, Project Grant Coordinator,* WCTS-TV (PBS), Washington, DC, 1990–1994
*Freelance News Reporter,* WOOW-FM (NPR) and WTTG-TV (FOX), Washington, DC, 1990–1992
*Co-Anchor, Reporter, Associate Producer,* WAVY-TV (ABC), Norfolk, VA, 1988–1990

### EDUCATION

B.A., English/Journalism, University of Virginia, 1988

# Roger Jacobson
1 Main Street
City, NY 11111
(201) 555-0111

CAREER OBJECTIVE: **Position in Emergency Management**

## SUMMARY OF QUALIFICATIONS

Five years in Emergency Management responsible for planning, inter-department coordination, communications and crisis leadership. Managed 135+ life-threatening events with efficient, speed, and appropriate responses. Experienced in dealing with media in crisis situations. Proven ability to unite departments utilizing excellent interpersonal and communication skills.

## PROFESSIONAL EXPERIENCE

*Emergency Services Planner,* U.S. Navy, 1980–2000
*(Promoted from Search and Rescue Officer, promoted from
Maritime Law Enforcement Officer)*

### Crisis Management
- Manager-in-charge of crisis situation overseeing 135+ life-threatening events including: burning ship, dangerous weapons barge aground on resort beach, bomb threats, emergency aircraft landings, fires, water rescues, disabled ships.
- Efficiently and quickly coordinate all necessary response departments to handle an emergency including medical, evacuation, current information communications, and appropriate response actions.
- Public Affairs Representative dealing effectively with local and national media handling large scale hurricane with loss of life. Produced press releases, conducted on-air radio and television interviews. Published related articles.

### Planning
- Three years as the Emergency Services Planner preparing for natural disasters. Responsibilities included: authored formal emergency plans, tested each plan for effectiveness, coordinated all federal, state and civil department's interactions, reevaluated and finalized plan.
- Planned emergency responses uniting federal, state, and local emergency response agencies to quickly deal with an instant disaster.
- Authored five emergency response plans from 30 to 300 pages in length.

### Technical Communications
- Establishing plans to access emergency communication networks in event of regional communications outage to link top officials to relief coordinators.
- Expertise in handling communications via dedicated phone systems, computer, and facsimile systems.
- Instructor in Emergency Operations Plans course for managers.
- Written hundreds of reports, plans, studies, and process analysis related to emergency services. Authored numerous communications plans.
- 100+ presentations to widely diverse audience on social issues and emergency planning.

## EDUCATION

Bachelor's Degree, University of Maryland, 1986

# Robert Charleston
1 Main Street
Braintree, MA 02100
(781) 555-1212
rjcharl@aol.com

*One of only a few resumés sent and it got him the job.*

CAREER OBJECTIVE: **Educational Technology Program Manager**

### SUMMARY OF QUALIFICATIONS

An innovative visionary integrating technology into education to provide new programming and educational experiences for K–12 students. Proven experience incorporating technology and new ideas into usable education methods achieving highly acclaimed and useful programs. Possess ability to train nontechnical teachers/staff/employees/parents and provide technical support for higher user satisfaction. Excel at program development, team motivation, project management, and achieving goals.

### PROFESSIONAL EXPERIENCE

*Instructional Technology Manager*—Internet Academy, Weymouth School District, 1999–present

*Technology Specialist/Multimedia Production Supervisor*—Hingham School District, 1995–1999

*Multimedia Producer/Consultant*—MacDonald Communications, Boston, MA 1987–1999

## Interactive/Online Program Development
- Established the US's first online K–12 program, creating a virtual school offering K–12 courses for Washington State students, currently seen nationwide as a leading model.
- Managed development of the virtual school, duties included: course creation, authoring HTML pages, establish multiple websites, design of user interface for interactive online courses, create marketing campaign and promotional materials, interviewed/registered students, establish help desk, manage and train faculty, budget management, software license agreements, and manage software development team.
- Created new live interactive cable television program airing math and science enrichment episodes weekly for two years. Target audience 8–12 year olds.

## Curriculum Development
- Authored and taught six online courses for 4th–8th grade students integrating math, science, language arts, and social studies. These serve as the model for all future online course development.
- Designed new, innovative projects and materials for students to increase their computer applications skills and develop their cognitive abilities.
- Served as consultant to teachers to incorporate and integrate technology skills into mainstream curriculum to improve learning retention and meet state learning standards.

*Editorial Note: Original resumé all appeared on one page*

Multimedia/Technology
- Produced live interactive cable television programs; produced dozens of employee educational videos; designed and installed new television studio and multimedia board room.

### EDUCATION

Master's Degree, Media Communications, Boston State University, Illinois, 1986
Master's Degree, Elementary Education, Boston State University, Illinois, 1985
Bachelor's Degree, Empire State College, New York, 1983

**COMBINATION**

# Nathan Muyen, MBA
1 Main Street
San Jose, CA 95000
(408) 555-1212
nmy@att.net

*This resumé landed the career changer four better-paying job offers in the new field.*

CAREER OBJECTIVE: **Power Marketer**

## SUMMARY OF QUALIFICATIONS

Twelve years of proven management in the energy field: electric power, natural gas, hydro, coal and transmission. Managed / negotiated 60% of electric / gas company's wholesale, utilities and municipalities contracts. Coordinated all RFPs and selection of utility and wholesale vendors. Built profitable relationships with key industry power managers. Developed innovative financial costing forecast models that resulted in company savings of $375 million. Recognized for relationship building, innovative pricing solutions, financial analysis, negotiation skills and program management.

## PROFESSIONAL EXPERIENCE

*Senior Engineering Program Manager / Analyst*—California Power and Energy, San Jose, CA 1985–present
(Promoted from *Senior Power Resource Engineer.*)

### Management / Finance / Marketing

- Twelve years managing 60% of all the power / gas utility's wholesale contracts ($300 million annual) including: marketing negotiations, contracts, financial analysis, budgets, strategic planning, client relations and power costing forecasting.
- Managed the buying / purchasing process of power from wholesale power producers. Directed the RFP (Request for Proposal) process, including review and final decision authority to select and negotiate the transactions.
- Served as company liaison between wholesalers, utilities, municipalities, public utility districts, power marketers on major power resource contracts. Coordinated all legal, financial and technical interactions between both parties. Developed solid and extensive relationships within the industry's wholesalers and utilities managers.
- Developed a new financial modeling process to forecast short and long term costs for power and natural gas. Using model, renegotiated 15 major fuel supply and power resource/utility contracts for a corporate savings of $375 million.
- Coordinated company's activities in the development of Independent Grid Operator (IndeGO) and California Regional Transmission Accociation (CRTA) with 21 transmission providers and other wholesale entities in order to regionalize the transmission system in California.

### ENGINEERING / TECHNICAL

- Broad experience in the electric utility field, with hands-on expertise in hydro, natural gas, coal, electric and transmission systems.
- Developed and managed the Open Access Same-Time Information Systems (OASIS) of company's transmission sales transactions, pricing options, transmissions availability information and reservation access.

*Editorial Note: Original resumé all appeared on one page*

- Developed new identification process for underground cable failure and corrosion with innovative solutions to mitigate the problems. Implemented systems throughout company service area.

### EDUCATION

MBA, Santa Clara University, California, 1989
BS, Electrical and Computer Engineering, California State University, 1985

### RELOCATION: AS NEEDED

# *Volunteer/Reentry*

If you are like most people who volunteer, you often disregard these valuable experiences. When I met Kimberlee, her very first question was: "Do you think anyone would hire me? I've never worked a day in my life." One look at her resumé will show you how she spent her time—volunteering. She achieved a lot, but until our meeting and Goldmining, she'd devalued it all.

In Jacqueline's case, she had been a booker for the Sheriff's Department years ago, but it was her desire to move into an advisory role that brought her to me. She had acquired a lot of valuable skills from her community activities, none of which she realized would matter to an employer before our coaching session.

Maria, an HR manager, told us: "We value experience and appreciate a person who has shown initiative through volunteer activities to obtain it." Employers evaluate experience, paid and unpaid, as an overall package. Donna, a senior vice president, told me: "Women tend to disregard life skills—scheduling, budgeting, organizing events, and charity work. Planning a fundraiser and having 200 people turn out is significant. Likewise, coaching a team demonstrates management leadership that's definitely needed in today's workplace."

As you look at the two clients' resumés that follow, what stands out are the skills and results these women achieved. We only include activities that present the skills important to the jobs they wanted. *Both women* put their enthusiasm behind their new resumés (as well as self-discoveries on specifics to sell to the employer) and *landed excellent jobs within a few weeks.*

# Kimberlee Hartword
1 Main Street
City, NY 11111
(201) 555-0111

CAREER OBJECTIVE: **Fundraiser**

## SUMMARY OF QUALIFICATIONS

Development professional with proven expertise in fundraising, strategic planning, organizational development, marketing, media relations, budget analysis, gift solicitation and donor relationships.

## WORK EXPERIENCE

### Fundraising

- Coordinated and chaired 3 day national conference, attracted 600 attendees. Budget $100,000. Only conference to make a profit in organization's history.
- Campaign team contributor raised $1.3 million on annual dinner, 600 attendees. Personally solicited gifts of over $500 with 80% success rate.
- Conducted 25 direct mail, phonathons, donor and membership campaigns exceeding goals on 75% of projects.
- Coordinated 45+ special events, including dinners, receptions, lunches, exhibits, auctions, conferences, concerts, exhibitions. Responsible for planning, lodging, catering, marketing, logistics, publicity, volunteer recruitment, and budgeting.
- United Nation's Host Committee Organizer. Planned logistics. Secured 12 corporate sponsorships. Coordinated volunteers.

### Administration

- Recruited, selected, trained, and scheduled hundreds of volunteers; clerical to board positions.
- Budget committee member deciding resource allocations on $3.6 million budget.
- Strategic planning on organizational growth and development.
- Built productive teams through effective leadership, motivation, accountability, recognition.
- Secured large corporate sponsors to underwrite special events.
- IBM computer skills.
- Grant writing.

### Marketing/Public Relations

- Produced brochures, booklet, flyers, pamphlets, media releases, PSAs, promotional video, radio commercial, and print advertisements.
- Wrote press releases that aired on WABC, WNBC, WCBS TV and numerous radio stations.
- Created repeated newspaper publicity generated through press releases and media contacts.

## WORK HISTORY

*National Secretary,* American Jewish Federation, New York, NY, 1992 to present
*Projects Coordinator,* Women's Organization, New York Region, 1984–Present

## EDUCATION

Bachelor of Arts, Skidmore College, Saratoga Springs, NY, 1981
Advertising Certificate, New York University, NY, 1996

**FUNCTIONAL**

# Jacqueline Grant
1 Main Street
City, NY 11111
(201) 555-0111

CAREER OBJECTIVE: **Program Coordinator**

## SUMMARY OF QUALIFICATIONS

Ten years experience dealing with youth-in-crisis situation and criminal behavior. Excellent communication skills to deal effectively with diverse populations. Strong program coordination abilities with proven expertise to organize programs, recruit volunteers, and produce positive results. Firm, but strong caring attitude to develop each individual's self-worth and self-esteem.

## WORK EXPERIENCE

### Community Relations
- Ten years experience processing juvenile and adult criminal offenders including: intake interview, assess physical condition, evaluate mental/emotional status, and make appropriate referrals.
- Effectively handled thousands of families in crisis situations to explain the situation, outline their rights, advise on options and resources available.
- Provided counseling to individuals and families to direct them to outside resources in a supportive caring way.

### Communication Skills
- Excellent interviewer having conducted thousands of interviews to gather information that is often difficult for individuals to disclose.
- Ability to effectively communicate to all individuals with skill in dealing with widely diverse populations.
- Trained 75 new staff in effective interview techniques.
- Proficient computer skills on IBM and Mainframe systems in word-processing and tracking spreadsheets.
- Strong written skills having produced thousands of reports, assessments, and correspondence.

### Youth Social Issues
- Excellent training on youth social issues, including drug and alcohol abuse, criminal behaviors, justice system, gang behaviors, and youth in crisis.
- Personal experience balancing full-time employment and sole responsibility for two children.

## COMMUNITY ACTIVITIES

- Recruited volunteers for various community service projects, using media, presentations, PSAs, press releases, and personal solicitation.
- 100+ presentations to groups from 15 to 1000, including Board of Education, parent groups, PTAs, community organizations, and churches.

## WORK HISTORY

*Booker,* Dade County Sheriff's Department, Miami, FL, 1990–1999

# *Relocation*

Relocating filled Peggy with anticipation, hope, excitement, and gut-wrenching fear—all at the same time! Moving to an unknown city with few if any contacts, and few job leads, can be overwhelming. When her husband's coaching job went to California, Peggy said good-bye to a job she loved and went with him. Then, her new job search began. She had excellent qualifications that we noted in her new resumé. Peggy followed the job hunting guidelines that I'd given her which quickly led her to a great new job. If you are moving, these tips will help you, too:

✔ Research the area thoroughly *before* you move. Subscribe to local newspapers and order telephone directories. Write to the Chamber of Commerce for employment information. Obtain the area's yellow pages and newspapers. Visit your local library and use their Internet/computer systems to locate listings and huge volumes of employment information. Compile a list of potential employers that would have the type of job you seek.

✔ Use a top-notch resumé. Strong cover letters are also essential. Demonstrate your abilities and accomplishments concisely and quickly using a local address whenever possible. Gather up letters of recommendation. Make copies of excellent performance evaluations and compile a portfolio of work samples, necessary evidence that will impress future employers.

✔ Build a new network. Labor studies state that 85% of all jobs are hidden or unadvertised. Newspaper ads list only 7 to 8% of an area's current job openings, so networking is essential to your success. Ask everyone you know for names of anyone living in your targeted location. Call your professional associations for state and city chapters. Check with your college for alumni who live in your new area. Many are eager to help. Reassure contacts that all you seek is guidance and that you don't expect them to know of, or offer you, a job.

✔ Implement a job search action plan with step-by-step weekly activities. The average job search takes time when you're someplace new. Today, many people must actually *move* to the new location before they find a job. Employers are reluctant to cover relocation expenses for all but the highest level employees. Once you've moved, meet new people by attending association meetings, group meetings, or school and church functions. Ask for help, ideas, and job leads.

✔ Take a job search class when you get to the new city. The instructor can be a good resource to introduce you to new companies and organizations. You might also look to meet with a career counselor who can point you toward several organizations, saving you huge amounts of time in the transition.

Relocating takes extra effort on your part, but Peggy did it and *fast*. Her resumé follows.

# Peggy Knolls
1 Main Street
City, NY 11111
(201) 555-0111

CAREER OBJECTIVE: **Position in Sales and Advertising**

## SUMMARY OF QUALIFICATIONS

Seasoned publishing professional with fifteen years in Sales and Advertising for major regional magazines and newspapers. Proven new business development due to excellent prospecting and client rapport building skills. Able to motivate staff to highest levels of productivity.

## PROFESSIONAL EXPERIENCE

*Account Executive,* Las Vegas Magazine, Las Vegas, NV, 1998–2001

- Doubled territory's sales in two years through cold calls, proposals, presentations, telemarketing, and building client relationships.
- Developed 30 new business accounts due to excellent prospecting and follow-through abilities.
- Built strong relationship with key accounts resulting in significant sales increases.
- Created new advertising section within magazine; sold 22 pages to new advertisers.
- Responsible for creation and sale of new thirty-six page magazine.
- Developed over 50+ marketing plans emphasizing a strategic plan to meet advertiser's goals through the magazine medium.
- Extensive traffic coordination between client, advertising agencies, and magazine.

*Advertising Manager,* The Real Estate Newspaper, Las Vegas, NV, 6/95–6/98

- Launched new weekly real estate advertising magazine, 36 pages, distribution of 220,000.
- Extensive telemarketing, cold calls, presentations, secured endorsement of Las Vegas Association of Realtors, yielded 22 advertisers for first issue, forty within 30 months.
- Built excellent client relationships that continually developed into increased sales revenues.
- Established the office functions including: billing, rack distribution, staff training, traffic ad flow, production deadlines, public relations, media campaign, and advertising campaign.

*Advertising Manager, promoted from Sales Rep,* California Progress, 1992–1995

- Manage sales staff, personally responsible for fifteen accounts plus a 40 account department.
- Extensive coordination over all advertising including: writing, proofreading, detail organization, layouts, designs, and productions.

*Public Relations,* Scenic Country Club, Carmel, CA, 1990–1992
*Classified Advertising Manager,* Jones Newspaper, Monterey, CA, 1977–1990

## COMPUTER SKILLS

Proficient IBM and Macintosh skills on WordPerfect. Quick learner on all software programs. Trained staff on computer software applications.

## EDUCATION

Three and one-half years in Business Administration, California State University

## *Consultants*

More and more professionals are abandoning employers to become consultants. Often, they need a resumé that shows their credentials, enabling them to land projects or assignments. David created a *consultant resumé,* designed to portray him as a systems expert. He always includes his resumé in the marketing materials he mails to prospective clients.

Carl used his resumé to illustrate his credentials as a consultant, and so did Daniel. Quite the opposite situation for Brad. He was tired of searching for work every few months when a contract ended. He wanted to move back into top management and become an employee again. Six years had passed since he'd managed a manufacturing plant, which downplayed the old jobs he'd left when he began consulting. We created a *resumé to return to work as an employee* that briefly introduced him and his strengths. It took some time for him to identify the companies he was interested in, as well as the correct person to contact. But that research paid off—today he's happily employed as a Plant Manager for a very progressive manufacturer.

# David Steinburg
1 Main Street
City, NY 11111
(201) 555-0111
dsteinburg@earthlink.net

CAREER OBJECTIVE: Consultant for ISO 9001:2000
Quality Management Systems

## SUMMARY OF QUALIFICATIONS

Thirty years at the forefront of quality/quality assurance systems management, planning, developing, and implementing efficient systems that surpass standards for achieving bottomline gains for Fortune 100 manufacturers.

## PROFESSIONAL EXPERIENCE

### Quality

- Served as a Senior Quality Assurance Manager for Fortune 100 international manufacturers in the automobile and computer services area.
- Developed a quality system using cross-functional teams. Established policies and procedures. Contributor to long-term strategic planning. Handled resource allocations, staffing and budgeting. Implemented quality systems. Negotiated with governmental agencies for compliance/program acceptance and conducted government proposal reviews.
- Audited over 50 national and international product suppliers for quality systems to meet client's quality standards. Identified each company's deficiencies, inaccurate documentation, configuration control problems, and contract compliance issues.
- Developed and implemented the entire quality assurance program for new equipment production plant.

### Management

- Project manager instituting a new internal employee audit of the entire Manufacturing Group's compliance to ISO 9001 for a major company. Developed the audit plan, initiated the 12 member cross-functional audit team, coordinated planning and audit process, and prepared final audit report for the client. Industry first. Eliminating outside regulatory auditors. Result: $250,000+ saved.
- Team contributor on the documentation and costing process for $1.6 billion proposed federal contract on quality assurance processes. Received contract and implemented the new system for the government.

## PROFESSIONAL CERTIFICATIONS

*ISO 9001:2000 Certified Quality Systems,* 2001

*ISO 9000 Certified Quality Systems-Auditor,* 1995

*Certified Quality Auditor,* American Society for Quality Control, 1994

*D1-9000 Certified Supplier Quality Auditor,* 1995

## EDUCATION

Bachelor of Science, Business Administration, Tulane University, New Orleans, LA

**COMBINATION**

# Daniel Lowe
1 Main Street
New York City, NY 11111
201-555-0111
dlowe@msn.com

*Editorial Note: Original resumé all appeared on one page*

CAREER OBJECTIVE: **Management Consultant—Wireless/Telecom Industry**

### SUMMARY OF QUALIFICATIONS

Results oriented professional with proven experience in the wireless industry as a consultant, program manager and business development director. Strategic and tactical leader with unique blend of technical and business acumen. Extensive R&D experience with keen global assessment skills of new products and services from conception to launch. Exhibit superior planning, organization and communication skills. Widely respected for the development and management of key customer/strategic partner relationships.

### PROFESSIONAL EXPERIENCE

*Management consultant,* Verizon Wireless, New York, NY 2001–Present
*Director Product Development, Network and Business Development,* Cellular Inc.,
New York, NY 1998–2001
*Senior Consultant,* Andersen Consulting, Chicago, IL 1996–1998
*Project Manager/Engineer,* MCI, Overland Park, KS 1991–1996

### Product/Program/Project Management

- Ten large scale wireless projects during the last decade that led to reduced cost and introduction of new products and services generating new revenue streams. Major duties included: general management of business unit, leadership of cross-functional teams; coordination of R&D efforts; establishment of strategic alliances, new product development plus adding/evaluating revenue streams with forecasting, budgeting, and developing pricing methodology.
- Managed day-to-day operations of a Verizon Wireless Business Unit serving partners and affiliates in a General Manager role coordinating business and technical operations, product development, technology development, engineering, operations, IT, documentation, and training. Results: added products, established policies and procedures/processes, significantly improved technical support, implemented staff training plus generated a 60% increase in annual revenues.
- Pioneered the R&D work combining wireless with the Internet utilizing an Intelligent Network approach that produced a patent-pending technology that will dramatically increase Information Services options Telecom Carriers will be able to offer end user customers.
- Served as committee member writing the Wireless Industry Standards

### Business Development

- Analyzed AT&T Wireless product sales and market trends, then conducted service assessments on potential new service offerings to determine feasibility of potential new revenues, product fit, expenditures, staffing requirements; summarized data into a strategic planning report for senior management.

- Extensive experience analyzing and establishing key strategic partnerships and then served as client account manager to these corporate customers. Also managed third-party vendor relationships.

### HONORS

Co-inventor on patent-pending application for the wireless and Internet convergence
*Who's Who in Science and Technology in America,* 2001 Edition
Served as Program Director for educational seminars and exhibits,
IEEE Conference Fall 1998

### EDUCATION

BSEE, Electrical/Computer Engineering, Michigan State University, 1991

# Brad Roche
1 Main Street
City, NY 11111
(201) 555-0111
broche@aol.com

CAREER OBJECTIVE: **General Manager for a Manufacturing Company**

## SUMMARY OF QUALIFICATIONS

Proven track record to lead manufacturing companies through turn-arounds, start-ups and achieve profitable results. Strengths include reengineering, high productivity development, strong team building, technical problem solving, innovation, and strategic planning.

## PROFESSIONAL EXPERIENCE

*Strategic Planning/Project Management Consultant,* The Roche Company, Seattle, WA, 1996–Present
- Provided leadership, project management, and extensive planning to start up new forest product plants and facilities ranging from $60–200 million.
- Created strategic planning modules for small- to medium-size companies; included analysis of competition, market penetration and long-range strategic plans to achieve market share goals.

*General Manager,* Allstar Glass, Bellevue, WA, 1990–1996
- Credited with turn-around of glass fabrication company with six prior years of unprofitability within five months. Redesigned material management methods, labor usage, increased productivity and individual accountability levels, plus improved product quality. Achieved annual sales of $13 million, 150 employees.
- Developed market and sales campaign and introduced proprietary new product line that increased new business and market share by redirecting sales force efforts to focus on high margin products vs. high volume. Results: continuous profitability 250% above industry average.

*Manufacturing Manager,* Weyerhauser Corp., Federal Way, WA, 1987–1990
- Reorganized plant and reengineered processes and labor systems resulting in 30% productivity increase, plus labor and material cost containment. Instilled high levels of quality management; emphasis on customer service.

*Division Engineer,* Five plants, Paccar, Renton, WA 1982–1987

## EDUCATION

Executive Management Certificate, University of Washington, Seattle, WA, 1996
B.S., Mechanical Engineering, University of Washington, Seattle, WA, 1982

# Carl Vancelote
1 Main Street
City, NY 11111
(201) 555-0111

CAREER OBJECTIVE: **Management Consultant**

## EDUCATION

Master's Degree, Graduate School of Public Affairs, University of Washington, 1985
Bachelor's Degree, School of Business Administration, University of Washington, 1965

## SUMMARY OF QUALIFICATIONS

Thirty years successful Boeing Company top management experience in managing large multi-discipline new business/product development/nationwide field marketing organizations. Personally contributed to acquisition of multi-billion dollar NASA and DOD contracts. Management consultant to U.S. federal/state/local and Canadian governments.

## PROFESSIONAL EXPERIENCE

*Director of Business Development,* Boeing Company, 1971–2002

### Program Development

Managed Boeing Aerospace and Electronics Company new business budget ($195M). Developed acquisition strategy resulting in contract award of space station, light helicopter, and F-22 fighter programs. Performed planning/implementation of Boeing new start businesses: Boeing Computer Services (BCS), Boeing Engineering and Construction.

### Management Consulting

Developed first Boeing Aerospace Company application of Continuous Quality Improvement (CQI)–Baldridge criteria to customer service activities; participated in subcontractor CQI evaluations. Provided organization/program planning service to: NASA, U.S. Dept. of Energy, U.S. Dept. of Housing & Urban Development, States of Washington and California, City of Seattle, Boston Housing Authority, British Columbia, Canada Treasury Board, and British Columbia Systems Corp.

### Marketing

Managed activities of 17 U.S. field marketing offices. Established contacts with U.S. federal government agencies and Congress in Washington, D.C. Developed annual international exhibit plan and directed advertising support. Developed marketing strategy for key programs.

### Instruction/Training

Course development, instruction, and lecturer for management courses to senior Boeing program managers, Dept. of Defense Management College and University of Washington School of Public Affairs. Recruited, evaluated and advised engineering, technical, scientific, management and clerical staff.

## PUBLICATIONS

- Journal of Systems Management
- National Contract Management Journal
- Defense Systems Management Review
- The Manager
- Air Force Comptroller
- Modern Purchasing

# Curriculum Vitae (CV)

Doctors and Ph.D.'s, as well as college and university educators, require a specialized resumé commonly referred to as a Curriculum Vitae or CV. This is a more thorough document outlining academic and professional achievements. It details your training, professional affiliations, honors, publications, and presentations summarizing all your credentials into two or three pages.

Unfortunately, most write a CV that is so poorly written it loses its effectiveness. Your CV has only one purpose: to effectively sell your professional skills to the reader *quickly* demonstrating your competence as a knowledgeable expert. To create a good CV requires time, energy, and analysis of your training, ability, and accomplishments. Having worked with hundreds of doctors, physicians, and academic professionals, I recommend these additional guidelines along with The Goldmining Technique to help you produce an impressive CV.

## Target the Curriculum Vitae to the Reader

It's important to keep in mind the person who will read your CV. A doctor would likely have a slightly different emphasis in each of the CVs: one for patients, a different version for colleagues or insurance companies, and still another when trying to land teaching jobs. This approach requires that you first write your CV for one targeted audience (e.g., your patients); then when the first document is finished, you need only make minor editorial changes to adapt it to another targeted audience (e.g., insurance providers).

### BE CONCISE

Strong content, good formatting, readable style, and a computer-generated, laser-printed document will establish your credibility and professional accomplishments. A common error is to create a monstrous CV of 8 to 12 pages. The CV itself should never exceed three pages, *two being ideal.* Anyone with numerous publications can use a short summation that might state: "46 publications in journals noting three or four of the most prestigious journals." Similarly, a short summation on given presentations would list only the most prestigious. An additional document should be developed that lists all the numerous publications and presentations that can be added to the actual CV when needed or called for.

## BE VISUALLY APPEALING

The CV's appearance must be highly professional! It should catch the eye. Watch for spacing and margins. Allow for lots of *white space* and *borders.* Make use of *italicizing,* CAPITALS, underlining, **bolding,** indentations, and • bullets • to emphasize important points. Use a computer and get a laser-printed copy to give it a sharp, polished look that instills confidence about your expertise as the reader glances at the document. The laser printer gives a rich, crisp sharpness to your CV while an ink jet or dot matrix printer looks dull and will not be as impressive.

## BE CLEAR AND PRECISE

Your CV should contain no abbreviations or acronyms. Be sure to spell out titles, degrees, city, and state. It must be a flawless document: no typos, mistakes, or misspelled words. *Proofread!* Computer spellcheckers often read words correctly that are spelled right (e.g., sea) but have the wrong meaning when you mean vision (e.g., see), not a body of water. They also don't tell you if a word is missing. Be perfect!

## USE QUALITY PAPER, BUT NOT LETTERHEAD

High-quality linen or woven paper in cream, white, or blank paper that matches your letterhead should be used. Actual letterhead is often too distracting and interferes with the CV's readability and professionalism. Since so many CVs are faxed, be sure that you keep several copies on white paper for clear fax transmission.

# The CV's Preferred Writing Style

## HEADING

Begin your CV with a centered heading listing your name, then your address and phone number listed directly below. Use either: Dr. Thomas Jones *or* Thomas Jones, MD. I prefer the Dr. format. A common mistake is to use Dr. Thomas Jones, MD; this is incorrect and a faux pas you should not commit. The preferred Ph.D. heading is Mary Brown, Ph.D.

## EDUCATION

Your academic training should be listed in two categories. First, would be any PostDoctoral Education. Under the PostDoctoral heading, I recommend you list your completed diplomate degree such as Board Certified Orthopedic Surgeon, then institute or conferring agency, city, state, and the year the degree was awarded. The term *Board Certified* is the universally accepted medical terminology that distinguishes those who have this advanced certification. Always list your highest degree first. Then after postdoctoral (or if you have no postdoctoral training), list your education. Start with your doctorate, then list completed master's or bachelor's degrees. I highly recommend that you do not list any community college associate degrees, as doing so devalues your doctorate and your overall impression to the outside reader. Under no circumstances should your high school graduation be listed.

## PROFESSIONAL EXPERIENCE

This section highlights your work history. List dates of experience and a few sentences under each subheading to describe your experience. Action verbs and short fragments—10 years in private family practice—work best. Be sure to include the types of cases you treat. If you are an author or instructor, statements such as "Taught twelve English composition courses at both community and four-year colleges" are both descriptive and clarifying to the employer, versus just saying instructor, with no details.

## PUBLICATIONS AND PRESENTATIONS

This lists starts with publications first, followed by presentations. It lists your most recent publication, then the next recent in continuous, reverse chronological order. If there's room, include this section on your CV, but if you have more than six listings, use a separate document. Be sure to follow proper journal and presentation listing form using reverse chronological order. The heading should state:

**Thomas Jones, Ph.D.**
**Publications and Presentations**

This separate document is commonly used for academic, consulting, and publishing purposes and does not always have to accompany the CV.

## PROFESSIONAL AFFILIATIONS

Here you list all associations and professional services you're involved with. Spell out the full name of all organizations.

## HONORS

List all awards and honors that relate to your degree/profession. Avoid listing Cub Scout Leader here as it belongs in the Community section.

## COMMUNITY SERVICE OR COMMUNITY ACTIVITIES

List related community activities: coaching, PTA, city council. Religious activities are not usually included in a CV. The entire community activities section is optional and not needed on CVs to companies, other professionals, colleges, or universities.

## CONTINUING PROFESSIONAL EDUCATION

This should include subject topics of courses you've taken that are important to remaining current in your field.

## PERSONAL DATA

This section is nice to add to the CV for physicians and dentists, especially if the CV is given to your patients. Include marital status (only if you're married), children, personal interests, and where you reside. Don't exceed more than two or three lines in this area. Educators should be careful *not* to include personal information, as it is deemed inappropriate and irrelevant.

## OTHER RELATED INFORMATION

For those in higher education, your CV will be screened for employment opportunities. Be sure to include research, writing, and teaching sections. While dissertations are important for newer graduates, after six or seven years they can be dropped (or briefly mentioned) since by then you'll be evaluated more by the work you've done since graduation. Don't forget to include committee work and any program coordination you've contributed to in your previous positions; that's important, too.

## SUMMARY

Your new CV will announce your expertise, credibility, and professional accomplishments to the world. This targeted approach impresses and distinguishes you from others who failed to see the importance and value in creating a universal calling card that quickly and clearly advertises exactly who they are. Once you start using your new CV, you'll realize how easy it is to impress patients, personnel managers, or potential bosses. Proposals, grants, papers, and insurance provider applications are just a few places where your CV is required. You'll find dozens of ways it can be used to demonstrate your expertise to others. A good CV is an excellent marketing and public relations tool to announce to the world your true qualifications—improve yours today and use it often!

# Glen D. Edmiston, Ph.D.

1 Main Street
City, NY 11111
(201) 555-0111
E-mail: edmiston@utexas.edu

CAREER OBJECTIVE: **Research Scientist**

## SUMMARY OF QUALIFICATIONS

Innovative chemist with a proven track record of developing research and achieving significant findings. Able to develop end result practical/industrial applications as part of research goals. Strong presentation abilities with twenty journal publications to date. Excel at laboratory management, staff supervision, training and project administration.

## EDUCATION

Ph.D., Inorganic Chemistry, University of California at Berkeley, 1996
Bachelor of Science Degree in Chemistry, Michigan State University, 1990
Ph.D. Dissertation: *"Transition-Metal Complexes with
Unusual Coordination Numbers, Oxidation States, and Bonding"*

## PROFESSIONAL EXPERIENCE

*Research Associate,* University of Texas,
Department of Chemistry, 1996–Present

### Research

- Developed a new modular template method for the synthesis of organic molecules containing sulfur and nitrogen. Created numerous model compounds that had various industrial applications.
- Investigated the properties of nickel, iron, and zinc complexes to better understand how metals function in metallo-enzymes to industrial applications with both large-scale cost and energy savings results.
- Conducted experiments using NMR, UV-visible and infrared spectroscopes, x-ray crystallography, GC-mass spectroscopy, electrochemical techniques, high vacuum line and dry-box techniques.

### Administration

- Managed research project with team of three research assistants including: project management, planning, scheduling, inventory, purchasing, equipment maintenance, laboratory supervision and staff training.
- Wrote comprehensive reports on data findings, project analysis and project results, including professional journal publications.

*Research Assistant,* University of California at Davis,
Department of Chemistry, 1991–1996

### Research

- Synthesized and characterized by X-ray crystallographic and spectroscopic (NMR, UV-vis) methods a wide variety of air-sensitive inorganic and organometallic transition-metal compounds.

## Instructor

- Instructed and supervised laboratory students on crystallographic concepts, instrumentation usage, crystallographic computing and quantitative analysis. Taught several university undergraduate chemistry courses including Inorganic Chemistry.

### PROFESSIONAL AFFILIATIONS

American Chemical Society

### HONORS

UC Berkeley Research Award Grant, 1995

### ABSTRACTS AND PRESENTATIONS

"*Thiolate-Containing Pentadentate Ligands for Modeling the Binding and Reactivity Properties of the Low-Spin, Non-heme, Iron (III) Site of Nitrile Hydratase,*" Edmiston, G.D., Barne, K., and Kollaches, M.N. Presented at the Symposium "Metal Ions in Biology and Medicine—Natural and Synthetic Approaches" December, 2000 meeting of the International Chemical Congress of the Pacific Basin Societies, Honolulu, Hawaii.

"*The Possible Role of Metal-Bound Thiolates in Biological Proton Transfer Reaction,*" Edmiston, G.D., Barne, K., and Kollaches, M.N. Presented at the 1999 summer meeting of the American Chemical Society, Washington, D.C.

### PUBLICATIONS

Twenty publications in chemistry journals including *Journal of the American Chemical Society, Angewandte Chemie, Inorganic Chemistry, Organometallics,* plus others. Topics centered on inorganic and bio-inorganic chemistry research finding. A complete list is available.

# Dr. James Barringer
Woodhaven Chiropractic Clinic
1 Main Street
City, NY 11111
(201) 555-0111

## Doctor of Chiropractic

### POST-DOCTORAL EDUCATION

Chiropractic Orthopedist, Board Certified, National College of Chiropractic, Lombard, Illinois, 2000. 1 to 2% of chiropractors nationally complete program.

Certified Chiropractic Sports Physician, Western States Chiropractic College, Portland, Oregon, 1998

### EDUCATION

Doctor of Chiropractic, Cleveland Chiropractic College, Los Angeles, California, cum laude, 1987

Bachelor's Degree, University of California, Davis, cum laude, 1983

### PROFESSIONAL EXPERIENCE

*Chiropractor,* Woodhaven Chiropractic Clinic, Costa Mesa, California.

Fifteen years in private family practice treating a full spectrum of chiropractic patients particularly with low back pain, headaches, auto and sports injuries.

*Founder and Director,* California Chiropractic Sports Council, 1997–present.

Established state certified Sports Chiropractor Program. Coordinated dozens of annual, professional and amateur sports events utilizing chiropractic physicians.

*National Football League Players Association Chiropractor,* 1995–Present

*Sports Chiropractor,* 1997–Present. Professional, Olympic and college athletes in baseball, football, volleyball, golf, bowling, and track treated. Special Events include: US Powerlifting West Coast Open, Special Olympics, Pro Golfer's Tour, Pro Rodeo Tour, Women's Triathlete. Olympic Trials—Physician, US Rowing Team, 2001

*Tournament Chiropractor,* National Pro Beach Volleyball Tournament, 1996, 1997

*Preferred Provider,* numerous insurance and managed care programs including: Kaiser, California Health, Chiropractor Network Services, HMO California, Pacific Health Plans, Metropolitan, Good Health, Traveler's Insurance, Independent Chiropractic Examiner, plus numerous other insurances. Contact Woodhaven Chiropractic Clinic for complete list.

### PROFESSIONAL PRESENTATIONS

Developed and taught dozens of classes for the community, companies and insurance providers. Topics included: Understanding Chiropractic Care; Exerball; Good-bye Backaches; Back Health; Back Safety; Health/Wellness Program—City of Costa Mesa; Chiropractic Care for Insurance Adjusters; plus Strength and Conditioning programs.

*Dr. James Barringer* *page 2*
*(201) 555-0111*

### PROFESSIONAL AFFILIATIONS

American Chiropractic Association
American College of Sports Medicine
California Chiropractic Association
California Chiropractic Sports Council
National Strength and Conditioning Association
American College of Chiropractic Orthopedists
American Public Health Association
National Athletic Trainers Association
American Massage Therapy Association
Chiropractic Rehabilitation Association
Diplomate, National Board of Chiropractic Examiners
Diplomate, Chiropractic Board of Orthopedists

### HONORS

Cleveland Chiropractic College—Cum Laude graduate

University of California—Cum Laude graduate

Outstanding Service Award—California Chiropractic Association, 2000

Award of Merit—US Powerlifting Team, 1999

Award for Outstanding Service—Cleveland Chiropractic College

### CONTINUING PROFESSIONAL EDUCATION

Cox Technique
Nimmo Technique
Diversified Technique
Gonstead Technique
S.O.T. Technique
Extremity Adjusting Technique
Acupuncture
Motion Palpation
Sports Injuries
Rehabilitative Techniques
Radiology
Personal Injuries
Impairment Rating

### PERSONAL

A.A.U. National Ranked Swimmer; Black Belt, Karate; Amateur Weight Lifter.
Married, two children. Residence in Huntington Beach.

# NEW COLLEGE GRADUATE RESUMÉS: UNDERGRADUATE AND ADVANCED DEGREES

## 8

One of the biggest mistakes I see with new college grads is that for some unknown reason they love to create two-page resumés. At the beginning of Chapter 11, "Creating Your Own Resume," I discuss at length the strategic advantages of using a one-page resumé. I recommend that every new college grad, whether searching with a B.A., medical degree, MBA, or even a law degree, use the one-page format for maximum impact. It really is a mistake to create a long laundry list of all the courses you took in college. Employers aren't interested and they'll skim over it—often to the point where they move on to the next person. If you follow the format I've outlined, and use bullets that demonstrate action and results, plus incorporate a SUMMARY OF QUALIFICATIONS section, you'll be way ahead of the game and gather more attention from prospective employers.

## Undergraduates

Nothing is more exciting or intimidating than graduating from college and having the world at your feet. You have so many options and choices, and it can all seem overwhelming. Before we get to the resumés, let's digress for a few moments, so I can share some job-hunting techniques that I've found work well for new grads launching careers.

A common mistake many make that will hinder their success tremendously involves the magnet companies like Microsoft, Nike, American Express, NBC TV, etc. These sexy, glamorous companies are magnets, attracting thousands of resumés each month. (Microsoft receives more than 25,000 resumés every month!) College students send countless resumés to no avail, because they never answer this big question—*specifically, what you can do for the company.* Employers hire people to do *particular* jobs. So your first step is to do some career research and select a few job titles and areas to focus your search on.

In Sarah's case, she had her heart set on working for the Liz Claiborne company. It was the place for her, she just knew it. Problem was, Liz Claiborne didn't know it. Prior to our session, Sarah had never defined what jobs she could do for them—or for anybody else, for that matter. Even when a family friend arranged for a telephone call with someone who worked at Claiborne, Sarah naively hoped the person would find her a job at the company. She never told the Claiborne manager about the types of jobs she could do, never asked questions about its marketing department, and was basically "starstruck." So, nothing happened after the meeting. It wasn't the Claiborne employee's job to figure out what career Sarah could do for them—it was Sarah's. Not having a clear idea of the types of jobs you want to do is a critical error MANY college students make.

I began to work with Sarah shortly after her Claiborne meeting. I helped her focus on identifying her stronger skills—writing, customer service, and planning events. That direction led her to hear about a retail marketing position, and within two weeks she was hired.

As I tour college campuses around the country giving speeches, eager grads often ask me, "Where are the HOT opportunities?" Most grimace when they learn the jobs are typically programming and engineering, as they know those jobs aren't for them. If you pursue a field in which you have a lot of interest (e.g., broadcasting, computers, fashion) it will lead to greater lifetime satisfaction. Follow your dreams, especially if you have a practical way to mix your interests and your career. The greatest number of opportunities exist within small companies, usually those with less than 100 people. These employers are found in Yellow Pages, want ads, and by asking friends and family for leads. Many good jobs are available with nonprofit organizations, also. Small offices can offer you more responsibility, so you'll learn more, faster, and those experiences will help propel your career along into future positions. Internships and temporary jobs will expose you to companies and fields that you may not have known existed, so take advantage of those opportunities too.

Pursuing a hot field is like racing after a magnet company—a lot of effort without achieving the results you hoped for. It's best to combine your interests and abilities in a job match when you're looking for career satisfaction. Spend time investigating career options; libraries (which now have most resources available online) and career centers have extensive career exploration resources available. The *Occupational Outlook Handbook* is a good place to start. As you narrow your future goals, identify two or three job titles. Interview people who actually perform these jobs to learn specifics and determine if they are good fits for you. Then, select the field or industry (i.e., healthcare, finance, retail, software, manufacturing, telecommunications, etc.) to target. Use the Internet—more and more job listings in various fields are popping up each day. But don't expect to "land the job online," for that's highly unlikely. Networking has been and remains the number one way people find new jobs.

One of the biggest complaints I hear from new grads is that they don't want to *network.* "I'm not going to hit on people or use them," that's the attitude—and also the problem. Fact—63% of all jobs are filled by contacts and referrals, according to the Department of Labor. Two-thirds! Networking is an effective tool—be sure it's a job-hunting strategy you use. Start with your college's alumni office—so many alums are happy to inform you about their jobs, fields, or companies. I recommend you utilize others' assistance before the other guy does and lands the job *you want.*

For interview coaching, I suggest you read my book *60 Seconds & You're Hired* (Penguin), which I've devoted to that subject. For more strategies on career exploration and help with job search techniques and landing the job of your dreams, I recommend my book, *What to Do with the Rest of Your Life,* published by Simon & Schuster. For cover letter help, my book, *Winning Cover Letters* (Wiley), will be very useful. It teaches a very effective technique that gets potential employers' attention. I also have numerous audiotape programs available. You'll find these and my books at my website: www.robinryan.com.

## GPAs

A question I'm often asked by college students is whether their resumés should include their GPAs. Josh, a College Recruiting Manager, advises, "GPAs are an important addition for a top achiever. Unfortunately, too many resumés come in where the GPA is less than desirable." Here's a general guideline: if your grade point is 3.2 or above, list it. If your major is higher (e.g., 3.2 cumulative, but 3.6 in your major) you might list the 3.6 major. GPAs lower than 3.0 should not be included. Play up skills and experience instead. If you personally helped finance your education, then note it by mentioning how much and through which type of jobs. That industriousness *is valued.*

## Note All Experience

Don't underplay the skills you do have. Include paid and unpaid positions on your resumé. Employers care about computer skills, research abilities, writing, public speaking, working well within a team, and customer service. So sell 'em what you've got!

Need some experience? If necessary, volunteer. Take temporary jobs and seek out internships to add a little substance to your package. Soon your career will be launched and you'll be flying high on the road to success.

There are times when *where* you did the work is not a selling point, but we do want to emphasize what you accomplished. For example, another client's experience in planning events came from organizing sorority functions. We dropped Melissa's reference to "sorority," as many employers often view the Greek system as "party central," in a negative light. She did have customer service and sales experience from retail summer jobs, so we added that—she had excluded them completely in her original resumé. *The new resumé we created landed her an events planning job just one week after she started using it!*

Now, take a closer look at these clients' resumés to learn more about how they got attention from employers. All these resumés produced interviews and were key in assisting the clients in landing terrific jobs.

**FUNCTIONAL**

# Sarah Jaffee
1 Main Street
City, NY 11111
(201) 555-0111
sjaffee@hotmail.com

CAREER OBJECTIVE: **Retail Sales Associate**

## SUMMARY OF QUALIFICATIONS

Enthusiastic, customer service oriented individual with extensive experience satisfying customer needs. Track record as a hard-working individual with record of dependability and punctuality. Strong exposure to clothing, fashion merchandising, and special events coordinator.

## EDUCATION

B.S., Apparel Marketing, State University of New York, Stony Brook, NY, 2001

## PROFESSIONAL EXPERIENCE

### Sales/Customer Service
- Two years working retail sales, cashiering, handling customer complaints, and arranging special events.
- Developed excellent customer service skills handling hundreds of customer complaints, resolving 98% of all problems to customers' satisfaction.
- Coordinate setup of customer purchased special event parties, served food, handled customer requests, complaints. Repeatedly praised by customers and managers for well-organized functions.

### Clothing/Fashion
- Co-chairman, winter fashion show representing six stores with twenty models, 200+ attendance. Duties included: corporate sponsorship, recruited models, wardrobe transfers and returns, and arranged musical background.
- Marketed spring fashion show and student designs via flyers, direct mail, and advertisements.
- Selected fabric and color, then personally produced 500+ draperies for college building windows.
- Upholstered 150+ sofas and chairs for dormitory furniture.
- Assisted designers, cutting patterns and fabrics for national sportswear manufacturer.
- Reorganized sample room, categorized by style number and season. Assisted coordinator with tradeshow and sales rep samples for national sportswear manufacturer.

## WORK HISTORY

*Seamstress,* Upholstery Inc., Bronx, NY, 1999–2001
*Service Agent,* Hertz Rent-A-Car, JFK Airport, Summer, 1998
*Concession Sales,* Woodland Parks, Brooklyn, NY, 1997–1998
*Retail Sales,* Town Photo, Brooklyn, NY, 1996–1997

> **Editorial Note: Original resumé all appeared on one page**

# Melissa LeBack

1 Main Street
City, NY 11111
(201) 555-0111
missyl@aol.com

CAREER OBJECTIVE: **Events Planner**

### SUMMARY OF QUALIFICATIONS

Events coordination experience with excellent organizational and time management abilities. Emphasis on customer service and sales with proven interpersonal skills to effectively resolve problems and deal with difficult, demanding individuals. Strong computer abilities, able to quickly learn new programs. Outstanding writing and editing skills with two published articles.

## Events Coordination

- Coordinated and assisted coordination of numerous college special events, for groups of 7 to 125 people, including receptions, special events, meetings, conference activities.
- Responsible for numerous details pertaining to special events, including: invitations, food preparation, press release, media relations, mailing lists, audio/visual equipment arrangements, room set-up and budget.
- Negotiated service bids for catering events emphasizing quality and best price.
- Provided on-site coordination and problem solving for smooth-flowing event activity.

## Customer Service/Sales

- Well-developed customer service skills. Deal effectively with demanding, difficult customers.
- Well trained in suggestive selling, repeatedly being recognized for meeting sales goals.
- Set up displays to promote and increase sales.
- Inventory on 2000+ items.
- Efficiently dealt with telephone orders, numerous special orders, filling mail orders.

## Communications

- Published two articles in London County Newsletter, quarterly distribution 400,000.
- Attended town meeting, public hearings to record notes for the Newsletter Editor.
- Wrote press release that resulted in an interview and printed article in city newspaper.
- Authorized guidebook brochure for Exhibit special event, computer produced.
- Researched numerous topics and wrote essays, reports, and letters.
- 40+ presentations to groups up to 125.
- Excellent grasp of grammar with good editing skills.

### WORK HISTORY

*Internship,* Museum and Art Gallery, London, England, Spring, 2002
*Sales,* The Gift Shop, Smithsonian Institute, Washington, D.C., 2001
*Sales,* The Gap, Northgate Mall, Arlington, VA, 1999–2000

## Computer Skills

Proficient IBM skills on WORD, WordPerfect, Excel, Typing 60 wpm

### EDUCATION

Bachelor of Arts, English Literature, GPA 3.6, University of Delaware, 2002
Foreign Exchange Student, Cambridge University, England, 2001–2002

## *Unique Approaches to Standing Out in Competitive Fields*

Teachers, reporters, newscasters, flight attendants, and advertising people all face a great deal of competition. So how exactly do you stand out with little to no experience when it seems like everyone on the planet is competing for the same job you want? Let's take a closer look at this predicament and how one client solved it—quite cleverly, in fact.

*Teachers are in great demand*—at least that's what the press says. But when Andrea Lohr began to job hunt in the nicer, suburban schools of Boston, she found it nearly impossible to land a job. The competition, she learned firsthand, was very steep.

Her first objective was to create a terrific resumé, so Andrea called me. Her goal was to remain in Boston, a city she grew to love while attending college there. The competition for jobs was "huge," she said, noting it seemed like every district was flooded with thousands of teachers looking for work. Andrea's big deficit was that she had no experience, outside of her student teaching.

**OLD**

# Andrea M. Lohr

## Objective

To obtain an elementary teaching position

## Education

**Boston College**    Chestnut Hill, MA
Masters of Education, Reading and Literacy, Summer 2000 G.P.A. 3.92
**St. Bonaventure University**    St. Bonaventure, NY
Bachelor of Science, Elementary Education, May, 1999
Magna Cum Laude, Education G.P.A. 3.94
**Oxford University**    Oxford, England
Attended Summer Classes for Undergraduate Degree, 1997

## Teaching Experience

**Student Teacher: Grades K–4**                                 **Spring, 2002**
*Bennett-Hemenway Elementary*                          *Natick, MA*
Assumed responsibilities as a Reading Specialist for grades K–4.
Prepared and taught language arts lessons for individual students, small groups and whole groups.
Modified lessons to accommodate a variety of learning styles and abilities.
Prepared and taught short- and long-term lessons and units.
Incorporated the MA State Standards in each lesson.

**Student Teacher: Grades 1 and 2**                          **Fall, 1998**
*Coudersport Area Elementary School*              *Coudersport, PA*
Taught in multiage classroom.
Created and implemented unit plans for a wide range of developmental levels.
Planned and taught lessons in all subject areas while incorporating PA standards.
Prepared and taught an in-service about multiage classrooms for prospective multiage teachers.
Participated in an Instructional Support Team.
Attended open houses, parent conferences and after school activities.

**Student Teacher: Grade 5**                                       **Fall, 1998**
*Allegany-Limestone Elementary School*              *Allegany, NY*
Taught in a departmental fifth grade classroom.
Prepared and taught hands-on science lessons and experiments for 4 classes each day.
Taught Spelling and Social Studies lessons each day.
Incorporated unique and effective classroom management and techniques.
Prepared all lessons according to NY State Standards.
Volunteered at a Christmas dinner for the elderly held at the school.

**E-Mail: Andrealohr@Yahoo.com**
PERMANENT   100 TROY STREET   SENECA FALLS, NY 13148 FAX (315) 568-0985
PRESENT   35 ORKNEY RD. SUITE 5   BRIGHTON, MA 02135 (617) 975-3136

**Practicum Experience: Grade 5**                    **Fall, 1997**
*Seneca Elementary School*                           *Salamanca, NY*
Team taught in a traditional classroom setting.
Prepared and taught lessons in math, social studies, language arts and
science.
Created a number of interactive bulletin boards that correlated with lessons.

**Direct Study Internship**
*Kinder-Kinetics Program Assistant*
Directed a motor development program for Montessori students with and
without disabilities.
Designed developmentally appropriate child-centered movement activities
integrating the academic content of mathematics and language arts.

## Awards Received

**A1 Northern Student Teacher Award,** Sole Recipient from the class
of 1999
**Kappa Delta Pi,** International Honor Society in Education
**Delta Epsilon Sigma,** National Scholastic Honor Society

## Activities

*Bona Buddies Programs:* Big brother/sister program for less fortunate
children in the Olean area
*Warming House* Volunteer: Soup located in Olean, NY, run by students
from St. Bonaventure University.
*St. Bonaventure Student Ambassador Volunteer:* Recruited prospective students through a variety of activities, such as hosting overnight
stays, giving campus tours, working open houses and college nights.
*Child Abuse Seminar:* Attended a seminar that grants certification in
child abuse detection.
*Bonaventure Education Association.*
*St. Bonaventure Women's Field Hockey:* Participated in the first two
years of this new women's club sport.

## Licenses and Accreditations

*NY State Certified Elementary Teacher (N–6)*
*Passed the Following Praxis Teacher Certification Exams* (Grants
certification for 17 states)
*Principles of Learning and Teaching: Grades K–6 (30522)*
*Elementary Education: Curriculum, Instruction and Assessment (10011)*
*Elementary Education: Content Area Exercises (20012)*
**Massachusetts Elementary Certification Pending**

## References

Confidential recommendations available upon request from the Career
Development Center, Room 216, Reilly Center, St. Bonaventure, NY 14778

**E-Mail: Andrealohr@Yahoo.com**
PERMANENT   100 TROY STREET   SENECA FALLS, NY 13148 FAX (315) 568-0985
PRESENT    35 ORKNEY RD. SUITE 5   BRIGHTON, MA 02135 (617) 975-3136

Here are some significant problems with Andrea's old resume:

✔ *Very hard to read.* The text font was microscopically small! So small that most employers would have skimmed it, if they read it all. Many missed most of her points. She crammed it to the side, making the headings the only thing that stood out. She used a "9" size font. I recommend using nothing less than a "12" for easy reading.

✔ *Lines interfere with scanning.* Many employers scan resumés and lines can be seen by scanners as page breaks. If that happened, her scanned resumé would become separate documents and would certainly be rejected, especially since the different sheets wouldn't even have her name on them. Don't use long lines at all and you'll solve this problem.

✔ *Never knew there was a page 2.* By looking at the first page, you'd never know another followed—one that had some key information on it. Employers often lose second pages. A one-page format is the ideal. You want your skills concisely and clearly available to the reader, not buried away, as was done here.

✔ *Terrific background and skills are lost.* Too long, too general, and too small type makes the candidate lose the strengths and achievements she's trying to sell. Always remember, your resumé is an advertisement and it must be effective and eye-catching during the brief 15- to 20-second initial review, or the employer will simply pass you by without another thought.

# Andrea Lohr

1 Commonwealth Ave. Apt. 3
Boston, MA 02135
(617) 555-0111
alohr@aol.com

CAREER OBJECTIVE: **Elementary Teaching Position and/or Reading Specialist**

### EDUCATION

Master's of Education, Reading and Literacy, Boston College June 2001 *GPA 3.92*
BS, Elementary Education, St. Bonaventure University, May 2000
(Magna cum laude *Education GPA 3.94*)

### SUMMARY OF QUALIFICATIONS

Recognized by former teachers, principals and students as a good teacher who incorporates creativity, computers and hands-on exercises to achieve better learning experiences for the students. Experience teaching grades 1–5, and also specializing in reading and language arts. Possesses solid classroom management skills and actively participates in after school functions.

### PROFESSIONAL EXPERIENCE

*Student Teacher—Reading Specialist,* Grades K–4, Bennett-Hemenway Elementary
Natick, MA      January–June 2001

*Student Teacher—Elementary,* combined grades 1 & 2, Coudersport Elementary
Coudersport, PA      August–November 1999

*Student Teacher*—Grade 5, Allegany-Limestone Elementary Allegany, NY
October–December 1999

*Practicum Experience*—Grade 5, Seneca Elementary School Salamanca, NY
August–December 1998

## Teaching/Curriculum Development

- Acquired solid teaching skills from four student teaching experiences providing daily classroom instruction on all subjects for elementary kids grades 1–5.
- Developed 5-grade science curriculum including numerous hands-on experiments teaching four classes per day, adjusting approaching and coursework to meet the varying learning levels of the different classes. Implementing new classroom management techniques and customized hands-on approach yielded a superior level of learning with noted student improvements.
- Developed daily lesson plans to meet state/school learning objectives for various elementary grades in language arts, math, social studies, science, art, and music, adjusted to individual class needs.
- Developed learning tools using computer and color printer plus incorporated Internet resources, having students use the computer in class to improve student skills.
- Created science and language arts unit programs incorporating central focus over extensive timeframes that develop cross-curricular skills such as reading, writing, art and math.

Reading
- Worked as a reading specialist to over 100 elementary children providing small group (2–5), one-on-one, and entire class reading courses.
- Prepared customized lessons for both needs-based and enrichment programs on phonetics, children's literature, and reading. Taught lessons.
- Developed MCAS enrichment reading plans as well as taught third grade students in preparation of this exam.

### SCHOOL ACTIVITIES

Provided decorations and served meals for school's Elderly Christmas Dinner.
Attended chorus concerts and other after school functions.
Participated in a teacher in-service seminar on multiage classroom teaching.

### AWARDS

St. Bonaventure Outstanding Student Teacher Award—2000 (*nominated by practicum school teacher, selected as top student teacher of the year*)

Andrea's new resume really emphasized her skills, accomplishments, and abilities in a noticeable way. We then discussed her big problem—getting noticed—at length. We decided that she'd create a sheet of color photos, showing her in action. She had some good ideas about putting it all together and creating a nice folder packet to hold letters of recommendation, a sample lesson plan she'd used, and her references list, resumé, and cover letter. A few weeks went by and Andrea mailed me the packet she created. It was outstanding—a very creative, eye-catching one that would definitely get her noticed. And it did. She landed several interviews at different schools in the greater Boston area, and every hiring manager commented on how terrific the packet was.

Her roommate, also looking for a teaching position, wasn't as creative and landed no interviews at all. So what made Andrea stand out in a sea of hundreds of applicants? Her packet! She took a lot of pictures during her student teaching. She laid them out on a page with a terrific design of her blowing bubbles. Inside each bubbled circle was Andrea "in action," teaching. One HR manager even called her "the bubble lady" when she came in for an interview. Her photo-covered cover page—glued to the front of her folder—also included a quote or two about teaching, plus her name and telephone number. Inside, she placed a brochure titled "Why Hire Andrea Lohr?" that she designed with colored brochure paper from a supply store. It quite effectively outlined her credentials and the benefits of having her as a teacher. Her resumé and cover letter were top-notch. She included a lesson plan, four glowing letters of recommendation, and another color copied sheet of photos of her teaching students various subjects. The entire packet was by far the best I've ever seen a candidate put together.

So was all her effort worth it? I'll let Andrea tell you. "I felt I had to be that creative to get noticed, because I'd heard thousands apply for a single teaching job in Boston. It was expensive to do, about $7 per packet, but I had to find a way to stand out. Many interviewers commented that it was ingenious to have the collage of me teaching on the front cover. It really caught their eye. In fact, I was searching on the Internet and saw an ad for teachers in Liverpool, New York, claiming they offered starting salaries that were among the highest in the country. So on a lark, I sent them a packet. They called and offered a screening interview. I went to a meeting with the Assistant Superintendent, who said she was shocked to learn I'd been called off my materials. She said, 'I don't think that's ever happened before—our recruiters meet teachers at job fairs, through contacts, or from referrals. I've never heard of someone just mailing in and getting an interview.' "

Everyone she interviewed with really commented on the packet. One even told her it was the first time he ever saw a teacher holding a six-foot snake, smiling about it, and calling it hands-on learning.

Demonstrating her creativity paid off for Andrea. She started at Liverpool Elementary last September as a $41,000-per-year first-year teacher. Her friends, the few that found full-time jobs, started at $28,000 or less. Yes, Andrea did a lot of extra work to get noticed. She recognized that her first teaching job would be the hardest one she'd probably ever have to get. But in going above and beyond, she won the job of her dreams, even with no professional experience.

## *Advanced Degrees, MBAs, Lawyers, etc.*

Many graduates go on to pursue a higher level of education. Many positions, such as doctor or lawyer, require additional degrees. Some weight is definitely given to grads for more competitive or highly ranked programs, but nothing beats illustrating what you've learned and done wherever you went to college.

Curtis was seeking his first job right out of law school. He had no other experience besides the required clerkships and an internship. This resumé really examined what he'd done in those jobs, in order to best sell the skills he had acquired.

Aggressive networking uncovered the job lead that landed my client Curtis his law position. *He beat out 210 lawyers!* Some "inside information" obtained from a contact allowed us to create a strong resumé and polish his interview skills to get the job.

Today, a larger number of working grads find themselves back in the classroom to pursue an MBA. Many of these people already have significant experience and years on the job before they even begin their MBA. That's true in Jack's case, in which his company actually paid his tuition as he pursued his degree. Once it was completed, he found the best way to advance was to leave his current employer and move on to a new one. That move, the first to capitalize on his MBA, also resulted in a BIG jump in salary.

# Curtis McIntyre
1 Main Street
City, NY 11111
(201) 555-0111
curtmc@aol.com

CAREER OBJECTIVE: **Attorney**

## SUMMARY OF QUALIFICATIONS

Strong legal research abilities with experience working within a major metropolitan city prosecutor's office. Excellent writing skills with good courtroom presentation style. Highly productive worker excelling under pressure. Thinks well on feet. Not easily flustered or intimidated. *Licensed to practice law in Arizona.*

## EDUCATION

J.D., Arizona State University, Tempe, AZ, 2001
(Personally financed 100% of law school education)
B.A., Economics, Tuskegee University, Tuskegee, AL, 1998
(Junior year abroad, one semester, Florence, Italy)

## PROFESSIONAL EXPERIENCE

*Legal Intern,* County Prosecutor's Office, Phoenix, AZ, Summer, 1999
- Assisted two deputy prosecuting attorneys with 120+ juvenile cases.
- Interviewed potential witnesses, drafted direct-examination and cross-examination questions.
- Wrote ten appellate briefs and numerous trial court motions.
- Researched legal issues including: suppression of evidence, double jeopardy, criminal procedure, and constitutional law.

## LAW SCHOOL ACTIVITIES

*Twelfth Circuit Lieutenant Governor,* Law Student Division, American Bar Association, 1999–2000
- Worked as membership coordinator promoting the student programs, developing marketing and fundraising concepts that raised membership by 20%; the largest divisional increase throughout the United States.

*Active Participant,* Client Advising, Trial Advocacy, and Moot Court Competitions.
*Co-Captain,* Intramural flag football team, and softball team member.

## COLLEGE HONORS

*Ford Foundation Scholar,* Top 10% of college class
*Dorm President,* Student Legislative Council
*Project Director "Project Hope,"* School's largest community service program

## WORK HISTORY

*Customer Service/Technical Support,* Electronic Systems, March–Oct. 2000
Other: Warehouse Worker, Purchasing, Shipping and Receiving, Waiter, Landscaper

## PUBLICATIONS

"The Impact of Personality Characteristics on Leadership Effectiveness Ratings," contained within *The Impact of Leadership,* Editors: Ryan, Smith, and Jones, 2000 Edition.

**COMBINATION**

# Jack Dieckman, MBA
1 Main Street
New York, NY 85282
(201) 555-0111
jacktheman@hotmail.com

### CAREER OBJECTIVE: **Program Manager**

### SUMMARY OF QUALIFICATIONS

Excellent organizational development skills to streamline procedures/processes/policies that enhance employee productivity and profitability. Proven program coordination experience with great attention to detail and follow-through. Strong training background including presentation and manual development. Good research ability; quick learner.

### PROFESSIONAL EXPERIENCE

*Manufacturing Tech,* Intel, Portland, OR. 1995–present (promoted from Program Coordinator) *U.S. Army,* Germany, 1992–1994

## Program Management

- Developed and managed the complete overhaul of the parts inventory and distribution process resulting in millions of dollars in department savings. Received superior service award for performance.
- Managed the security program for high tech company including: staffing; planning: implementation of policies and procedures; crisis management; coordination of the emergency response team.
- Coordinated sophisticated security operations management of high risk, remote multisite high tech facilities.

## Marketing

- Extensive coursework on in-depth market research including: creation of survey, survey distribution, written report of statistical analysis, recommendations on business viability, risk level, customer penetration, targeted marketing and business plan, plus profit forecasting.

## Training

- Developed new training program for Intel contract workers that included: employee orientation, policies and procedures, and safety topics. Program allowed company to quickly adjust workforce to meet manufacturing needs.
- Wrote, edited and distributed three new employee training manuals to detail performance and handling of policies, procedures and job operation duties.
- Taught 50+ employee training programs and classes on job performance issues and employee orientation.
- Taught several "train-the-trainer" programs for the military staff. Created curriculum and all training materials.

### COMPUTER SKILLS

Proficiency utilizing Word, Excel, PowerPoint, Lotus, databases

### EDUCATION

MBA, University of Portland, Portland, OR 2002
BS, Oregon State University, Corvallis, OR 1991

# EXECUTIVE RESUMÉS:
## CEO, VP, CFO, COO, GM, PRESIDENT, AND OTHER SENIOR EXECUTIVES

*Results. Accomplishments. Measurable Achievements. Notable Outcomes. Demonstrated leadership to meet and beat the goals. That's what employers truly care about!*

Top executives are responsible for the success or lack thereof of the entire organization. When a search committee is looking to hire a key person such as yourself, your past record comes under close scrutiny. I've worked one-on-one with many top-level executives, all terrific on the job, but not so terrific at selling themselves to new employers. Their resumés were often ridiculously long—one CEO was quite proud of his eight-page resumé, until it failed to produce any inquiries. Others give a great deal of space and detail to positions held 10 to 15 years ago, positions that have little impact on the current level desired. Some give a "skills" laundry list, or a "qualifications" list, highlighting job functions, like this one taken from a client's old resumé:

### Qualifications

| | | |
|---|---|---|
| General Management | Strategic Planning | Mergers/Acquisitions |
| International Operations | Distribution | Organizational Development |
| Sales/Marketing | Product Launches | Business Development |

When I questioned a client about why he made this list on his resumé, he said he simply used the template the national outplacement company gave him and *voilá!* He created this. Unfortunately, these duties or job functions demonstrate no actions or results. This was a critical error, he admitted after analyzing why no employers responded to this resumé.

I recently conducted a survey of 78 top executives—CEOs, presidents, board chairs—on promotions, promotable people, and exactly what it takes to make it to the top (and stay there). When questioned about what qualities they look for when hiring or promoting a top executive, the decision makers were very forthcoming. They felt the person must *produce results* (most important) and *excel at what they do.* They look for *good team builders* and team players who *add a lot* to the executive group. They, surprisingly enough, wanted an *honest person who acts with integrity.* This was noted as a very important trait. They need a *strategic thinker* and *problem solver,* someone who was *continuously improving themself, their job, their department/area, and their company as a whole.* (A complete copy of this servey is on my website: www.robinryan.com.)

Sounds simple. You've done that. You know you have the accomplishments and the skills to get the job done. But a generic resumé won't open doors. You need a more savvy, strategic marketing tool. One that clearly and concisely demonstrates your previous successes. Remember, CEO really stands for Creative Energetic Overachiever, proven by the fact that every year one-third of all CEOs are fired and need to resourcefully locate a new job. The yardsticks for the top jobs can be difficult to measure up to and achieve.

Today's workplace is unpredictable, unstable, full of mergers, layoffs, and fabulous opportunities. I've seen many senior executives mourn the loss of a great job, only to find an even better one, with an even higher salary, six months later. Some move on to head new companies, some simply start their own businesses, and others go to much larger organizations, usually landing a position a few steps down from the top job.

Whether you are making this change because you want to or have to, it's a key opportunity to secure something you'll love doing every day. Your resumé is an important introductory tool that must command attention. Allow me to have you eavesdrop on one of my consulting sessions, where CFO Michael Money and I worked on his old resumé. We went through the Goldmining Technique™ and he learned a great deal about how to state, describe, and market his accomplishments.

Michael Money was a CFO and Vice President who created a one-page, very general, boring resumé before we met. Not surprisingly, he received no response after sending it out. He missed the major concept basic to all resumé writing, demonstrating ACTIONS = RESULTS!

I cannot stress enough that the entire Goldmining Technique™ is based on uncovering important job duties and your actions performing them, plus noting the significant results you achieved. Michael Money's new resumé clearly demonstrates the major impact utilizing this process can achieve.

# Michael Money
135 Colbert Street
Ft. Lauderdale, FL 88850
(816) 222-5555

OBJECTIVE    To contribute to the growth and profitability of a company as a member of the management team.

EXPERIENCE

1993–Present    CFO and Vice President    Marina Boat Centers

A large retailer of pleasure boats, parts, accessories and service with multiple locations in the U.S. and Canada. Responsible for entire accounting operations and profitability of company. Specific responsibilities include data processing, human resources, profit sharing and supervision of accounting department. Have increased profit by creating more efficient and effective processing systems in the accounting department. Successfully implemented two computer conversions. Created information systems that provided store managers with better understanding into the operations of their stores, leading to higher profitability. Responsible for all banking relationships.

1988–1993    Assistant Controller    Waterworld Enterprises

A multi-faceted corporation involved in manufacturing and service industries. Responsible for administering entire accounting function including financial statements, budgets and corporate tax returns. Implemented and developed cash management system. Updated data processing system. Set up cost accounting system. Established internal control procedures. Hired, trained and supervised accounting staff. Assisted in acquisition and integration of new businesses.

1984–1988    Supervisor    Ernst & Young, Certified Public Accountants

Provided accounting, auditing, tax and management advisory services to retail, wholesale, manufacturing, real estate companies. Demonstrated skills in staff supervision and training, analyzing and identifying cost saving procedures, effective tax and financial planning. Knowledge of electronic data processing accounting systems.

PROFESSIONAL LICENSES/

MEMBERSHIP    Certified Public Accountant

Florida Society of Certified Public Accountants

American Institute of Certified Public Accountants

COMMENT    Conscientious team player who enjoys challenging opportunities.

Here's an analysis of the main problems with Michael Money's OLD resumé:

✔ *Too general!* Did not mention any figures or percentages in his statement of "having increased profits." Without the answers to "how much" and "how" it's just a weak puff statement. Overall, it reads like a simple job description—nothing more.

✔ *It stresses dates, not his prominent job titles.* In fact, your eye is actually drawn to the dates of employment in his old resumé. You almost overlook the titles "CFO" and "Vice President" when you quickly scan over the resumé. Employers sort through stacks of resumés very fast and much is easily missed.

✔ *Memberships mean you paid your dues.* By no means is it influential or a big deal. As for professional licenses, his "CPA" license is buried—the title needs to be added directly after his name at the top of the resumé as it is a very important credential in performing his job.

✔ *Lacks summary of qualifications.* He really missed the boat, so to speak, when he used the small heading "comment." This section needs several more sentences to entice employers to request an interview.

✔ *No college degree is listed.* All CPAs have a college degree, a prerequisite before obtaining their CPA license. He just "forgot" it, he later told me, when I questioned him about why it wasn't listed on his resumé.

✔ *Long paragraphs make it hard to catch accomplishments quickly.* The old-fashioned resumé style he used, with its long, descriptive paragraphs, is often a major detriment in today's fast-paced, skim-the-resumé-in-15-seconds workplace. You need the impact only short phrases and bulleted statements can provide.

## What Goldmining™ Did for Michael Money

Michael faced a saturated market of highly qualified finance people. Many were victims of layoffs, providing extensive competition for plum CFO jobs that just a few years before remained open for months. In the current environment, it's not surprising his talents didn't stand out on his old resumé. We agreed to change his format to a modified *Combination* style that added his two previous jobs to the tail end of his Professional Experience. I felt it was important to retain them, particularly since he'd been a supervisor for one of the big accounting firms. But the level of experience was so early in his career that it really didn't deserve any descriptive lines. We used the space to emphasize his CFO duties, the job he was currently seeking. Michael quickly identified (using the Skills Area list in Chapter 8) his major experience headings as: Financial, Computer Systems, and Human Resources.

My next objective was to get his mind thinking about ACTIONS = RESULTS. *How big was the company he ran? What had he increased? Exactly how did he increase sales and by how much? Where did he save time or money? What other improvements had he made?* I grilled him for definitive numbers and percentages. We put the last few years of his career under the microscope and culled out the important, influential facts. Two hours later, we created his new resumé. He was amazed at the improvement. "You've really opened up my eyes today," he said. "It's obvious to me now that by putting forth the actions and accomplishments, I'm telling the employer important contributions that they can expect if they hire me. I'm ecstatic over the difference."

Within days of mailing out the new resumés, employers noticed him. Michael got several interviews and was very selective. His current job was OK, but he longed for a new challenge. When a company came along that really needed new leadership to turn it around (over two years it had consistently lost money), he took on the challenge.

# Michael Money, CPA
135 Colbert Street
Ft. Lauderdale, FL 88850
(816) 222-5555

CAREER OBJECTIVE: **Chief Financial Officer**

## SUMMARY OF QUALIFICATIONS

Proven track record leading a company's financial direction to improved sales, profitability and growth. Excellent computer systems expertise to maximize efficiency and produce high levels of productivity. Responsible for building a team environment company-wide resulting in significant growth in sales, profitability and employee longevity.

## PROFESSIONAL EXPERIENCE

*Vice President/CFO,* Marina Boat Centers, Miami, FL, 1993–Present

### Financial

- Directed the financial operations of 10 retail store chain with United States and Canada operations, annual sales of $60M. Duties include: financial analysis, cost accounting, budgets, forecasting, strategic planning, cash management, banking relations, investments, computer systems, all accounting functions (A/P, A/R, payroll, financial statements), human resources. Contributed significantly to company's expansion including opening new stores, implementing financial analysis/cost accounting/strategic planning processes, creating a total team concept company-wide, re-targeted sales price points that generated increased sales, improved efficiency in service departments, results increased sales $18M.
- Reorganized the labor needs based on sales volume/store performance/job functions resulting in improved efficiency, cost-savings reduced labor costs 10%. Profitability increased 1.25%.

### Computer Systems

- Implemented new point-of-sale computer system networking all stores, correcting troubleshooting problems of nonworking system over two-year period. Negotiated entire hardware/software system purchase. Results increased financial data for analysis, cost accounting and strategic planning.
- Developed processes, customized software to maximize efficiency of computer system.
- Trained managers on system usage.

### Human Resources

- Created employee policies and procedures handbook, documenting first-time-ever manual covering all 200+ employees.
- Administered employee profit-sharing plan, employee benefits, compensation, payroll, employee legal conflict/disputes and terminations.

*Assistant Controller,* Waterworld Enterprises, Fort Lauderdale, FL, 1988–1993

*Accounting Supervisor,* Ernst & Young, Miami, FL, 1984–1988

## EDUCATION

Bachelor of Science, Business Administration/Accounting, William and Mary College, Williamsburg, VA, 1984

Within a year, not only was the company doing well and profiting, Michael Money was benefiting, too. A major bonus and stock options had him rolling "in the money."

Michael told me another benefit he received from the Goldmining Technique™—one I think you'll find valuable, too—came from analyzing what he'd accomplished. By thinking about where his actions had resulted in important cost savings, he realized exactly what he'd done to improve the bottom line, as we documented his actions in his resumé. During our consulting session, Michael achieved clarity on his achievements, and became more adept at discussing them during job interviews, another result of the Goldmining Technique.™

In this chapter, several other resumés follow that were used by high-level executive clients. You'll notice they all clearly illustrate the "Action = Results" formula. All of these people's resumés got them terrific interviews and helped them land great jobs.

I've also included some special situations, like Ed's. He had been CEO of a $25 million company and wanted to move up and on to a bigger challenge. His next job turned out not to be a CEO position, as he originally had targeted. Instead, he became a CFO, but at a major, much, much larger organization. There are times, as Ed found, that a step down in title is essential for a step up in responsibility, prestige, size, and salary, too. The move proved to be perfect and he's now primed to eventually move on to a "biggie" CEO job one day soon.

Sam Williams faced another obstacle. He had fabulous experience and a very strong track record, but no college degree. Since his whole career had been one straight upward path for a manufacturer, it was never a problem. When he began to job hunt, he listed a few job courses under EDUCATION that pulled his resumé down and weakened it significantly. Our decision to drop the Education heading completely resolved that problem and allowed him to move forward on his track record alone.

Travis Black had been a client for many years. Seemed like every time he wanted to change jobs he'd call me up for help with a new resumé and another strategic job-hunting session. He flew to his CEO position in only eight years. That top position was with a new start-up online company—with terrific salary and stock options—and life was grand until the dot-coms all crashed and burned when the venture capitalist money dried up. An entrepreneur at heart, he did some consulting while he looked for a new high tech CEO job. What caught his eye, though, was a cool job in Microsoft upper management (but far from the CEO spot). The job entailed combining business analysis and developing new businesses. It was exciting, interesting, and a challenge he couldn't resist, so he took it on and found it exceeded his expectations. Even though he doesn't run the whole show, he's head of his division and has a great deal of autonomy to make things happen. He said he's definitely found a home—at least for a while. His salary is now more than he ever thought he'd make and he admitted that the dot-com crash, in retrospect, wasn't the worst thing that ever happened in his life. Now he realizes it gave him the confidence and push he needed to move into that select group of folks earning well over $100K. In other words, he turned the company closure and job loss "lemons" into "lemonade."

All these clients were talented people who used moves to advance their lives. Upon analysis of these other examples, you'll understand how using the action = results worked for them and will also work effectively for you.

# Edward Rhone, CPA, CMA

1 Main Street
Chicago, IL 11111
708-555-0111
erhone@hotmail.com

CAREER OBJECTIVE: **CEO**

## SUMMARY OF QUALIFICATIONS

Results-oriented leader with proven expertise in business development, achieving higher levels of growth and profitability. Strong financial ability managing turnarounds and high risk projects achieving profitable results where failure loomed. Excel at strategic planning, fostering profitable business growth, streamlining costs and operations plus developing a cohesive highly productive team that exceeds growth.

## PROFESSIONAL EXPERIENCE

*President and CEO,* promoted from CFO, Sterling Investments, Ltd. Chicago, IL
1998 to present

- Spearheaded a company turnaround revamping all operations and implementing new financial systems that achieved profitable results in 12 months. Developed company from $10M annual revenues to current level of $25M, exceeding 12% profitability every year.
- Developed new business, negotiated profitable deals on new construction projects and major renovation projects leading to significant corporate growth, while reducing internal overhead to maximize profits.
- Created a five-year strategic plan mapping out strategic direction, assessing growth opportunities, controlling risk and planning cash management for long-term financial health.
- Developed a leadership team that promotes professional growth of employees that work together to meet or surpass goals.

*Chief Financial Officer,* Simone Properties Chicago, IL 1997–1998

- Managed all financial operations for real estate developer/operator, $40M annual revenues. Duties included: cash management, forecasting, general ledger, accounts payable, accounts receivable, risk management, banking.
- Streamlined and reorganized the entire accounting process resulting in 1000 man hours saved, improved accuracy and faster financial reporting.
- Installed new computerized accounting system.

*Educational Program Director,* Becker CPA/CMA Review Course Chicago, IL
1994–1997                    Instructor: 1990 to present

- Managed the development of educational training program to become one of the nation's top programs.
- Taught hundreds of financial accounting, cost accounting, and management theory courses.
- Co-author of the 1000-page certified management accounting manual used as the core resource for national accounting educational program.

*VP Finance,* JMR Limited Chicago, IL 1991–1994
- Restructured real estate developer/contractor organization implementing new strategic plan, new financial and computer systems, and hiring and training staff. Results led company from $10m to $40M in annual revenues within 18 months.

*VP Finance,* promoted from Controller, Prime Corporation Chicago, IL 1983–1991
- Full financial responsibility for this diversified developer, whose operations included development, construction, marketing and operation of offices, apartments, condominiums and single-family homes.
- Total financial responsibility for three corporations and 25 partnerships, annual revenue of $50M.
- Secured financing and negotiated loans on 25 different multimillion-dollar real estate development projects.

*Senior Accountant,* Midwest Instrument Co., Chicago, IL 1982–1983

*Staff Accountant,* Hagen Pernell, CPAs, Chicago, IL 1981–1982

EDUCATION

BA, Accounting, University of Illinois, 1981
CPA Certification 1982
CMA Certification 1996—award for second highest score in United States

**COMBINATION**

# David Christiansen, MBA
1 Main Street
New York, NY 11111
(212) 555-1211
Email: dachris@ix.netcom.com

*Editorial Note: Original resumé all appeared on one page*

CAREER OBJECTIVE: **Vice President—Aviation Company**

## SUMMARY OF QUALIFICATIONS

Fifteen years in aviation leadership providing strategic planning, management, and new business development that consistently achieved profitable results. Involved with improving the information/computer network systems resulting in greater efficiency and higher levels of productivity. Excel in new business development and client relationships, as well as significantly expanding product sales and increasing market share that resulted in bottomline profits.

## PROFESSIONAL EXPERIENCE

*Assistant VP,* Aviation Underwriters, New York, NY 1988–present
(Promoted from *Assistant Branch Manager,* promoted from *Underwriter*)

### Management/Operations

- Managed the daily operations for an aviation-only insurance organization for 14 years. Duties included: branch administration, strategic planning, information technology management, operations, customer relations, new business development, budgets and forecasting, risk analysis, staff supervision and oversee pilot training program.
- Administered the pilot training program for continuous certification providing in-flight instructor/check pilot approval for over 200+ pilots.
- Developed, implemented and upgraded entire corporate information technology for 9 branches to improve efficiency, productivity and product quality resulting in a much higher level of customer satisfaction.
- Provided strategic planning and leadership to assist in company's branch growth by 30%.
- Negotiated and analyzed hundreds of contracts for risk analysis and liability with total authority to determine acceptable and unacceptable terms.

### New Business Development/Client Relations

- Created new strategy and approach to Canadian business identifying potential markets and niches, developing new business plan, wrote business operations manual, established friendlier policies and procedures that fostered significant growth in the Canadian marketplace.
- Developed region's marketing plan to strengthen relationships with customers, expanded the market share targeting high-margin products.
- Served as brand manager on new product launch including all strategic planning, goal setting, promotion, developing potential customer list, staff training, and overseeing sales.
- Managed all major accounts dealing directly with customers, accounting for 40% of all branch revenues.

## EDUCATION

MBA, Seton Hall, South Orange, NJ, 1993
BS, Business Management, SUNY Buffalo, NY, 1988
Certified Pilot in 1985, Commercial multiengine rated from 1990, Status: current
Certified Instrument Flight Instructor, Status: current and active

# Eric Van Haren
1 Main Street
Atlanta, GA 11111
(404) 555-5555
ericvan@aol.com

CAREER OBJECTIVE: **Chief Operating Officer**

## SUMMARY OF QUALIFICATIONS

Superior track record as Chief Operating Officer, leading commercial print company to greater profitability with a 46% increase in annual revenues. Excel at strategic planning, streamlining operations, cost cutting while developing new business and maximizing profits. Visionary team builder who can motivate others to produce results.

## PROFESSIONAL EXPERIENCE

*Chief Operating Officer,* Peachtree Press, Inc. Atlanta, GA 1991–present
*(Promoted from Director of Manufacturing, promoted from Production Manager)*

- Managed the entire operations for $65M commercial print company including: financial management, manufacturing, strategic planning, forecasting, budgets, human resources, distribution, facilities, computer systems, website/online sales, policies & procedures, labor negotiations, vendor relationships plus contract negotiations.
- Increased revenues during last three years by acquiring new plant; streamlined prepress process with new equipment purchase, reduced costs, reduced print cycle time, increased capacity and product quality, plus developed new business. Results: increased annual revenue by 46%.
- Reorganized both plants/operations; decreased staff; consolidated tasks; installed new equipment; eliminated some sub contracting. Results: saved 1 million dollars annually.
- Instituted new technology changes moving from conventional prepress operation to digital operation to Direct-To-Plate process. Handled all purchasing and implementation of new systems. Results increased print speed, quality, reduced waste and attracted eight new large corporate accounts that dramatically increased bottomline profits.
- Negotiated vendor contracts. Obtained better prices, better terms, and eliminated unnecessary contracts. Results: saved $526,00.
- Established highly successful web based Internet business as part of global operations to capture e-commerce business. Established sophisticated website that allows for customer sales, service, account access and order tracing all online. Results are producing a fast growing, high profit revenue stream.
- Served as liaison with union handling union contract negotiations, communications, policies & procedures, and any union/management issues.

## EDUCATION

Bachelor's Degree, Rochester Institute of Technology, New York 1987

# Tom Lee
1 Movie Star Lane
Los Angeles, CA 91111
(310) 555-0011
tlee@aol.com

CAREER OBJECTIVE: **General Manager**

## SUMMARY OF QUALIFICATIONS

Proven track record of station management in both top and midsize television market-places developing large viewership and strong advertising base. Keen ability to develop programming that attracts desired demographic groups while streamlining operations to grow and improve profitability each year. Excel at team development that continuously meets or beats goals.

## PROFESSIONAL EXPERIENCE

*General Manager,* KSCA TV (#2 market), Los Angeles, CA 1993–2002

### Management
- Established new television station for Los Angeles marketplace; responsibilities included: programming, operations, sales, personnel/hiring, promotions and facilities construction. Achieved 98% penetration within the marketplace selling a multicultural Asian channel.
- Achieved start-up station profitability within 18 months; then doubled revenues for each of three years; followed by increasing annual revenues by 21% for remaining years until sale of station in 1998.
- Set up the entire new station facilities including: design, construction, and transmission operations for studios and offices. Negotiated contracts and terms, saving over $3 million.

### TV Programming/Sales
- Developed original concepts for television station to establish a niche in a broad competitive marketplace. Achieved large viewership, profitable annual return, and strong advertising base within 18 months.
- Continuously realigned programs to increase viewership and capture more market-share.
- Created sales/promotion/marketing campaign to attract viewers and advertisers using newspaper and radio ads, special events/tradeshows, direct mail, and promotional contests.

*Station Manager,* KNMZ-TV (64th market), Albuquerque, NM 1988–1993
- Organized all the operations, production, engineering, promotions, public affairs, traffic, creative services art, film and video departments for new start-up independent channel to achieve coverage throughout state.
- Coordinated the design, layouts, equipment purchase, and new construction of studios and station facilities. Negotiated contacts achieving significant savings.

*Director of Engineering,* Educational Television Services, Arizona State University, 1985–1988

## EDUCATION

Bachelor of Science, Arizona State University, Tempe, AZ 1987

**COMBINATION**

# Bryan Novelle
1 Main Street
San Francisco, CA 94111
(415) 555-1111
bryann@msn.com

CAREER OBJECTIVE: CEO

## SUMMARY OF QUALIFICATIONS

Proven leader with superior record in international mergers/acquisitions and business expansions that resulted in significantly increasing profitability, streamlining operations, decreasing costs, while gaining greater market share Excel at product launches, improving profit margins, international and national sales plus developing organizational team and employees that meet or exceed goals.

## PROFESSIONAL EXPERIENCE

*President,* Progeny, Inc. San Francisco, CA 1997–present
*President,* Cencon International, Menlo Park, CA 1991–1997
*Senior Vice President, Sales and Marketing,* Roche Corp., Palo Alto, CA 1981–1991

### Leadership

- Directed the international expansion of company through acquisitions and mergers, utilizing strategic planning, targeted marketing and product rollouts, increasing annual sales from $15 to $70 million in four years, establishing significant market share and doubling profits.
- Led the international division through a profitable expansion, merging three companies to create a significant market share dominance in Europe in twelve months. *Results: more than tripled annual sales to $50 million, while doubling profits to 10%.*
- Planned and managed the company's first product launch for first-time expansion into Japanese marketplace while establishing an operating company in Japan. *Results: achieved $10 million in sales within 2 years.*
- Merged two competing Canadian companies, then led the acquisition team to achieve increased sales and market share while consolidating functions and streamlining operations. *Results: saved 25% in operational costs while doubling profits.*

### Sales/Marketing/Business Development

- Launched Roche's biggest new product in company history that eventually achieved $1 billion in sales.
- Managed the growth expansion of all national sales and marketing from $50 to $500 million over ten years. Duties included: successful product launches, team development, sales management, strategic planning and implementation of innovative marketing techniques.
- Consulted with start-up company on its product development, sales forecast, marketing plan and partnering options.

- Managed the business development of a new franchise area, building and opening several operating units within the greater Puget Sound marketplace, and then sold the enterprise.

### EDUCATION

Bachelor of Arts, English, University of California, Los Angeles, CA 1973
Executive Program, Stanford University Graduate School of Business,
Palo Alto, CA 1985

**COMBINATION**

# Travis Black, CPA

1 Main Street
Seattle, WA 98100
(206) 555-1111
travis@consulting.com

CAREER OBJECTIVE: **CEO**

## SUMMARY OF QUALIFICATIONS

Possess a unique and proven set of high tech, accounting, and business operations skills that are innovative and visionary, producing solutions that foster company growth and expansion. Excel at creating new and never-before-done systems that work well and surpass goals. Superior strategic planning skills and ability to develop and hire teams that produce results. Enjoy challenges, cutting edge technology and risk taking.

## PROFESSIONAL EXPERIENCE

*Consultant/Owner,* Consulting LLC, Seattle, WA Nov. 2000–present
*(start-up computer consulting business)*
*CEO,* Optical Express LLC, Seattle, WA August–November 2000
*Online company, operations stalled due to collapse of financing and venture capital money for online companies.*
*Director of Finance,* Cyberspaces, Inc., Kirkland, WA May–July 2000
*Online company, projected financing ended or disappeared*
*Client Manager,* Townsend Associates PS, Bellevue, WA 1994–2000
*CPA firm exclusively serving the high tech industry*
*Staff Accountant,* Moss Brown, CPAs Seattle, WA 1992–1994

### Finance

- Managed numerous high tech corporate accounts proving financial, tax, accounting, strategic planning and business operations services. Also handled mergers and acquisitions, due diligence and equity compensation plans.
- Developed new high tech accounting tools for clients. Developed accounting policies and procedures and reporting templates that acquired and streamlined financial data addressing issues such as revenue recognition, forecasting, budgeting, taxes (state and federal), and subscription accounting.

### Computer Systems

- Served as IT manager for rapidly growing CPA firm. Selected hardware and software, purchased and installed systems customizing to company needs. Built and maintained servers and workstations.
- Provided specialized consulting to Microsoft on the program design for an update to Microsoft Money. Provided financial accounting recommendations and usability guidance, some of which was incorporated into final product.

## COMPUTER SKILLS

Systems expert on Windows 2000 Server, Windows 2000 Professional, Windows NT, Microsoft Exchange Server, Windows 98, and Microsoft Office. Expert user level skills in accounting, tax preparation, and financial planning software.

## EDUCATION

Bachelor of Arts, Accounting, Washington State University, Pullman, WA 1992

**COMBINATION**

# Sheila McFarland, MBA
1 Main Street
Fort Worth, TX 75000
(214) 555-1211
smcfarland@att.net

CAREER OBJECTIVE: **Chief Executive/Operating Officer**

### SUMMARY OF QUALIFICATIONS

Top executive with proven track record to advance company growth while improving profitability and increasing employee performance to meet and surpass organizational goals.

### PROFESSIONAL EXPERIENCE

*CEO/General Manager,* Hair Experts, Dallas, TX 1993–2001

*Assistant Treasurer,* MCI, Dallas, TX 1976–1993
(Promoted from *Director of Finance,* promoted from *Accounting Manager*)

## Leadership
- Created strategic plan and implemented comprehensive business/operations/marketing plan that grew stores from 16 to 52, doubling employees to over 700 and grew revenues from $3M to $19M while tripling profitability over the eight years of responsibility.
- Developed business concept that achieved regional store/brand recognition within highly competitive industry.
- Created manager and store employee policies and procedures, hiring strategies, and training programs on business operations, customer service, employee retention, staff motivation, technical techniques/advances. *Results: achieved skilled labor force with highest retention rate in industry.*
- Managed the reorganization of accounting, client records, and billing operations consolidating eight MCI regional offices into three. Duties: operations, strategic planning, finance, budgets. Coordinated with union for the outplacement of 800 staff positions over two-year period.

## Finance/Computer Systems
- Provided financial management (on a daily basis at MCI and as top executive at Hair Masters). Overseeing capital and expense budgets—$300M annually, daily financial operations, financial statements and systems.
- Implemented new sophisticated point-of-sale computer system for all stores. *Results: increased manageability of the business, reduced inventory and expenses, increased retail sales by eliminating nonperforming product lines while quickly identifying hot products.*

### EDUCATION
MBA, Southern Methodist University, Dallas, TX 1976
BS, Baylor, Waco, TX 1975

# Braden Halforn, CPA

1 Main Street
Philadelphia, PA 97000
(215) 555-1122
bhalforn@accessone.com

CAREER OBJECTIVE: **Vice President Finance/Treasurer**

## SUMMARY OF QUALIFICATIONS

Proven track record demonstrating superior financial leadership to increase profits, contain costs and streamline operations with a $100M international company. Excel in establishing favorable banking relationships that yield lower interest rates and better terms. Able to establish policies, procedures and processes that increase efficiency and save time. Recognized for developing cohesive team that meet or exceed expectations and goals.

## PROFESSIONAL EXPERIENCE

*CFO,* PFS-RMC Management LP, Philadelphia, PA 1998–present

### Financial Management

- Managed all accounting and treasury functions for a $100 million, 1,000 employee international organization. Responsibilities included: financial management and reporting, treasury, forecasting, budgets, cash management, strategic planning, banking/foreign currency transactions, human resources, and information systems.
- Led organization to improve the profit margin from 25% to 30% while dealing with a declining product sales price.
- Reorganized cash management strategies and investment program that resulted in cost savings of over $500,000 annually through reduced interest and bank service fees.
- Streamlined financial operations and reporting that reduced the general ledger process time from 90 days to 10 days. Results: dramatically improved the executive team's ability to manage and plan company's worldwide operations.
- Evaluated, analyzed and implemented significant process, policy and procedural changes to reduce both equipment maintenance and workman's compensation costs by $3 million annually.
- Established a new satellite information system to create an instantaneous financial reporting system on worldwide operations that contained costs, and expedited resolution of expenditure problems.

### International Business

- Broad experience operating business in foreign countries, numerous currencies with varying complex political organizations.

*Senior Audit Manager,* Grant Thornton, Baltimore, MD, 1985–1998
- Coordinated several initial public offerings, debt offerings, secondary offerings and business combination filings for emerging fast growth companies in US and Europe. Supervised SEC annual and quarterly reporting.

*Accountant,* Ernst & Young, Baltimore, MD 1983–1985

## EDUCATION

BS, Accounting/Business Management, Pennsylvania State University 1983

**COMBINATION**

# Linda Northrup, MBA
1 Main Street
Louisville, KY 40200
(502) 555-1211
lnorthrup@aol.com

CAREER OBJECTIVE: **Chief of Operations**

## SUMMARY OF QUALIFICATIONS

Proven track record as a "hands-on" operations manager with demonstrated experience in streamlining operations, building highly productive teams, improving efficiency, delivering cost reductions and significantly increasing bottomline profits.

## PROFESSIONAL EXPERIENCE

*Chief Executive Officer,* Southern Price Stores, Louisville, KY 1984–2002
(Promoted from *Chief of Operations,* promoted from *Director of Purchasing,*
promoted from *Human Resources Manager*)

### Operations

- Analyzed entire business operations and implemented a new turnaround restructuring plan due to a permanent market downturn. Streamlined operations, eliminated eight positions, improved efficiency, eliminated poor-selling products, increased profit margins. Continually added process and distribution improvements. *Results:* Achieved $340,000 annual savings, returning company to profitability status by next calendar year.
- Established a new private label products program that produced $1M in new sales within six months; achieving expansive growth of $10.5M over five years.
- Implemented new policies and enhanced safety program with better employee training resulting in a 48% decrease in job-related injuries plus reduced worker's compensation premium 23%.

### Management

- Streamlined entire accounts payable process, eliminating three positions and improving the tracking and payment system to eliminate double billings and errors, saving $100,000.
- Developed new computerized forecasting program that implemented more just-in-time inventory processes resulting in inventory reductions of $1.2M while also improving service levels.
- Directed the procurement/resale process on over 20,000 items serving 200 stores. Established seasonal product variations, category product mix and negotiated best vendor pricing. *Results:* Expanded gross margin profit by .5%.
- Directed short- and long-term strategic plans that capitalized on market trends/changes using key financial analysis to establish better product mix, resulting in improved profitability.
- Negotiated the sale of entire company; inventory stock and facilities, in 1999. Located buyers, negotiated all offers, secured top bid and handled transaction process.

## EDUCATION

MBA, Emory University, Atlanta, GA 1995
BS, Business, University of Kentucky, Lexington, KY 1984

# Sam Williamson
1 Main Street
Columbus, OH 43000
(614) 555-1211
Sam_wil@msn.com

CAREER OBJECTIVE: **Vice President or Director of Manufacturing**

## SUMMARY OF QUALIFICATIONS

Demonstrated manufacturing operations leadership for billion dollar medical diagnostic equipment company achieving high levels of quality, major cost reductions, productivity enhancements and increased profits. Strong success record on analyzing problems and processes, then implementing change. Strengths include: Problem Analysis, Strategic Planning, Process Change and Implementation, Productivity Enhancements with an eye for cost reductions.

## PROFESSIONAL EXPERIENCE

*Director of Manufacturing/Business Planning,* Dade Behring, Inc.,
Columbus, OH 1990–present
(Promoted from *Director of Manufacturing,* promoted from *Production Manager*)

### Operations Management and Planning

- Served as team director in establishment of a new manufacturing culture based on self-directed teams, continuous improvement, product enhancements, and cost reductions. *Results: achieved 20% increase in productivity and $3.5 million increase in bottomline profits.*
- Managed a product production turnaround through entire process including: analysis, problem definition, planning, restructuring, implementation, and enhancements. *Results: achieved 26% productivity increase with $2 million in annual cost reductions.*
- Designed new parts repair center for a complex medical diagnostic equipment start-up product including: analysis, planning, regulatory approval, staffing, training, implementation, forecasting and production. *Results: repair center saved over $13 million during life of product.*
- Led quality improvement effort in high volume consumables process utilizing SPC tools. *Results: achieved $300,000/year cost reduction in material and labor.*
- Directed the restructuring of product production process on 6-month order backlog problem. Implemented new processes, new organizational structure, improved communications, increased productivity while maintaining quality standards. *Results: increased production from 18 units to 30 units per month, maintaining same cost per unit and similar quality levels.*

### Project Management

- Headed a "bridge product" team to resolve current product's end of life, offering bridge product to fill two-year gap before completed regulatory approval allowed launch of new product. *Results: secured and maintained company's 28% global market share.*
- Directed the strategic planning and implementation of relocating a product family's manufacturing to new plant (3,500 miles away) plus closure of old plant. *Results: achieved 43% cost reduction with no supply or service impact for customer.*

**COMBINATION**

# Raymond Peters, CPA
1 Main Street
City, NY 11111
(201) 555-0111

CAREER OBJECTIVE: **Chief of Manufacturing Operations**

## SUMMARY OF QUALIFICATIONS

Unique background blend of financial management and international manufacturing operations. Achieved significant cost-savings, increased profitability and expansive growth. Joined 75 year old company and in ten years took sales from $5M to $17M in competitive marketplace. Excel at strategic planning, productivity enhancements and employee motivation to maximize productivity and profits.

## PROFESSIONAL EXPERIENCE

*Vice President of Operations,* Melvin Foods, Smithe, TX, 1990–Present
*(Promoted from Controller)*

### Operations

- Directed the operations, financial management, distribution and human resources for international food manufacturer. Growing from $5M to $17M annual sales.
- Responsible for entire mail order fulfillment and customer service, expanding from $1.5M to $5.5M in sales. Recognized as having one of the lowest fulfillment costs in mail order industry.
- Researched, selected and purchased new expansive phone system to efficiently handle call volume, eliminating lost sales. Old system averaged 18,000 incomplete calls. Estimated sales increase: $200,000 annually.
- Construction project manager involving feasibility studies, purchase, design layout, on-site supervision of $1.3M, 75,000 sq. foot inventory/distribution center.
- Negotiated repeated contract concessions from international distribution carriers including: loading allowance, quantity discounts, price reductions, labor cost reductions, drop shipping/zone skipping. Annual savings of $135,000.
- Implemented new employee quality standards emphasizing personal accountability and autonomy resulting in 10% increase in profitability.

### Financial

- Provided financial leadership managing $15M annual sales including: general ledger, A/P, A/R, payroll, treasury functions, budgets, taxes, cost-accounting, cash management, benefits administration, risk management and all human resource functions.
- Streamlined Operations, Distribution, Inventory, Banking expenses, implementing cost-savings procedures. Total ten year savings of $1.2M.
- Implemented new, efficient cash management policies and procedures based on accurate forecasting and budgeting dealing with cyclical revenues.
- Expert witness providing financial documentation in company prosecuting lawsuit, winning final settlement of $600,000.

## COMPUTER SYSTEMS

Managed three hardware/software total company conversions to a UNIX system. Prepared long range strategic plan, projections, forecasts and budgets.

## EDUCATION

B.B.A., Accounting, University of Texas, Austin, TX, 1983

# Gayle Farino
1 Main Street
City, NY 11111
(201) 555-0111

CAREER OBJECTIVE: **Shopping Center Manager**

## SUMMARY OF QUALIFICATIONS

Twelve years producing profitable, measurable results in marketing and shopping center management. Handled four new mall openings, two expansion openings and more than fifty new merchant launches. Achieved up to 18% sales increases for upscale, urban shopping center *each year* during a seven year period. Notable strengths include strategic planning and implementation, merchandising, promotions and consumer trends.

## PROFESSIONAL EXPERIENCE

*Regional Marketing and Sales Manager,* The Townsend Co., Baltimore, MD, 1988–2000   *(Promoted from Shopping Center Marketing Manager)*

### Marketing and Sales
- Managed national region with four shopping centers and $255 million in annual sales. Duties included: strategic planning, market research, development and implementation of institutional and co-op advertising programs, vendor relations, creation of incentive/promotional programs, merchandising, community events and public relations.
- Obtained between 2% to 18% sales growth for prominent urban shopping center every year for the seven years the center has been open.
- Conducted extensive assessments and training for merchants to increase sales, customer service, improve merchandising, and target customer demographics to maximize store sales.

### Management
- Handled multimillion dollar marketing and advertising budget.
- Coordinated operations and crisis management such as floods, earthquakes, public relations scares to expediently resolve situations to tenant and customer satisfaction.
- Organized more than 300 large-scale special and merchandising events plus hundreds of smaller events including: concept development, strategic planning, targeted market segments, sponsorship solicitation, supervision and follow-through, promotion, media relations, and achieving proforma-based results.

### New Business Development
- Opened four new shopping malls and two major mall expansions/renovations, covering all aspects of planning, promotion, advertising and marketing.
- Handled 50+ new merchant launches, developing media relations appeal, coordinating events, celebrities, providing on-site promotions, coordinated operations, security, special zoning requirements and coordinated area resources needs.

## HONORS

*Maxi Award,* International Council of Shopping, Marketing, 1999
*Chairman,* Marketing Committee, Downtown Baltimore Association, 1999–2000

## EDUCATION

Bachelor of Arts, Georgetown University, Washington, D.C., 1978
Certificate, Marketing Director, International Council of Shopping Centers,
University of Michigan, 1990

**COMBINATION**

# Ben Warisond
1 Main Street
City, NY 11111
(201) 555-0111

CAREER OBJECTIVE: **Vice President of Business Development**

### SUMMARY OF QUALIFICATIONS

Proven business development leadership within high-tech, growth-oriented companies. Excel at strategic planning, business acquisition analysis, negotiations, licensing/ distribution/partnership agreements to advance market position and sales. Build cohesive teams that always achieve and often surpass corporate goals.

### PROFESSIONAL EXPERIENCE

*Director of Business Development,* Microsystems Inc., Portland, OR, 2000–Present
*Technology Director,* Teknosystems, Beaverton, OR, 1982–1991 and 1993–2000
*Director of Engineering,* Medical Technology Systems, Portland, OR, 1991–1993

## Business Development

- Directed the new business development for a high tech company, annual revenues $265M. Duties included: technology licensing, strategic planning, mergers and acquisitions, distribution agreements, negotiations, product/market research, financial analysis, and product development.
- Identified, negotiated and acquired a technology company whose strong product line complemented current products allowing for more extensive and profitable market penetration as a result.
- Negotiated and implemented a joint venture corporation which develops new software products complementing the current product offerings.
- Established strategic partnerships with other companies to develop new products.

## Engineering

- 15 years in hardware and software engineering technology including: program management, circuit design, sensors, instrumentation, team development, computer networks, real-time systems, digital signal processing, and data acquisition.
- Expanded the company's intellectual property portfolio through acquisitions and patent assignment agreements.

## Management

- Negotiated numerous partnerships, acquisitions, equity interest, license agreements, and distribution agreements.
- Managed multi-million dollar budgets, major product development programs, corporate financial analysis, and acquisition candidate valuations.

### EDUCATION

Ph.D., Electrical Engineering, Massachusetts Institute of Technology, 1978
MS, Electrical Engineering, MIT, 1976
BE, New York University, Magna Cum Laude, 1974

## *More Tips for Executives*

✔ *Use a one-page resumé.* The world is fast-paced and electronic. Long resumés get broken apart and lost. By emphasizing your accomplishments concisely and quickly, you'll appear to be an executive who gets things done. Since your background may be lengthy, focus on the duties that apply to the job you want and your last five to seven years of work.

✔ *Avoid repetition.* Most lengthy resumés are very repetitive, stating the same skills over and over again. Say it once and edit out those excessive details too many executives include. Lengthy, generic descriptions make you look disorganized, scatterbrained, and slightly arrogant, as if every single thing you've ever done is noteworthy. A concise, comprehensive overview is much more impressive in the hiring world.

✔ *Recruiters aren't the hiring decision makers.* Many recruiters want a very detailed history of your background, plus all your salary information. Never disclose your salary—use broad ranges to allow more room for negotiations. (For more advice, read my book *60 Seconds & You're Hired!* which extensively covers salary negotiations. Also, keep in mind that to get their commission, an external recruiter needs to find the "perfect" candidate, therefore they are highly critical and selective. Rejection should never be taken personally. Just keep networking and talking to the real decision makers—CEOs, VPs, Board Chairs—whoever is on the selection committee.

✔ *Create a nice package.* Be sure your cover letter, resumé, and other documents that demonstrate past achievements, plus copies of your awards and/or letters of recommendation, are all easy to read and in a professional looking format. Use nice, weighty, matching paper that's rich looking for both your resumé and cover letter.

✔ *Get up to speed about electronic resumés and online searches.* Chapter 10 covers this area and has key advice to follow. Most employers report they believe top executives, or at least the talented, dynamic, and highly qualified ones, *aren't* looking on the Internet, but instead are searching for these positions in more traditional ways. The job may be posted on the company website, but a paper resumé or networked meeting are still the ways in the door.

✔ *Present a polished, professional, "I'm a leader" look.* As the workplace has gotten more casual, workers have gotten more sloppy. We now have HR departments sending out memos to reverse the "casual" look, which got out-of-control, specifically telling employees how to dress up a bit more. One client, Thomas, said he learned a very hard lesson on this whole issue. His company was a casual workplace, and Fridays were Polo and Dockers days. When he had a late morning call to meet some board members searching for a company president, he didn't give a second thought to his attire. That is, until he went to the restaurant and the board chair greeted him in a $2,000 custom-tailored black suit. When he saw everyone at the table dressed equally well, Thomas quickly realized his mistake and explained about "Casual Fridays." The board chair said, "Yes, we don't do that," rather briskly, and my client said he knew he was sunk from there. Always have a suit or sports jacket with you to "dress up" if the unexpected happens. For women, pant suits are terrific for the workplace. They are comfortable, look professional, and are great for business meetings and daily wear, but wear a real suit—one with a skirt—for job interviews. For men and women, conservative colored suits (navy is a great choice) that fit well (no squeezing into something a size or two too small!) are a must.

✔ *Above all else, clearly demonstrate your actions and the results achieved.* The CEO survey I recently did said that the bottom-line "results" must be stressed clearly and succinctly. They are the factor that influences the decision makers to call you. The importance of being recognized for achieving notable results is covered at length in my career advancement audio talk program *The Power of Branding You,* available on my website at www.robinryan.com.

# RESUMÉS FOR THE ELECTRONIC WORLD: INTERNET, EMAIL, FAX, AND SCANNING

## 10

*E*lectronic resumés is the term often used when referring to resumés sent over the Internet. By going online, you can place your resumé on bulletin boards, employer websites, and recruiter sites, as well as email your resumé to interested parties. These high tech job hunting avenues are multiplying. Every day, more and more organizations expand their recruiting efforts and advertise for a wide range of positions on the Internet.

Numerous professional associations and colleges have now jumped on board with web pages carrying employment listings. The immediacy of reaching targeted professionals has been a major draw, attracting thousands of employers and recruiters nationwide to begin placing jobs on the Internet. The cost is often a small fraction of the cost of a Sunday newspaper ad. This has been a significant factor in why companies use the Internet and other electronic media, especially faxing.

There's no doubt the Internet plays a role in the job market, but it has NOT proven itself to be "THE WAY" to land a job.

The candidates are out there, posting and emailing their resumés, then sitting back and WAITING for a call that most of the time never comes. On the other end, employers are inundated with thousands of computer files that are code-discombobulated from the electronic transmission, filtered into an empty file, or otherwise lost. Many hiring managers complain that there are many electronic candidates, but that those candidates are often unqualified to perform the advertised jobs—that the ease of Internet use encourages people to apply for everything and every job opening, without regard to whether they even have the basic skills to perform the job.

Many employers repeatedly say high quality candidates aren't "posting" their resumés (with the exception of some very specific niche sites). Many hiring professionals and human resources managers have concluded the Internet will never replace or make obsolete hiring managers who scan resumés, looking not for keywords but for candidates with track records and solid skills.

This rang true for me when a hiring manager shared this story with me last week. He said, "We were looking to hire a Director of Facilities Systems—a key, well-paid position. HR advertised the position in our major newspaper and placed it on our website. After two Sunday ads, we got about 50 resumés, not of the caliber I'd hoped for. I was given four dozen electronic resumés, reviewed my options, and hired an internal candidate. I immediately notified HR to stop recruiting. Three weeks later, our company's webmaster called, wondering *when* I was going to pick up all the resumés I'd received. I was surprised, and said I thought I had them. Our webmaster replied, 'You've got over 700 here.' I was dumbfounded. Lots of people applied that I never saw, and well, the new guy was three weeks into the job and doing OK. Still, it overwhelmed me that so many people were looking, and what hiring manager would ever have time to screen them?"

If only the candidates had sent a paper (hard) copy, too, they would not have been "forgotten" in a database somewhere. If you follow my advice, you'll leave nothing to chance, or more commonly, internal company disorganization. Sending a backup hard copy also ensures you'll get a second look, improving your chances of being picked from the crowd.

As you visit websites, pay close attention to specific directions outlining company technology. Many allow you to paste your resumé into a site form. Others simply expect you to send it as an attachment. It's important to remember that all employer and recruiting sites *vary!* One site can view resumés with bullets, boldface, and italicizing, but another can't. Whenever possible, use your entire resumé, but be savvy and realize that technology varies from system to system, so you'll need to accommodate and customize to fit the particular site's format.

## *Internet Resumés*

This client's resumé really demonstrates his technical expertise in producing CD-ROMs and interactive games. We designed Patrick's resumé to be used or easily adapted for email, and also as a hard copy for snail mail.

His background and qualifications are strong. Patrick's goal was to advance his career, seeking an even bigger challenge. He said: "I don't want an opportunity to pass me by because I'm not out in the market-place advertising my skills. I know I always have to be aware and passively looking." His resumé captured a lot of attention. Since many high tech companies recruit on the Web, he found several good companies and sites to place it on.

Take a close look at Patrick's resumé:

# Patrick Foster
1 Main Street
City, NY 11111
(201) 555-0111
pfoster@aol.com

CAREER OBJECTIVE: **Multimedia Product Manager**

## SUMMARY OF QUALIFICATIONS

Proven leadership in multimedia and film production creating dozens of commercially successful products. Demonstrated excellence in strategic planning, marketing, and technical production skills. Built key business partnerships with Fortune 500 clients. Displayed strong interpersonal and communication skills working with diverse clients. Produced from concept to roll-out CD-ROMs, films and interactive products.

## PROFESSIONAL EXPERIENCE

*Executive Producer,* Interactive Publishing, Seattle, WA, 1996–Present
*(Promoted from Project Lead, Producer)*
*Producer,* Universal Studios, Hollywood, CA, 1993–96
*President,* Foster Films, Los Angeles, CA, 1987–93

### Strategic Planning and Business Development

- Part of senior management taking start-up company from 2 CD-ROM titles to 20 with international distribution, increasing revenues by 1,000% over 30 months.
- Contributed to new business development, planning, contract negotiations; securing Fortune 500 clients as partners in product development and distribution.
- Wrote client proposals acquiring a large percentage of the proposed business.
- Significant contributor and writer on five year business plan.
- Resolved conflicts and negotiated with clients and vendors to arrive at win-win situations. Negotiated fees, product features, ownership of derivative content and other terms.

### Project Management and Product Development

- Managed company's largest partner deal securing clients, developing CD-ROM content, coordinating all client liaison, technical design, supervising team, managing budgets and production schedules. Return on investment was 200% in first 90 days of release.
- Produced 60 documentary films, full-length video releases, and hundreds of commercials, industrial/training/sales videos.
- Produced 6 cross-platform CD-ROM reference titles and 4 new releases within 29 months. Each release used the most innovative technology available. All were profitable.
- Earned a reputation for meeting impossible deadlines, shipping 5 out of 6 titles on time. All 6 CD-ROM projects came at or below budget.
- Handled product development from concept, content acquisition, interface design, production, testing.

### Multimedia Technology

- Hands-on experience with programming and production tools for CD-ROM development and digital video editing including: Lingo, Hypercard, Photoshop, Project,

Filemaker, Painter, Premiere, After Effects, DeBabelizer, plus numerous others. Both Win and Mac OS.
- Produced 100+ films, CD-ROMs and video releases.

### Awards

1999, International Milia for the Best How To Title.
PC Magazine's Pick Hit of the Month.
1999, Winter CES Innovations Award, and numerous others.

### Education

B.A., Film Production, University of Southern California, Los Angeles, CA 1989

Patrick's credentials were excellent and really stood out with his new resumé. He was very creative, with strong organizational skills. His resumé clearly outlined what he had done, which was a great deal. High tech is a very competitive field requiring a resumé that shows proven skills and accomplishments, and that also gives the impression of a nimble, resourceful person who adapts to change very quickly. Hiring managers who reviewed his resumé could get a feeling that "this guy gets the job done." His resumé was written to exude confidence and competence. It was a winning combination.

## Job Search Tips for Using the Internet

✔ *Skip mega sites.* Monster.com and HotJobs.com are very large and have hundreds of thousands of job listings all over the universe. Unfortunately, no index makes it easy to screen to identify your desired job. I listed myself on the site and got a huge list of potential "management" positions, most of which I neither wanted (wrong job) or wouldn't move to (I like living here in Seattle). You can spend a great deal of time on these mega sites, getting job listings advertising everything from taxi driver and pizza delivery person, all the way to rocket scientist, with a million different jobs in between. This won't yield the results you need, specifically, landing a new job, and it's not worth all the effort it requires. I always find in my job search seminars that many people visit these mega sites. But I've only found three rare people who actually found jobs this way.

✔ *Avoid posting on general bulletin boards and recruiting sites.* This is often easy to do, a cut-and-paste procedure. Many are visited by recruiters, but jobs here are often closed or nonexistent. These sites do not lead to landing good jobs.

✔ *Create your electronic resumé in the only software almost all companies accept—MS Word.* A word of caution: Most home PCs use Works, not Word, and if you use Works, no human resources firm will ever be able to open your file to read it. Therefore, only use Word.

✔ *Post your resumé on niche sites.* Niche sites (often called *vertical sites*) are racing to demonstrate that they are the best places to find job leads and get your resumé to hiring managers. Accountants can go to their CPA societies, which now offer a niche site for their profession. This is true for techies, doctors, lawyers, and many other professionals. These sites are useful—so ask colleagues or a reference librarian to identify good ones related to your field and job title.

✔ *Frequent employer websites often.*   Companies, nonprofits, and governmental agencies are expanding their websites to include employment opportunities. These are terrific places to job hunt—people often get interviews when they see an ad on the company site and apply for a specific job opening. Many company websites are their name (i.e., www.starbucks.com or www.ford.com). If you can't find a specific company using just the company name, consult a search engine or a reference librarian to determine the exact URL, or web address, for the company you are interested in.

✔ *Research companies, salaries, business trends, and new careers.* The Internet offers a wealth of easy-to-access information that can help you find companies to apply to. You'll easily uncover reams of specifics on new fields and industries, with job descriptions and useful career training requirements for jobs that might interest you. You'll also find salary surveys to get a clearer idea on what your specific skills are worth.

✔ *Home pages aren't effective.*   Many techies have begun to create elaborate home pages—the "me as a candidate" page. People rarely see them. Once you land an interview, your site may get a visit, but using your time and talents to find leads will yield much better results then creating a "me, I'm great," site.

✔ *Portfolios and samples do well on CD and disc.*   Graphic artists, marketing and advertising people, photographers, producers, broadcasters, etc. may find these tools useful. Keep the hiring manager and company's style and culture in mind, though. One woman complained that she'd made a fabulous CD portfolio. She showed it to me—it was very avant-garde, trendy, and cutting edge. I thought her mistake was sending it to traditional companies, which wanted more wholesome images. She also "forgot" that lower-tech people (and hiring managers) might not have the knowledge or software to open her disc. This is a take-off on the video clips that news broadcasters have created for years. One key fact is not to be forgotten here, as you burn CDs with your best creative examples, your written resumé and cover letter must be strong enough to get the hiring manager to go the extra step to open your accompanying CD or disc, or watch your video. Sending them alone is expensive and ineffective—too many managers say they never open discs or CDs that come without enticing letters or resumés. Overburdened decision makers say time is too short and the number of submissions they receive too many to watch 'em all. One other smart strategy: make sure your very best example is the first one on the disc or tape, since you'll often only get a brief peek.

✔ *Don't bother using resumé blasters.* The person who does well with this service is the person who sells it to you. The premise is that for a fee the blaster will send hundreds of your resumés to who really knows where. These don't work—many seminar participants have attested to that. Your resumé won't get to the hiring managers you're seeking, so save your money and don't use these services.

## *Email an Extended Summary of Qualifications*

When you are emailing your resumé as an attachment to an employer, remember that different operating systems and software can transform the beautiful resumé on your computer into "gobbledygook" code on the employer's computer. If you post the resumé inside an email, it will greatly alter the formatting, making it difficult to read or quickly scan your skills. Like it or not, hiring managers give your resumé 15 seconds, and for electronic ones it's often less.

**Always create electronic resumés in MS Word to maximize readability.**

I use a technique for my clients that solves these problems and has been cited by hiring managers as an excellent idea. Kathy Han, a Fortune 500 Human Resources Director, had this to say about my technique, "This is really a novel idea. Wow! It sure would work here, where we receive hundreds of resumés on our site every day. The information is compact, specific, enticing and contains the necessary contact information. This is one technique I'll use myself, because it'll work, and I think, be quite effective." Clients report it has worked very well for them and so I highly recommend you use this as your "secret weapon" when job hunting via the Internet.

The technique is an EXTENDED SUMMARY OF QUALIFICATIONS. It is a lengthier version of your resumé's qualifications summary—10 to 20 sentences that summarize your top credentials, accomplishments, and skills to perform the job you want. So, instead of unformatting or filtering out your attached resumé (which is essentially what scanning or fire walls can do), this short advertisement, covering your basic accomplishments, skills, and experience in short sentences with some key words thrown in as well, *will* get through. Look at how we took Patrick's resumé and created his extended summary.

## Extended Summary of Qualifications

SUBJECT: MULTIMEDIA PRODUCT MANAGER POSITION

Award winning developer and publisher of multimedia, film, CD-ROM and interactive game products. Eleven years' experience as producer of films, video and interactive products. Proven track record of creating dozens of commercially successful products. Tasks included: developed titles and story concepts, negotiated contracts, secured partnerships, created marketing campaign, supervised product production. Projects brought in at or below budget.

Expertise utilizing most programming and production tools for CD-ROM and digital video editing. Excel at strategic planning, creating joint venture partnerships, forecasting market trends and consumer buying patterns.

For a complete resumé, work samples, or to discuss a specific opening, contact:

Patrick Foster
1 Main Street
City, NY 11111
(201) 555-0111
pfoster@aol.com

Your EXTENDED SUMMARY can be emailed directly to hiring managers or placed on employer and employment websites, plus professional bulletin boards. Be specific—tout accomplishments, but don't oversell. Remember, you'll need to be able to back up these statements later. We simply took the best that Patrick had to offer and put it out there. And yes, the phone did ring and his email squealed with employers saying, "We're interested—tell us more."

Here are a few more things to remember when using this technique. Be sure your address and phone number are in the email. If you also send a complete resumé with it, as an attachment, I recommend you use only widely accepted software, particularly WORD. Some employers say that up to 50% of all attachments are unreadable. The preceding guidelines make the transmission an easier and hopefully more successful process. To be safe, I recommend you also send a copy via postal mail, too.

## *Scanning*

Patrick (and many other clients) also asked me about the scanners many companies use. Correcting him, I said, "You mean that personnel uses?" (The actual boss doesn't scan, HR does.) Patrick wondered what he needed to do to his resumé to meet the "send resumé suitable for scanning" requirement in the Time Warner ad he brought me. Scanning is an electronic tracking system that uses imaging technology to store your "data" or "resumé" on the company's computer system. Used almost exclusively by very large companies and organizations, this allows personnel to count and perform keyword searches to extract resumés that are a direct match to the keywords entered. Keywords often include specific job titles, years of experience, education, and/or specific job skills, defined by a "keyword," such as "budgeting" or "web design."

If you are overwhelmed by how you'll get noticed, realize that electronic scanners process data on hundreds of thousands of resumés. Your chances of being hit by lightning are better than figuring out the perfect keywords to use to be a match. Two different managers can conduct a search for the same desired employee, but one types in Buyer, the other types in Purchaser, and they will get totally different matches. Scanners are popular at magnet and very large companies, as well as governmental agencies. On the grand scope—95% of all employers are small companies and don't use scanners. That said, there is a trick to the keyword thing and I recommend you do exactly what I advised Patrick to do.

At the bottom of your electronic resumé, add a heading entitled "key-words" and paste in all the major words that could produce a match for your skills, as well as a list of all your potential job titles. Notice what we added to the bottom of Patrick's resumé, entitled "resumé with keywords section."

# Patrick Foster
1 Main Street
City, NY 11111
(201) 555-0111
pfoster@aol.com

CAREER OBJECTIVE: **Multimedia Product Manager**

## SUMMARY OF QUALIFICATIONS

Proven leadership in multimedia and film production creating dozens of commercially successful products. Demonstrated excellence in strategic planning, marketing, and technical production skills. Built key business partnerships with Fortune 500 clients. Displayed strong interpersonal and communication skills working with diverse clients. Produced from concept to roll-out CD-ROMs, films and interactive products.

## PROFESSIONAL EXPERIENCE

*Executive Producer,* Interactive Publishing, Seattle, WA, 1996–Present
*(Promoted from Project Lead, Producer)*
*Producer,* Universal Studios, Hollywood, CA, 1993–96
*President,* Foster Films, Los Angeles, CA, 1987–93

### Strategic Planning and Business Development

- Part of senior management taking start-up company from 2 CD-ROM titles to 20 with international distribution, increasing revenues by 1,000% over 30 months.
- Contributed to new business development, planning, contract negotiations; securing Fortune 500 clients as partners in product development and distribution.
- Wrote client proposals acquiring a large percentage of the proposed business.
- Significant contributor and writer on five year business plan.
- Resolved conflicts and negotiated with clients and vendors to arrive at win-win situations. Negotiated fees, product features, ownership of derivative content and other terms.

### Project Management and Product Development

- Managed company's largest partner deal securing clients, developing CD-ROM content, coordinating all client liaison, technical design, supervising team, managing budgets and production schedules. Return on investment was 200% in first 90 days of release.
- Produced 60 documentary films, full-length video releases, and hundred of commercials, industrial/training/sales videos.
- Produced 6 cross-platform CD-ROM reference titles and 4 new releases within 29 months. Each release used the most innovative technology available. All were profitable.
- Earned a reputation for meeting impossible deadlines, shipping 5 out of 6 titles on time. All 6 CD-ROM projects came at or below budget.
- Handled product development from concept, content acquisition, interface design, production, testing.

## Multimedia Technology

- Hands-on experience with programming and production tools for CD-ROM development and digital video editing including: Lingo, Hypercard, Photoshop, Project, Filemaker, Painter, Premiere, After Effects, DeBabelizer, plus numerous others. Both Win and Mac OS.
- Produced 100+ films, CD-ROMs and video releases.

### AWARDS

1999, International Milia for the Best How To Title. PC Magazine's Pick Hit of the Month.
1999, Winter CES Innovations Award, and numerous others.

### EDUCATION

B.A., Film Production, University of Southern California, Los Angeles, CA 1989

### KEYWORDS

| | | |
|---|---|---|
| Multimedia Product Manager | Multimedia Producer | Executive Producer |
| Producer | International Distribution | Multimedia Director |
| Creative Director | Contract negotiations | Documentary films |
| CD-ROM | Written proposals | Wrote proposals |
| CD-ROM Product Manager | CD-ROM Publisher | Multimedia Product |
| Interactive Service Manager | Interactive Games Producer | Manager |

Here are some other tips to follow. Try to contact the company for more specifics. Verify there really is a current job opening and not a major cattle call for "future possibilities" that will probably open up five years from now. Ask for specific guidelines on their system, which should outline whether bullets, italics, asterisks, slashes, etc. can be used. Systems vary, so ask or check company websites for a list of guidelines before you send. One cardinal rule is avoid lines—scanners almost always read these decorative additions as page breaks.

Don't stop there. Use your network and detective skills to obtain the name of the hiring manager in the department you're interested in. Mail (via the post office) an entire resumé directly to that person with a well-written cover letter. The other option is to send an EXTENDED SUMMARY, with a cover letter inquiring about current needs, inside an email sent directly to your potential boss. You'll get far better and faster results using a targeted letter sent to a hiring manager than waiting for the mega computer in HR to pop out your resumé. After all, personnel doesn't hire, so getting your resumé in front of the real decision maker—your future boss—is the objective.

## Faxing

"Just fax it," is a common phrase. The big question is: Did it get there? Was it in a legible, readable form? Don't ever assume it was. If you know who it's going to, mail a hard copy. If not, wait a day or two and refax it to ensure the employer got it. Never, ever fax a resumé longer than one page. The likelihood that pages will get separated is very, very high, many HR advisors say.

Before you ever fax your resumé, fax one to yourself first. Analyze it. Is the font easy to read? If not, use Arial and be sure your font size is at least 12. Be doubly sure contact information—name, address, email and phone number—is large and CLEAR so it can be easily read and the employer can reach you.

# CREATING YOUR RESUMÉ

## 11

L et's develop a powerful resumé that effectively advertises your unique value and worth to employers.

One human resources manager I helped in writing her resumé told me: "A resumé is nothing more than a slick piece of advertisement. But an important piece. Once I saw mine, I would have hired myself." Your resumé is your sales piece. It's all the employer has when they start the screening process. I want to emphasize that in Goldmining, we uncover the *facts, truths,* and *accomplishments* that can honestly and accurately be backed up during the interview.

I've already shown that hiring managers really notice these resumés. You've reviewed the seven-step Goldmining process, and now we are going to work through it step-by-step as you create your masterpiece of self-promotion. You can do this! It'll be easier than you think, so let's get started. It may be very helpful for you to use my computer resumé plus cover letter templates that have all the formatting predone in MS Word. Find these on my website at www.robinryan.com.

## The One-Page Resumé

"Show me a successful track record that's well documented with how you can do the job," advises a senior executive at one of the country's most popular companies. "Eliminate the unrelated details and generic, nonspecific sentences. You must be concise as you show how your past experience relates to our present openings," says Randall, a human resource consultant. At least 100 hiring managers from our survey echoed this same objective.

"Job hunters send resumés in with no idea about the position. They mail in for anything and everything under the sun. No wonder they fail. It's the short, concise, one-page resumé with bullet-by-bullet accomplishments—that's the best way to impress me," says Jean, a senior executive who heads a large department. "Keep to one page," wrote several other employers. Pete DeBottis, a top administrator, pointed out: "Too many professionals list reams of minutiae which have little bearing on performing the position [for] which they have applied. I see this as a serious, serious obstacle to being hired." We asked the employers on our survey what they preferred: one, two, or three pages? Everyone said *no more than two pages, even for top executives.* The vast majority felt that one page is best. Hands down, for staff positions, *one page was the top preference.* Managers, professionals, and executives faced a serious problem when they elected to use a two-page version. "Be crisp and focused," advised Joseph, a department director. "Give me good info in an organized manner. Don't make me search for anything." Too often a longer resumé is not a *better* resumé. It's cluttered with irrelevant facts or old, outdated skills you've long since stopped using. Employers are interested in your abilities to manage and lead today, not in reading two paragraphs on the first job you held 20 years ago.

## The Strategic Advantage of Using a One-Page Resumé

Rationale:

1. Don't waste precious seconds (you're lucky to have more than 20 seconds) over three sheets of paper. You forget there's a cover letter to look at, too.

2. Employers are most interested in your experience over the last five to seven years. That's what must be stressed, not a long description on the first entry-level job you've held. Now that you're at the VP level, they want to see what you've accomplished as a leader. That means most of the emphasis must be on the last job or two. A combination resumé is often the perfect style to achieve powerful one-page results for upper, senior, and top management.

3. Details and specifics won't get *lost*. Results matter: what was achieved; how much was saved; what was increased; decreased. Use clear descriptions telling how large, adding numbers and statistics. All of these influence the selection process the most.

4. Professional easy-to-read formats are essential. Longer versions tend to be crowded and drag on with excessive irrelevant descriptions not essential to performing the job that needs to be done or are simply quite repetitive and dull.

5. The Summary of Qualifications, which speaks volumes on consolidating the best you have to bring to the job, really stands out and pulls the employer in for a closer look.

Two pages or one? Can a senior executive with 20 years consolidate it into one page? Does she or he need to? I think so. Although the survey data reports that two pages are acceptable to some, I called several hiring managers to try to get a deeper understanding. Here's what I found out. It seems very few HR professionals like the longer version. Many said they felt that when the resumé was too long (two or three pages), there simply was too much information, irrelevant information, or it was poorly organized. The employer *missed* credentials and big things which can eliminate a candidate during that crucial initial 20- to 30-second glance through the stack. Many admitted that they never even looked at page two, let alone page three.

From a strategic standpoint, I make the following conclusion and recommendation:

---

A *one*-page resumé is the preferred length to concisely advertise your top skills and experience to perform the requirements of the specifically targeted job, so that the hiring manager is convinced they must meet you after only spending 15 seconds looking at your resumé.

---

# *Select the Correct Format Style for You*

## Chronological

### Name
Address
Phone
email

CAREER OBJECTIVE: _____

SUMMARY OF QUALIFICATIONS

PROFESSIONAL EXPERIENCE

*Current/Last Job,* Company, City, State, Dates

- 
- 
- 
- 

*Next Job,* Company, City, State, Dates

- 
- 

*Next Job,* Company, City, State, Dates

- 
- 

EDUCATION

Optional headings: Computer Skills, Awards/Honors, E-Mail Address

## Combination

# Name
Address
Phone
email

CAREER OBJECTIVE: _____

SUMMARY OF QUALIFICATIONS

PROFESSIONAL EXPERIENCE

*Current/Last Job,* Company, City, State, Dates
*(promoted from "job title," if applicable)*

Skill Area
- 
- 

Skill Area
- 
- 

Skill Area
- 
- 

EDUCATION

Skill Area lists are found in Chapter 8.

# Functional

## Name
Address
Phone
email

CAREER OBJECTIVE: _____

SUMMARY OF QUALIFICATIONS

PROFESSIONAL EXPERIENCE

Skill Area

- 
- 

Skill Area

- 
- 

Skill Area

- 
- 

WORK HISTORY

*Current/Last Job,* Company, City, State, Dates

*Previous Job,* Company, City, State, Dates

*Previous Job,* Company, City, State, Dates

EDUCATION

Skill Area lists are found in Chapter 8.

# *Let's Write!*

The seven-step Goldmining technique™ is an easy formula to follow. (An electronic version of this in MS Word is available on my website at www.robinryan.com.) Let's walk through it.

## Step One

**CAREER OBJECTIVE:** _____

Just fill in the job title you're looking for (e.g., Teacher, Vice President of Marketing, Technical Writer, Dental Hygienist, Project Manager, Systems Analyst, Restaurant Manager, or so forth).

## Step Two

**EDUCATION**

There are several acceptable ways to address this section, truthfully and in a positive light. The accepted format is degree first, then your major (optional), university/college, city, state, and year (optional). List degrees in reverse chronological order beginning with the highest degree first. Several examples are listed including one to be used when currently pursuing a degree. The last option can be used when you started a program but never finished it.

*Doctor of Philosophy,* Chemistry, University of Washington, Seattle, Washington, 1991

*Master of Science,* Business Administration, Boston University, Boston, Massachusetts, 1986

*Bachelor of Science,* William and Mary College, Williamsburg, Virginia, 1994

*Bachelor of Arts,* English, Pepperdine University, Malibu, California, presently attending

*Bachelor of Arts,* History, Iowa State University, completed three years

*Graduate Studies,* Business Administration, Marketing, Organizational Planning, Boston College 1991

Now complete your Education section:

| Degree, | Major (if applicable), | College, | City, | State, | Year |
|---|---|---|---|---|---|
| Degree, | Major (if applicable), | College, | City, | State, | Year |

## Step Three

### PROFESSIONAL EXPERIENCE

Identify from your old resumé or job description the important abilities
you have that specifically relate to doing the job title you are targeting.
Start with your current or last job. Note and underline each major ability,
skill, or accomplishment here.

_____

_____

_____

_____

_____

_____

_____

_____

## Step Four

Now we must examine what were the ACTIONS you did, and then note the
RESULTS. Here's a list of some of the probing questions and statements
you'll need to answer when writing out your Professional Experience.
Keep in mind that most statements should try to achieve this ACTIONS =
RESULTS concept.

✔ List all your areas of responsibility.

✔ Note how large the organization was.

✔ Give specific information using examples and statistics.

✔ Did you save time?

✔ Did you save money?

✔ How many?

✔ How much?

✔ What was important about that?

✔ What exactly did you do?

✔ What was the result?

✔ Did you increase anything?

✔ Did you improve anything?

✔ Did you decrease anything?

✔ What?

✔ How?

✔ Give me another example.

✔ Let's get a dollar figure for that.

**Action:** _____

**Result:** _____

**Action:** _____

**Result:** _____

**Action:** _____

**Result:** _____

**Action:** _____

**Result:** _____

**Action:** _____

**Result:** _____

**Action:** _____

**Result:** _____

**Action:** _____

**Result:** _____

**Action:** _____

**Result:** _____

**Action:** _____

**Result:** _____

## Step Five

### MORE ON PROFESSIONAL EXPERIENCE

Now we must write out sentences for the major duties that link the ACTIONS and then the RESULTS achieved together into the sentence that will be incorporated into the resumé (example follows).

- Coordinated the new direct mail/marketing campaign that produced a 5% sales return, national average is 1–2%.

A list of action verbs is located in Chapter 8 to help you select the best descriptive words to start out your sentences.

All sentences are written in the *past* tense. Complete for current/last job held.

- _____
  _____

- _____
  _____

- _____
  _____

- _____
  _____

## Step Six

Repeat steps three through five for all previous jobs. Also do this for Computer Skills, Honors/Awards, and Volunteer or Community Service work.

Now, select the strongest ones that best illustrate your abilities to perform the needed job duties. Fill in the Professional Experience section with your best selling points. Then ask a friend to look it over and grill you to be sure you've answered these questions: "How did you do it?" "What resulted?" Use this friend to help edit and finalize your resumé to perfect it to be your very best advertisement possible.

## Step Seven

### SUMMARY OF QUALIFICATIONS

Now read through your new resumé. Drawing from both your experience of performing the job and insider/networked information, identify your top selling points. The important ones have got to be mentioned here. The number of years of experience is a good one to include.

List the major points you need to mention.

1. _____

2. _____

3. _____

4. _____

5. _____

Now create a few sentences (check out our samples to help you), and write your SUMMARY OF QUALIFICATIONS.

_____

_____

_____

_____

_____

_____

Now put it all together, and you've done it. Two final suggestions: (1) Always get someone else to read the resumé and confirm that it really *sells* you. They will verify that you have strong accomplishments and ACTIONS = RESULTS. (2) Always *proofread!!* No typos or mistakes. Employers said that spelling and typos were the biggest resumé killers and a faux pas you just cannot afford to make if you want to succeed. So make it your very best effort. Every hiring manager we surveyed selected typos and spelling mistakes as the worst possible error you could make. It stopped them from reading, and they trashed the resumé. I cannot stress enough that you need to make this advertisement of yourself *absolutely perfect.*

# *Formatting and Layout Guidelines*

Typing your resumé to look professional and attractive can be easier and aided by computer technology. Here are some layout and typing guidelines to make your resumé look terrific.

**Software:** Use MS Word

**Margins:** 1 inch top, bottom, and sides

**Font size:** 12-point or higher

**Font:** clean, easy to read. Arial is a good choice.

**Letterhead:** Centered on page,
Name, bolded in a slightly larger font size (14-point) than address (12-point).
Address
Phone: Home number and/or cell. Not work
Email: Home only, not work

### Tony Treasury, CPA
1 Main Street
City, WA 98111
(425) 555-1112
ttreasury@msn.com

**Headings:** Centered and bolded. Career Objective, Summary of Qualifications, Professional Experience, Education, Awards and Honors, Computer Skills. Career Objective: Position or title desired.

**CAREER OBJECTIVE: Vice President Finance/Treasurer**

**Work History:** Job title in italics, then company/city/state/dates of employment in regular text.
Example: *VP Finance,* Big Company, Boston, MA 2000–present
**Job function:** Use subheads, bolded and underlined.
Example: **International Business**
**Bullets:** Align all bullets under heading, as follows

Financial Management

- Managed all accounting and treasury functions for a $100 million, 1,000 employee international organization. Responsibilities included: financial management and reporting, treasury, forecasting, budgets, cash management, strategic planning, banking/foreign currency transactions, human resources, and information systems.
- Streamlined financial operations and reporting that reduced the general ledger process time from 90 days to 10 days. Results: dramatically improved the executive team's ability to manage and plan company's worldwide operations.
- Evaluated, analyzed and implemented significant process, policy and procedural changes to reduce both equipment maintenance and workers' compensation costs by $3 million annually.

**Education:** Degrees and licenses. Center whole section.

**EDUCATION**
MBA, Finance, Harvard University, Cambridge, MA 1994
BS, Accounting, University of Massachusetts, Boston, MA 1983

# References

Employers can be influenced *a great deal* by what your references say. You need to select people familiar with your work, not personal or family friends. I recommend that you choose three people (no less) or no more than four. Call and ask their permission to be a reference *before* you use their name. In selecting and adding references to make a positive impression on the employer, follow these guidelines.

✔ Pick people you've worked with—former bosses, department heads, clients—that were pleased with your work. Exclude mentioning any boss who will give you anything but a rave review.

✔ Select current references. If they are 8 to 10 years old, they are too outdated to be of much value, and employers may wonder if you're hiding bad performance at more recent jobs.

✔ Obtain correct address, phone number, and identify the relationship, for example, former supervisor, major client, and so on.

✔ Mail the person your current resumé with a thank-you note that points out some of the key points they'll likely be questioned about. This is a good refresher and will produce a better endorsement when the person's called.

✔ Obtain letters from departing bosses and performance appraisals to use in future job interviews.

✔ References are usually brought into the interview and given then. Unless you are specifically asked to mail them in the ad, don't bother to add them in with your resumé. They'll just clutter up your package.

# *What to Do about Bad References, No References, or Not Wanting Employers to Call Your Current Boss*

These issues pose a problem you are needlessly worrying about. *Never,* ever, use the name of a former boss who disliked or had conflicts with you. Just never give their name and no one will call them. Find another manager or top executive who will say good things, and use that person as your reference. One CEO told me, "I think it's a huge mistake using old, dated references. I need people to speak to your current level of employment, not something you did ten years ago."

Some company policies require managers to only verify employment, but not elaborate beyond that. You'll need more to convince a new employer to hire you. Performance appraisals and letters on a job well done can be substituted, but potential employers will still want to talk to someone. Maybe a manager who left the company will help. Current bosses might be willing to give "personal references" to get around company rules and say a little more if you ask them to. Always ask your bosses or former bosses if they can be contacted at home as a personal reference for potential employers to call. Many will agree, especially for a good worker or someone they needed to lay off. Another option is to look outside your company to a customer you frequently work with or another executive you've done joint projects with. Perhaps someone who's worked with you on a volunteer project would be a good choice. They must be able to attest to your work, so skip social friends—they're not helpful. It's up to you to provide references who can be open, so be resourceful.

I often tell clients to never underestimate what references will say about you. If you have any concerns or questions in your mind, here's a good way to alleviate them. Get a friend to pose as a potential employer and call for a reference. Have the friend take notes and report back to you. Strong, glowing feedback is what you need. Now you know *exactly* what is being said. If it's not positive, find another person and use them as your reference. Overlooking these steps can cause you to lose a job you are qualified for, want, and have worked hard to gain.

Let me tell you what happened to Linda. I was hiring for a new Assistant Director. She did well in the interview and claimed she had strong skills in her resumé. So I called her company and asked for the supervisor she listed. The boss liked Linda, but when questioned about her accuracy and job abilities, he gave her a pretty poor recommendation, and consequently I didn't offer Linda the job. Most employers do their homework, so select your references with care. Choose people familiar with your work, not personal or family friends. I recommend you choose three people. Call and ask their permission to be a reference *before* you use their name. If it has been a few months or longer, call to confirm that their phone number, email, and address are still correct.

Now create your reference sheet by completing the following form. Be sure to bring this sheet to all interviews and leave it with employers.

## REFERENCE LIST
for
# Mary Brown
1 Main Street
City, NY 11111
(201) 555-0111
e-mail: MBrown@aol.com

*Sample:*    Cindy Johnson, former supervisor
Project Manager
The Boeing Co.
MS: 2122
Seattle, WA 98100
206-555-1212
cjohnson1@boeing.com

Reference Name: _____

Title: _____

Address: _____

_____

Phone: _____

email: _____

Reference Name: _____

Title: _____

Address: _____

_____

Phone: _____

email: _____

Reference Name: _____

Title: _____

Address: _____

_____

Phone: _____

email: _____

# *Printing, Paper, and Envelopes That Send an Influential Message*

The results of our hiring manager survey were crystal clear about these options. Here's what they said they preferred:

| | |
|---|---|
| Printing | Computer-generated, laser-printed. Font size, 11 to 12 text, 12 to 14 headings. Font recommendations: clear, clean, easy to read. Arial or Helvetica are excellent choices. |
| Paper color | White, off-white, ivory, in woven or laid finish with a rich feel and texture. Use the same paper for resumé and cover letter. Don't use any fancy design or create letterhead with lines across the page, which can be a problem if the resumé is scanned. |
| Envelope | Typed or laser-printed is best. Beautiful penmanship is acceptable if addressing by hand. Does not need to match paper. No advantage to using large brown 9½″ × 12″ envelopes or overnight service. Recommendation: Business size. Use professional looking return-address-labels or laser print. |

# HELPFUL RESOURCES

I want to make the writing process as easy as possible for you, so I've included some helpful lists that I've developed. George, a CEO, pointed out that the most effective way to impress him or one of his managers is to: "Use short, powerful phrases that are directed to the right aspects of the available position. These should be supported by specific examples of personal accomplishments." These lists (and, of course, all the previous resumé examples) should aid you in achieving George's goal and that of most employers: short, powerful, influential phrases that illustrate ACTIONS = RESULTS.

| | |
|---|---|
| **Skill Areas** | Allows you to quickly pick out the two or three major experience groups when you are writing either your **Functional** or **Combination** resumé. I've tried to identify almost any area you might need, but adapt one to fit your set of specific skills if nothing here is a perfect match. |
| **Action Verbs** | Start all your sentences with a powerful verb. They denote the ACTION, making it easier to lead into the RESULT. I've grouped them by area to make it faster to select the perfect description of your accomplishment. |
| **Transferable skills** | Denotes many important talents you possess that are relevant from job to job or field to different field. So often we just forget all these important traits, but don't let that happen to you. |

# Skill Areas

Functional and combination resumés use skill areas to identify the major experience group. Following is a list of numerous skill areas commonly used. Typically two to four skill areas are highlighted.

| | |
|---|---|
| Account Management | Editing |
| Accounting | Employee Relations |
| Administration | Engineering |
| Advertising | Environmental |
| Advocacy | Field Research |
| Analysis & Evaluation | Film & Video |
| Bookkeeping | Financial Analysis |
| Budgeting | Financial Management |
| Business Management | Financial Planning |
| Community Relations | Forecasting |
| Career Development | Fundraising |
| Client Services | Graphic Design |
| Communications | Hiring |
| Community Service | Human Resources |
| Computer Programming | Inspection |
| Computer Skills | Interviewing |
| Contracts & Agreements | Inventory Control |
| Corporate Administration | Management |
| Counseling | Investigation/Research |
| Curriculum Development | Labor Relations |
| Customer Relations | Language Interpretation |
| Customer Service | Market Research |
| Data Processing | Marketing |
| Decorating | Media |
| Display | Mediation |
| Drafting | Merchandising |

Multimedia

Negotiations

Office Administration

Office Skills

Outreach

Performing Arts

Photography

Policy Making

Presentation

Print Coordination

Process Improvement

Product Development

Product Management

Production

Program Design

Program Management

Project Management

Promotion

Public Relations

Public Speaking

Publicity

Publishing

Purchasing

Quality Assurance

Quality Improvement

Reengineering

Real Estate

Records Management

Recruiting

Reporting

Research & Development

Resource Development

Restaurant Management

Retail

Sales

Statistical Analysis

Strategic Planning

Supervision

Systems Analysis

Teaching

Technical Skills

Technical Writing

Telecommunications

Testing

Training

Visual Arts

Word Processing

Writing

# *Action Verbs*

| MANAGEMENT SKILLS | |
|---|---|
| Accomplished | Hired |
| Activated | Implemented |
| Adjusted | Improved |
| Administered | Incorporated |
| Advised | Increased |
| Analyzed | Initiated |
| Assigned | Interviewed |
| Attained | Invented |
| Chaired | Investigated |
| Conceptualized | Led |
| Conducted | Managed |
| Consolidated | Negotiated |
| Contracted | Organized |
| Coordinated | Oversaw |
| Decreased | Planned |
| Delegated | Presided |
| Designed | Prioritized |
| Developed | Produced |
| Devised | Recommended |
| Directed | Recruited |
| Established | Reorganized |
| Evaluated | Reviewed |
| Executed | Scheduled |
| Facilitated | Strengthened |
| Formulated | Supervised |

| COMMUNICATION SKILLS | |
|---|---|
| Addressed | Directed |
| Arbitrated | Drafted |
| Arranged | Edited |
| Authored | Educated |
| Collaborated | Enlisted |
| Corresponded | Explained |
| Developed | Formulated |

| | |
|---|---|
| Influenced | Publicized |
| Interpreted | Reconciled |
| Lectured | Recruited |
| Mediated | Spoke |
| Moderated | Stipulated |
| Motivated | Taught |
| Negotiated | Translated |
| Persuaded | Wrote |
| Promoted | |

## RESEARCH SKILLS

| | |
|---|---|
| Accumulated | Identified |
| Calculated | Inspected |
| Catalogued | Interpreted |
| Clarified | Interviewed |
| Collected | Investigated |
| Critiqued | Organized |
| Designed | Reviewed |
| Diagnosed | Summarized |
| Evaluated | Surveyed |
| Examined | Systematized |
| Extracted | |

## TECHNICAL SKILLS

| | |
|---|---|
| Assembled | Operated |
| Built | Overhauled |
| Calculated | Programmed |
| Computed | Remodeled |
| Constructed | Repaired |
| Designed | Solved |
| Devised | Surveyed |
| Engineered | Trained |
| Fabricated | Troubleshooter |
| Formulated | Upgraded |
| Maintained | |

## TEACHING SKILLS

| | |
|---|---|
| Adapted | Explained |
| Advised | Facilitated |
| Clarified | Guided |
| Coached | Informed |
| Communicated | Initiated |
| Coordinated | Instructed |
| Developed | Persuaded |
| Educated | Researched |
| Enabled | Simulated |
| Encouraged | Trained |
| Evaluated | |

## FINANCIAL SKILLS

| | |
|---|---|
| Administered | Developed |
| Allocated | Forecasted |
| Analyzed | Managed |
| Appraised | Marketed |
| Audited | Planned |
| Balanced | Prepared |
| Budgeted | Projected |
| Calculated | Researched |
| Computed | |

## CREATIVE SKILLS

| | |
|---|---|
| Acted | Illustrated |
| Advertised | Instituted |
| Conceptualized | Integrated |
| Created | Introduced |
| Demonstrated | Invented |
| Designed | Marketed |
| Developed | Originated |
| Directed | Performed |
| Established | Planned |
| Founded | Presented |

| | |
|---|---|
| Produced | Shaped |
| Recommended | Sold |
| Revitalized | |

## HELPING SKILLS

| | |
|---|---|
| Assessed | Expedited |
| Assisted | Facilitated |
| Clarified | Familiarized |
| Coached | Guided |
| Counseled | Referred |
| Demonstrated | Rehabilitated |
| Diagnosed | Represented |
| Educated | Served |
| Effected | |

## ADMINISTRATIVE OR DETAIL SKILLS

| | |
|---|---|
| Approved | Manipulated |
| Arranged | Modified |
| Calculated | Monitored |
| Catalogued | Operated |
| Changed | Organized |
| Classified | Prepared |
| Collected | Processed |
| Compiled | Purchased |
| Computerized | Recorded |
| Dispatched | Retrieved |
| Executed | Screened |
| Formulated | Specified |
| Generated | Synthesized |
| Implemented | Systematized |
| Informed | Tabulated |
| Inspected | Validated |
| Maintained | |

# *Transferable Skills*

These are skills that are important and can be used in any job or field. You may possess many of these abilities and yet not recognize that these are actual skills and talents employers want to know about. Spend a few minutes and mark each skill you possess.

| *Attributes/Abilities* | *Occupational Skills* |
| --- | --- |
| Administering | Able to accomplish tasks by directing work flow, implementing decisions, enforcing regulations, and coordinating tasks. |
| Advising | Feel competent to give advice or offer an opinion or recommendation about a particular problem or situation. |
| Analytical | Problem solving, analyzing, researching, diagnosing, systematizing, organizing, assessing, troubleshooting, appraising, judging, evaluating, investigating. |
| Analyzing | Able to examine and evaluate data and present alternative actions in relation to the evaluation. |
| Arbitrating | Able to help diverse groups work together by mediating between contending groups. Skilled at bargaining and reconciling. |
| Artistic abilities | Dealing creatively with colors, spaces, shapes, dimensions, ceramics, arts, music, drawing. |
| Assessing needs | Able to determine what is lacking and develop a plan to rectify the deficiency. |
| Budget managing | Can work competently with money, specifically in understanding and preparing budgets. Keeping financial records. Develop forecasts/projections. |
| Communicating | Able to exchange information in a clear, understandable manner, either verbally or in writing. |
| Computer | Proficiency using Macintosh and/or PC systems. Software user ability. Programming capability. Hardware design. Systems analysis and installation. Troubleshooting. |

| *Attributes/Abilities* | *Occupational Skills* |
|---|---|
| Coordinating | Able to determine time, place, and sequence of operations or action to be taken on the basis of analysis of data. |
| Correcting | Able to point out and rectify errors. |
| Counseling | Can advise others through the sharing of ideas, opinions, advice, guidance, or emotional support. Coach toward improved behavior or performance. |
| Creating | Able to develop new ideas or processes. Highly imaginative with many innovative ideas. Able to translate ideas into concrete written or visual form to share with others. |
| Creativity | Applying theory, developing, designing, being an idea person, inventing, planning models, creating, creative imagining. Producing new products or programs. |
| Data collecting | Able to gather, collate, or classify information about data, people, or things. |
| Decision making | See clearly what needs to be done and make a judgment or form a conclusion on that matter. |
| Defining problems | Able to isolate and describe a problem in order that steps may be taken to rectify it. |
| Delegating | Can appoint or assign others to handle various tasks or assignments. Willing to let go of parts of a project rather than always trying to do everything personally. |
| Developing ideas | Adept at creating order out of chaos. Able to take a thought from the idea stage through to completion. Idea person. Highly creative. Resourceful. |
| Documenting | Able to prepare written records of collected data. Can also involve classifying, recording, and filing of the data. |
| Establishing objectives | Able to determine a goal or goals to be worked toward. |

| *Attributes/Abilities* | *Occupational Skills* |
|---|---|
| Establishing priorities | Can sort tasks according to order of importance and/or urgency. |
| Evaluating | Able to appraise or determine the quality of, the worth of, and/or the effectiveness of a program, person, or organization. |
| Forecasting | Able to estimate or calculate, in advance, various actions or occurrences (generally based on analysis of data). Financial projections based on research and past performance. |
| Guiding | Able to direct or lead the way to a particular goal or objective. |
| Implementing | Able to bring an idea or plan into reality. Provide for or serve as the tool for this implementation. |
| Improving | Able to make a condition, situation, product, or process better. |
| Influencing | Able to affect the thoughts and actions of others and produce the desired results. |
| Inspecting | Able to examine a piece of work carefully and critically to detect flaws and/or determine errors. |
| Interpret | Speak, write, understand, and translate a different language. |
| Language | Public speaking, instructing, teaching, communicating, editing, writing, training, interrupting, translation, debating, reading, copying, talking, speaking, educating others. |
| Leadership | Organizing, affecting change, leading, initiating, controlling, coordinating, taking risks, managing people, projects, or programs. |
| Leading | Able to direct or guide groups by assigning specific duties and maintaining harmonious relations. Manage projects, programs, or teams. |
| Learning | Have acquired knowledge of a subject or obtained a skill by study, experience, and/or instruction. |

| _Attributes/Abilities_ | _Occupational Skills_ |
|---|---|
| Listening | Effectively hear what the speaker is attempting to communicate. Use active listening skills to draw people out and help them express their thoughts. Hear accurately. |
| Managing people | Help build a team through recognizing and utilizing the skills of others, by directing and supervising others in their work and being responsible for those workers. |
| Managing program/ and project/products | Direct the process, resources, coordination, work to achieve desired results. |
| Manual | Constructing, assembling, building, operating equipment or machinery, fixing, repairing, typing, showing dexterity or speed, data entry. |
| Money managing | Can plan finances and direct cash flow. Keep financial records. Tracking systems. Develop and maintain. |
| Motivating | Able to encourage and inspire others to perform at higher levels. |
| Negotiating | Able to exchange ideas, information, and opinions with others to formulate policies and programs. Arrive jointly at decisions, conclusions, or solutions. |
| Number skills | Accounting, doing cost analysis, keeping financial records, calculating, counting, taking inventory, purchasing, statistical analysis, compiling research data. |
| Organizing | Able to structure or form people or groups into a coherent whole; to set up and administer structure for the unit. |
| Performance abilities | Lecturing, demonstrating, getting up before a group, performing, acting, playing music, making people laugh, singing, presentations. |
| Persuading | Able to influence attitudes and ideas of others in favor of a desired product, service, or point of view. |

| *Attributes/Abilities* | *Occupational Skills* |
| --- | --- |
| Persuasion | Selling, behavioral modification, promoting, negotiating, influencing others, persuading, manipulating, reconciling, motivating, counseling, advising. |
| Planning treatment | Able to determine a method of treating or dealing with a particular problem or situation in order to achieve specific results. |
| Problem solving | Able to visualize and implement solutions to bring about changes. |
| Process improvement | Able to examine, streamline, develop, or design more efficient or effective ways to perform a task or function. |
| Program design | Able to plan a program. Outline the framework of a new program. |
| Program developing | Able to bring a program or plan into existence. |
| Program implementation | Able to provide the means for putting a program into action. |
| Promoting | Able to interest others in and/or sell ideas, goods, programs, projects, or services. |
| Reasoning | Showing foresight, policy making, planning, visualizing in the third dimension, perceiving, balancing factors, strategic planning, global thinking. |
| Recruiting | Able to enlist new membership, employees, subscribers, and so on. |
| Referring | Upon receiving requests for assistance, able to send or direct people to appropriate sources of aid and/or information. |
| Reporting | Able to prepare either a formal or informal account or statement describing the results of a particular occurrence. |
| Representing | Able to serve as an agent or substitute for others and authorized to work and speak in their behalf to accomplish desired results. |

| *Attributes/Abilities* | *Occupational Skills* |
|---|---|
| Researching (Original) | Have undertaken careful, systematic study and investigation in some field of knowledge to discover or establish facts or principles. |
| Responding abilities | Applying what others have developed, following through, being a detail person, focusing. |
| Revising | Able to update, correct, and/or improve a product. |
| Scheduling | Able to prepare a coordinated, timed plan for procedure on a project, which entails making arrangements for events and processes as well as making sure goals or promises are delivered on time. |
| Selecting | By using certain standards of excellence or quality, able to choose between various products, services, or people. |
| Self-starter | Possess an inner drive that causes or directs working toward a particular goal or moving in a particular direction. |
| Staff developing | Help build or improve the quality of a staff through training, counseling, guidance, and goal objectives. |
| Summarizing | Able to make a brief, concise statement presenting the substance, general idea, or main points of a subject. |
| Supervising | Able to determine or interpret work procedures for a group of workers, assigning specific duties to them, maintaining harmonious relations among them, and promoting efficiency. Ability to motivate workers. Build a cohesive, highly productive team. |
| Teaching | Able to give instructions or lessons enabling others to learn (via explanation, demonstration, and/or supervised practice) how to do something or learn about a specific subject. |

| *Attributes/Abilities* | *Occupational Skills* |
|---|---|
| Thinking | Able to understand how parts make up the whole and appreciate how an isolated item fits into an overall plan. Find new approaches to daily tasks and problems. Love learning. Problem solving. |
| Visual | Observing, examining, inspecting, diagnosing, determining, deciding, showing attention to details, filing, assessing, graphic designing. |
| Working with others | Enjoy working with other people. A good team player. Bring enthusiasm and energy into group efforts. Enjoy encouraging others and developing rapport. Great interpersonal skills. |
| Writing | Can clearly communicate a mood, information, or idea in writing. Involves a strong command of language and grammar usage. |

# THE PATH TO SUCCESS

*Dream Big—*
*the future is what you make it.*
*—ROBIN RYAN*

What does it take to achieve success? To land the job of your dreams? To feel the thrill of victory when the employer calls to say, "The job is yours"?

Surviving a layoff and living through a termination are two of the toughest career challenges you can face. Wanting something better, whether more recognition or responsibility, a higher salary, or more prestigious title, can be the impetus that puts you on the job search trail. The path to success is clear, but many fail because they do not put forth the effort and actions, nor will they take the risk. Your job search is an exciting self-discovery process where you come face-to-face with your own unique value and realize how much you do have to offer an employer. Once you set your goal and determine to land a better job, there's no stopping you. The bigger your dreams, the bigger the rewards.

Dennis, an engineer, told me: "I was petrified when I first heard the potential layoff rumors. Realizing that a major downsizing was inevitable, I went to work. I was surprised that the job market had changed so much during the last 10 years since I'd looked for a job. I sure had to move way out of my comfort zone. I had to examine my skills and learn their true value in the marketplace. I created a new resumé in which Goldmining drew out the best I had to offer. I tried to network. I used the Internet to reach employers. As D-day approached, I put tremendous effort into my search. I look back on it now, a year later, and see so many of my coworkers who got laid off still aren't working. No one seemed to believe that a downsizing would truly come to pass and hit them. None of them worked the hours a week I did to seek out a new opportunity. As my impending layoff loomed just weeks away, I landed the job with Hewlett-Packard and am happily enjoying both the work and the $20,000 more I make in salary today."

No job search is ever easy. Lots of hours and effort go into the process. Rejection is part of the game, the awful part, but still a part of it. But the end results, as Dennis says, are more than worth it. I've outlined the steps that lead to success: *Risk, Dream Big, See Your Value, Act, Focus, Persevere,* and *Commit.* Go for it! Soon you, too, will be enjoying a great new job!

## Risk

You'll never get to enjoy a great job without putting yourself out there, exposing yourself, and taking some chances. Everything worth obtaining means stretching beyond what you have achieved to push for something else, something more. The risk is worth it when you consider the potential reward of a better job, better company, more satisfaction, nicer benefits, and a higher salary.

## Dream Big

No major goal was ever achieved by not first clearly deciding to go after something you want. Why can't you land the perfect job? Why can't you have a more challenging job if you want it? Why can't you feel worthwhile, enriched, and satisfied every day you go to work? The only thing stopping you is *you.* Set a goal that's high as the sky. Push yourself; you can get it all!

## See Your Value

You can never tell others until you accept and see for yourself how valuable your own talents and skills are. Goldmining will uncover many hidden strengths and talents. Remind yourself of these and praise yourself often. Note what you did well, what you'd like to improve, and how you'll do that. Stay focused on the positive. Eliminate "black cloud" people from your life. These are the folks who walk through life and seem to attract bad things. They are always so negative and will kill your self-marketing efforts with doubts and negativity. Continuously remind yourself of your value and develop friends and supporters who praise you often, those who *want* and *believe* in your success.

## Act

Dreams are just fantasies without a clear-cut action plan to get there. Set the goal, write out the steps, and work at it every week. Even if you have a job, you must devote 5 to 10 hours to your search efforts. If you are unemployed, you'll need to devote 30 hours to proactive job hunting pursuits. Move outside your comfort zone and talk to more people, research more employers, write better letters, and polish your interviewing skills to achieve your goal. It'll never happen without concentrated effort and actions on your part.

## Focus

Concentrate on the goal by visualizing the success in your mind. See yourself working at the new job. Become obsessed with obtaining it. Pay attention to newspaper articles that discuss companies' plans for growth or new product launches. Look for job leads and ask everyone you meet about their job and company. Prioritize your time to make job hunting activities important. Visualize your success: the new job, office, perks, and the nice things the new salary will buy. Don't get distracted or procrastinate. A clear focus and a success objective must be your motivators.

## Persevere

No success will come without calculated effort. Calvin Coolidge said it best: "Nothing in the world can ever take the place of persistence. Talent will not; nothing is more common than unsuccessful men with talent. Genius will not; unrewarded genius is almost a proverb. Education will not; the world is full of educated derelicts. Persistence and determination alone are omnipotent."

# *Commit*

Go for it! I know you can and will succeed! I've had the privilege of working with so many other clients and coaching them on to success. In this book, I've shared that insight with you. Now, simply follow this last piece of advice and before long *you* will be enjoying the rich rewards from your brand new job:

*Make a commitment to achieve your own success.*

*Try harder.*

*Reach higher.*

*Believe you can do it.*

*Then do whatever it takes to make it happen.*

*—Robin Ryan*

# MORE CAREER HELP AVAILABLE

Robin Ryan has written other valuable career books that are excellent resources to aid you in your career change. Her books, available in bookstores, from online vendors like Amazon.com and barnesandnoble.com, and on her webwsite at www.robinryan.com, include:

*60 Seconds & You're Hired!* (covers interviewing and salary negotiations)

*Winning Resumés* (CD templates available)

*Winning Cover Letters* (CD templates available)

*What to DO with the REST of Your Life*

Robin Ryan is also the author of *The Power of Branding You* audiotape series.

She offers career counseling, resumé writing services, interview coaching, and assistance with salary negotiations via telephone consultations. For corporate clients she provides outplacement, spouse relocation, and executive coaching services.

A popular national speaker who has presented over 1,200 speeches, seminars, and keynote programs, Robin is available to speak to your group, company, or organization.

Visit her website for more details about her speaking and career coaching services at www.robinryan.com

You can also sign up for her email newsletter, "Career News You Can Use," at her website, www.robinryan.com.

To contact Robin Ryan, call her Seattle office at (425) 226-0414.

Email her at robinryan@aol.com or

Visit her website at: www.robinryan.com.

# INDEX

## About Robin Ryan, Author, National Speaker, and Career Coach

Robin Ryan is the prize-winning author of six books including *60 Seconds & You're Hired!, Winning Resumes, Winning Cover Letters,* and *What to Do with the Rest of Your Life.* Ryan has appeared on more than 700 TV and radio programs including *NBC Nightly News with Tom Brokaw, Oprah,* CNN, and CNBC, and appears regularly on Seattle's KOMO TV and Radio, Bloomberg Radio, and also on Fox TV's *Mornings Live* show. A consistent contributor to national magazines and trade publications, she's been featured in *Money, Newsweek, Fortune, Business Week, Cosmopolitan, Good Housekeeping,* and *McCall's.* She's appeared on the pages of most major U.S. newspapers including *USA Today, The Wall Street Journal, The New York Times, Los Angeles Times, Boston Herald,* and *Chicago Tribune.* She has also been a career columnist for *The Seattle Times* for six years.

A licensed vocational counselor for 20 years, Robin Ryan has an active career-counseling practice based in Seattle, where she offers telephone consultations to assist clients with career changing, resumes, job search, interviewing, salary negotiations, and other career issues. Additionally, her work includes outplacement consulting, executive coaching, and spouse relocation advising. Ryan is the creator of the audiotape series *The Power of Branding You.* She holds a master's degree in counseling and education from Suffolk University, a bachelor's degree in sociology from Boston College, and is former director of counseling services at the University of Washington. A popular national speaker, Ryan has taught more than 1,200 seminars and keynote programs, contributing to the career success of millions of people.

You can contact Robin Ryan at 425-226-0414.
Email: robinryan@aol.com
Websight: www.robinryan.com.